Critical theory and epistemology

Critical theory and contemporary society

Series editors:
David M. Berry, Professor of Digital Humanities, University of Sussex
Darrow Schecter, Reader in Critical Theory, University of Sussex

The *Critical Theory and Contemporary Society* series aims to demonstrate the ongoing relevance of multi-disciplinary research in explaining the causes of pressing social problems today and in indicating the possible paths towards a libertarian transformation of twenty-first century society. It builds upon some of the main ideas of first generation critical theorists, including Horkheimer, Adorno, Benjamin, Marcuse and Fromm, but it does not aim to provide systematic guides to the work of those thinkers. Rather, each volume focuses on ways of thinking about the political dimensions of a particular topic, which include political economy, law, popular culture, globalization, feminism, theology and terrorism. Authors are encouraged to build on the legacy of first generation Frankfurt School theorists and their influences (Kant, Hegel, Kierkegaard, Marx, Nietzsche, Weber and Freud) in a manner that is distinct from, though not necessarily hostile to, the broad lines of second-generation critical theory. The series sets ambitious theoretical standards, aiming to engage and challenge an interdisciplinary readership of students and scholars across political theory, philosophy, sociology, history, media studies and literary studies.

Previously published by Bloomsbury

Critical theory in the twenty-first century   Darrow Schecter
Critical theory and the critique of political economy   Werner Bonefeld
Critical theory and contemporary Europe   William Outhwaite
Critical theory of legal revolutions   Hauke Brunkhorst
Critical theory of libertarian socialism   Charles Masquelier
Critical theory and film   Fabio Vighi
Critical theory and the digital   David Berry
Critical theory and disability   Teodor Mladenov
Critical theory and the crisis of contemporary capitalism   Heiko Feldner and Fabio Vighi

Forthcoming from Manchester University Press

Critical theory and legal autopoiesis   Gunther Teubner
Critical theory and contemporary technology   Ben Roberts
Critical theory and sociological theory   Darrow Schecter
Critical theory and feelings   Simon Mussell
Critical theory and demagogic populism   Paul K. Jones

Critical theory and epistemology

The politics of modern thought and science

ANASTASIA MARINOPOULOU

Manchester University Press

Copyright © Anastasia Marinopoulou 2017

The right of Anastasia Marinopoulou to be identified as the author of this work has been asserted by her in accordance with the Copyright, Designs and Patents Act 1988.

Published by Manchester University Press
Altrincham Street, Manchester M1 7JA, UK
www.manchesteruniversitypress.co.uk

British Library Cataloguing-in-Publication Data is available

ISBN 978 1 5261 0537 0 *hardback*
ISBN 978 1 5261 3962 7 *paperback*

First published by Manchester University Press in hardback 2017

This edition first published 2019

The publisher has no responsibility for the persistence or accuracy of URLs for any external or third-party internet websites referred to in this book, and does not guarantee that any content on such websites is, or will remain, accurate or appropriate.

Typeset by Out of House Publishing

*To my mother,
Christina Marinopoulou,
who encouraged me towards irreverent dialogue ...*

It is through wonder that men now begin and originally began to philosophize; wondering in the first place at obvious perplexities, and then by gradual progression raising questions about the greater matters too, e.g. about the changes of the moon and of the sun, about the stars and about the origin of the universe.

Aristotle, *Metaphysics* 982b 10–15

Contents

List of figures   viii
List of tables   ix
Acknowledgements   x

Introduction   1

1 Phenomenology and hermeneutics   18

2 Structuralism and poststructuralism   51

3 Modernism and postmodernism   81

4 Systems theory   111

5 Critical realism   139

Conclusions   167

Bibliography   177
Index   185

Figures

2.1 The process of knowledge according to consideration   72
3.1 Foucault and Habermas on modernity   85
3.2 Foucault's structuralist account of power relations   95
4.1 Luhmann and Habermas   133
5.1 The dialectical process in Hegel and Bhaskar   150

Tables

1.1 Basic characteristics of phenomenological and dialectical approaches to knowledge   29
1.2 The concept of truth in Husserl and Heidegger   39

Acknowledgements

A book usually has a very long gestation period, during which the writer realizes that team work is required, rather than solitary research alone, as the writer initially thought. Although the usual suspect for a book's flaws or failings is only the writer, there were some excellent things, too, that took place during a very long route that started long before the signing of any contract.

I owe particular thanks to the series editor, Dr Darrow Schecter. He gave me the opportunity to participate in such an innovative and creative process as the publication of the book series on critical theory. His generous trust towards my work multiplied my sense of responsibility. Marie-Claire Antoinne (thank you so much!) and Michelle Chen were valuable supporters of the present project.

To Professor Dr William Outhwaite, I owe more than words permit me to acknowledge. Everyone who has worked with him is aware that he is one of the most progressive and erudite scholars nowadays. No matter how hard I try, everything I write seems insufficient to compensate for the privilege of being in dialogue with him.

Professor Dr Jürgen Habermas' response to my questions was an immense help, and I owe him grateful thanks. Particular thanks are due to Professor Emeritus Dr Dimitrios Andriopoulos. His advice and academic suggestions have been of great value to me throughout the years. A special note of thanks is owed to Professor Dr Gerasimos Kouzelis for encouraging me to present my research work at the National and Kapodistrian University of Athens.

I am grateful towards Associate Professor Dr Gerassimos Moschonas for all the persistent (and perhaps irritating) questions he answered, and most of all for encouraging uncoerced dialogue, as all inspired scientists know how to allow to 'happen' and promote. I remain indebted to Professor Dr Stefan Müller-Doohm who offered me his generous scientific assistance in multifarious ways, and taught me many invaluable things. Professor Dr Gonda Van Steen encouraged my research in every way she could without ever frowning upon my constant outrageous requests. I am especially grateful to Professor Alexander P. D. Mourelatos for his advice and generosity. I am also grateful to

ACKNOWLEDGEMENTS

Dr David Straw and Dr Simon Mussell because their expertise supported the completion of the book and deeply appreciate the constant help and criticism of Eirini Patsi (congratulations for all your successes!), whose unwavering support and cooperation proved invaluable.

There is always the inner circle.

My mother, Christina Marinopoulou, an outstanding school teacher showed understanding and most of all encouraged my efforts immensely, when for years my permanent answer to her questions and requests was the negation: 'I have work, I have to study'.

Vicky Kontou allowed me to be her lifelong friend and confidant, showed me in many ways what inner strength and determination towards an aim mean, and supported the completion of the present book with her generosity and discretion towards my constant refusals to participate in a cherished friendship for the sake of my work. I am immeasurably grateful for her toleration of all my anxieties.

Dr Eva Klinkisch merits special thanks. Many times she outdid herself with words of encouragement along with deeds of kindness. Friendship and conversations with her on political theory and philosophy have always been very important to me.

I would also like to thank my friends, who happen to be excellent colleagues too, Senior Researcher Dr Alexander Afouxenidis, Associate Professor Dr Manos Spyridakis, Dr Leonidas Vatikiotis and Assistant Professor Dr Akis Leledakis for their guidance and friendship throughout many difficulties I faced.

The present book would not have been an enjoyable process without the previous people and their serious approach to good humour during an era of barbarous economic crisis affecting our lives in Greece. I am grateful towards them for all the profound discussions, honest confessions and, mostly, for all the things we laughed about together so often, and continue to do so.

I mentioned above that the writing of this book has been a very long process. Nevertheless, very few things in life compare to the sheer joy of reading, writing and to the adventure of exploring knowledge regardless of short- or long-term results.

Introduction

Die Aufklärung, die ein radikales Verstehen bewirkt, ist immer politisch.
Jürgen Habermas, *Hermeneutik und Ideologiekritik*[1]

[T]he sciences are too important to be left exclusively to scientists, and indeed they have not been.
Norman Stockman, *Antipositivist Theories of the Sciences*[2]

Is there a winter of epistemological discontent?

Epistemology should be the axe that breaks the ice of a traditionalism that covers and obstructs scientific enlightenment. This is an idea inspired by the work of Franz Kafka.[3] *Critical Theory and Epistemology* is a comparison of the major epistemological concerns in the twentieth century with critical theory of the Frankfurt School. I focus on modern epistemology as a theory of and about science that also addresses the social and political aims of scientific enquiry. I also trace the course of modern epistemology's development which was initiated by Kant. His novel and differentiated understanding of critique is the cornerstone of modern epistemology. He examined how the latter can transubstantiate into dialogue that does not follow the idea of an all-inclusive process that allows affirmations and negations to co-exist. The book also explores the possibility of juxtaposing modern epistemology with critical theory, and offers a critique of the Kantian base of critical theory's epistemology in conjunction with the latter's endeavour to define political potential through the social function of science. Modern science appears to be something more than abstract hypotheses. It also appeals to *what is practical* for the people, and looks to *how* theory can become praxis. As such, it simultaneously touches upon two issues: the first concerns the *content* of science, and the second focuses on the *method* that science adopts.

The core argument is that critical theory bears the potential to redefine itself, as well as modern epistemology, through the Kantian critique of the *a priori*, which critical theory transforms into a concrete argument about dialectics and political epistemology. Kant's concept of the *a priori* signifies a perspective that helped to mark out modern epistemology. For Kant, the *a priori* was the primary conception of scientific critique without necessarily relying on the 'help' of experience. The same concept created an innovative approach that the Frankfurt School incorporated in order to extend the same problematics into the formation of a rational scientific and social reality. Both Kant and the critical theorists defined modern epistemology intrinsically in terms of what is critical, rational and modern. Then, they related their definitions to the social and political function of science. Science is neither apolitical nor asocial. If it claims to be such, then it refuses to take responsibility for its consequences within society. Can you imagine a doctor who refuses to consider the social impact of medicine, or a historian who does not acknowledge the influence of history on the education system?

The critique that the book deploys on the epistemological tendencies of late modernity suggests that the main distinction between Kant and the critical theorists lies in their understanding of rationality. Such a critique can be characterized as the 'battle' of modern epistemology for or against the scientifically, socially and politically rational. Thus, arguments of modern epistemology, as articulated by phenomenology, structuralism, poststructuralism, modernists and postmodernists, systems theory and critical realism, can certainly be considered 'modern' in historical terms, but in essence their concerns are of a pre-modern and pre-scientific nature. The following chapters elucidate this critique.

Critical theory situated science within the quest for social and political rationality. It indicated that science's normativity – which answers the question 'what should science do?' – orients itself in relation to the *a priori* potential of society. The latter for critical theory transforms itself into concrete political vindications for society and science. Critical theory dealt extensively with the potential for political vindications through the *a priori* perspective.

Adorno's *Gesamtgesehen,* that differentiates from any total and, therefore, totalitarian conception of what science is, along with Horkheimer's dialectical approach to science through interdisciplinarity and Habermas' notion of communicative rationality (that emphasizes scientific dialogue) in science, find themselves in marked contrast to the following:

(a) the *a priori* notion of phenomenology that never influences social rationality;
(b) Bourdieu's view of reason and structures as an unexamined relation of science to the world;

(c) Deleuze's lack of potential for new politics;
(d) Foucault's critique of science deprived of any notion of dialectical rationality;
(e) Luhmann's systems theory, where the total eclipse of scientific reason prioritizes action and not the normativity of the sciences; and
(f) Bhaskar's dialectics, which becomes relativistic through polyvalence where 'anything goes' in science and consequently in society and politics, despite its initial political anxieties.

All the latter tendencies find themselves clashing with Kantian and critical theory's epistemology because they distort epistemology and science into something 'asocial' or 'apolitical', where either *a priori* conceptions or action per se are all that matter for science.

Although my critique might appear at first to be based on the rejection of modern trends in epistemology, the comparison between modern epistemology and critical theory I explore is based on the conception that what is modern in the epistemological critique begins mainly with Kant's transcendentalism. Kant's conception of the transcendental never lost its timely character and influence in science, even if scientists and epistemologists recognize but dare not admit that transcendental critique cannot be ignored or marginalized precisely because it generates claims for rationality and commitments to action.

Moreover, this book's arguments focus on the idea of dialectics as both a process and a method. By questioning what *form of process* dialectics is, epistemology realizes that dialectical arguments are formed *a priori* without losing sight of what occurs in social and political reality. For the latter reason, epistemology cannot avoid having a political character; science is socially produced, and carries social and political implications. Dialectics is also *a method* because it derives from the exchange of argumentation between scientific subjects. Since dialectics has social consequences, it needs *accountability criteria* in order to be socially acceptable. Dialectics is accountable to society *because* it brings with it certain political consequences. Along the way, it also renders epistemology a scientific field that discusses the political character of scientific development.

The following chapters explore the concept of dialectics as the negation of the irrational and, furthermore, as the open field of epistemological conflict between rationality and irrationality. Throughout the chapters, my view of what constitutes scientific dialectics is condensed into the following five theses, which are not hierarchically ordered:

1. Dialectics constitutes a process of exchange of arguments, which are potentially oppositional or conflictual in nature.

2. The main point of the dialectical process is the part of negation, namely the function through which dialectics elucidates and enlightens scientific and social rationality. Therefore, dialectics is not a requirement of scientific advancement, but rather a condition of science.
3. Dialectics is a linear process, which does not allow or include anything or any deterministic objective. However, it evolves and innovates, both within itself as well as within science and social rationality.
4. Being in the methodological and processual position to facilitate social and scientific rationality, dialectics contributes both to the formation of a normative theory and to the potential for rational praxis.
5. Social and scientific subjects participate in the dialectical process that occurs in the social lifeworld and the scientific public sphere. Thus, scientific dialectics bears the potential to construct both social critique as well as political innovation.

Hence, I investigate to what extent conceptions of accountability criteria in the sciences, that are prioritized by dialectics in critical theory, are reshaped or ignored by phenomenology (in Husserl) and hermeneutics (in Gadamer), modernism and postmodernism (in Foucault and Lyotard), systems theory (in Luhmann) and critical realism (in Bhaskar), creating an epistemological deficit that lacks consistent arguments with regard to normative theory and rational praxis. On the other hand, critical theory of both the first and second generations appears to formulate a political argument that is committed to rational praxis, transcends both Kant and traditionalism, and creates 'space' in twenty-first-century epistemology, which remains open for renewal, through the political potential of its arguments.

The main aims of twenty-first-century epistemology of critical theory become the following: formulate a theory of normative rationality; reclaim commitments to rational praxis; and educate the sciences to maintain dialectics as their pivotal scope and method of advance. Such epistemological aims would probably also advance epistemology towards realizing its political potential to influence society.

The above-mentioned epistemological trends, which are compared with critical theory, replaced or selectively abstracted essential epistemological points of the social function of scientific dialectics. Therefore, they became traditional, deficient in their epistemological concerns, and dystopian when applied to science or society. The following chapters trace what became particularly problematic in modern epistemology:

- for Husserlian phenomenology, it was the avoidance of any connection with praxis;

INTRODUCTION 5

- in Bourdieu's structuralism, it was the concept of structure per se that indicated determinism;
- in Foucault's modernism or Lyotard's postmodernism, it was the premodern idea of the sciences and the dialectical 'silence' or general distrust of dialectics;
- in Luhmann's systems theory, it was the system as structure that reverted to pre-critical perceptions of the sciences; and
- in Bhaskar's critical realism, it was the lack of consistent critique that resorted to pre-modern conceptions of science.

In the course of my research, I realized that, far from any prejudices or preconceptions, many epistemological theories of modernity that ignored dialectics and its normative character reached scientific, social and political impasses. The following chapters examine such epistemological as well as methodological *culs-de-sac*. When considering the sciences, I always have the impression that they make reference to society and politics. As in the social and political sphere, where consensus of all participants appears important but not a condition *sine qua non*, the same is also valid for the sciences. It is not consensus that necessarily distinguishes a creative scientific process; rather, it is dissensus that sciences have to promote through dialogue.

The main aim of the book is not to trace particular differences in method, methodology and scope among multiple disciplines. It is to explore the evolution of arguments in the major fields of modern epistemology that question what constitutes 'science' and 'the scientific'. It is, by all means, a field of research that involves methods, methodology and consistency in argumentation. However, in my understanding sciences can be realized in themselves, each as a particular type of science, because they all involve the same procedure without which they can no longer be called sciences. That procedure is *dialectics*. Scientific dialogue among disciplines, namely exchange of argumentation, does not indispensably lead to consensus. It safeguards the position of disciplines as scientific and not religious or authoritarian fields. Science takes root when people start asking questions and attempt to find answers by means of dialogue.

Dialogue within and about scientific arguments serves to contradict and expose mythical and dogmatic thinking. It also has the capacity to purge orthodox or absolute convictions of any arbitrary meaning. Modern epistemology examines the diversity among scientific fields and approaches, but it also focuses on a common understanding of dialectics that recognizes the thesis and the antithesis of arguments, which are not necessarily followed by a synthesis of the antithetical parts. I intend to clarify that whenever modern epistemology failed to acknowledge the meaning of dialectics for the sciences, there was always a particular reason and interest behind such a failure that associated science with mythical or dogmatic beliefs.

The fundamental theme on which the book is based is a questioning of the contents, methods, methodology and aims of science in its different disciplines, and in the dialogue developed among epistemological theories. In dealing with modern epistemology, I examine the significance of dialectics not only as a method but also as the content of modern scientific theories. Furthermore, I attempt to answer the following questions: (a) to what extent is scientific enquiry inspired by the political questions of people as individuals and of societies as a whole?; and (b) how does science develop into certain scientific and political concerns?

In such a manner, we come closer to understanding what constitutes the scientific, philosophy, truth, and whether modern epistemology paves the way for a political epistemology in the twenty-first century. Science is not dogma, religion, or politics. Its basic function should be to provide a forum for open and uncoerced dialogue where a point of dispute arises. Science is neither a fixed understanding nor a vague assumption, but a scientific moment occurs when a question or a negation is formulated and asserted. A first approach, therefore, would concentrate on the idea that science incorporates dialectics, and as such is not the resigned apology of scientism (where, for example, science itself is the sole purpose of research), relativism or scepticism (where everything is reduced to mere ambiguity).

Critical theory's epistemological arguments were marshalled in a vehement critique of positivism, which marked its claims as a reaction against rational normativity, or as the new empiricist epistemology safeguarding scientific orthodoxy. By rejecting all subjective understanding according to consciousness and by prioritizing the empirical data (but what sort of empirical data and according to which criteria – the ones of time, space, historicity, or of the human senses?) as objects of knowledge, positivism questions the significance of dialectics for cognitive processes and resorts to causal explanations for its epistemological method and aims. The following sections of this chapter attempt to explore, among other things, the relevant exchange of arguments between critical theorists and positivists.

In an intriguing interview,[4] Horkheimer stated that philosophy can no longer be considered progressive because it is in the service of science; thus distorting the task of philosophy, as well as that of science. The constant problematic, which I examine as either implicit or explicit in epistemology, is whether scientists are falling silent over what takes place in science, or in the political or social sphere. It appears that philosophy has to incorporate the concerns of an epistemology orientated towards the political, the political significance of scientific research and arguments, and transform itself into an epistemology with a political perspective, namely into a political epistemology. Later in the twentieth century, Horkheimer's argument found a similar elaboration in one of Marcuse's statements on science.[5] Marcuse argued that there is certainly a part of philosophy, science and technology that is neutral. Nevertheless, owing to its social position, science takes a firm ideological stand.

Science and philosophy, by questioning what is true and valid, do not merely fill the void left by dogmatism and mythology, which stretches into the realms of society and politics, by creating prejudice and suppression; they set dialectics and dialogue itself at the centre of their process. The negation in dialectics has to be followed by something else, too, and that can be the enlightenment of the negation, not necessarily in the form of a synthesis with the thesis, but by arguments about the potential, the 'other' and the alternative, both in science and society.

The opposite reading of science and philosophy, and, moreover, of the social and the political as separate systems of autonomous being, is a rather pre-modern idea. Because of being pre-modern, it is also pre-scientific and, therefore, scientifically and politically primitive. The ongoing innovations of modernity in science and society laid the foundation not only for an innovative science, but also – and not consequently – for the promise of social progress and development. In order to understand what is modern, we probably have to affiliate it with what is scientific, and to question what is dialectical. If I were to draw a hypothetical line between what is scientific and modern, and separate them from the pre-scientific and pre-modern, that line would be dialectics itself. The following chapters attempt to make the dialectical line, and the criteria it bears, clear and persuasive.

The first generation of critical theorists: Horkheimer, Adorno, Marcuse

The following analysis of the three major thinkers of the Frankfurt School does not intend to draw differences or indicate similarities in their work. It does not even aim at offering a historical exegesis of their influences and legacies. Instead it aims to approach the basic *questions* that the first generation of the Frankfurt School expressed and attempted to answer, particularly in relation to epistemology and the social and political potential of the sciences.

The Frankfurt School's method of exploration (which refers to the first generation) is primarily based on the observation that historical and descriptive accounts might be very important methods of research. However, they still manage to miss the essence of critical theory's arguments, which entail the examination of reason and dialectics with regard to science and epistemology. Dialectics, for the Frankfurt School, was not merely a method of research; it was the subject matter of science transforming itself into interdisciplinarity and consummating dialogue among scientific disciplines. It generated dialogue with social science and posited society as the subject, namely the agent or the acting subject, of science itself.

For Horkheimer, Adorno and Marcuse, there existed a recurrent epistemological concern, namely that science contributed to the freedom of humans from social prejudices and political irrationality during modernity as well as to the formation of rationality for society. Nevertheless, science steadily transmuted rationality into irrational methodology, method, purpose and a ruthless domination of humans over nature that would culminate in the domination of man over man. Thus, the scientific crisis was, for modernity, an unavoidable dead end.

The critical theory of the Frankfurt School challenged instrumentality whereby human beings also become mere instruments along the lines set out by modern science. The methodology of positivism, which the Frankfurt School attacked, focuses on sciences (in the plural) as systems of knowledge that are separate among themselves and in relation to society, thus constructing a false sense of autonomy for scientific work. Within such systems, each science or scientist aims at articulating an inner set of instructions, according to which deductive statements are produced, and through which theory is dissociated from practical rules and praxis itself for the sake of producing immediate scientific results. The problematic concept of 'application' thus arises, leaving the scientists unprepared to criticize the scientific outcome in any alternative way, and unable to decide between the realm of 'pure' theory and 'pure' praxis as if there could ever be any theory without praxis and vice versa.

In order to deal with what constitutes science, epistemologically speaking, critical theory tackles the problem of scientific laws. The answer remains straightforward: whereas natural sciences facilitate the formation of scientific laws, it is rather unfeasible to expect the same degree of certainty in the humanities and social sciences. The sciences and, moreover, epistemology cannot merely be a description, nor can they be a rule, method, or methodology. They have to exert critique and influence on something else. Both are consistent with a definite method, which does not presuppose the socially autonomous formation of scientific theory and praxis, but derives from society itself. If science is disconnected from what takes place within the social realm, then it is also silenced and rendered socially indifferent or even fruitless. For critical theory, science for the sake of science did not seem a very plausible way towards scientific advancement. In fact, the reverse was the

INTRODUCTION

case: science becomes valid for both the scientific and the social realm when it stands critically in relation to what takes place socially and convinces people of its eternal relevance.

Science, for the first generation of the Frankfurt School, encompasses foremost the potential for critical reason, formulated because uncoerced dialogue among the sciences has taken place, thus signifying the dynamics of interdisciplinary dialectics. It is crucial for the Frankfurt School to note that dogmatism, positivism and deterministic laws of understanding the scientific and, successively, the social, create a scientific deficit whereby the sciences are unable to react to social and political crises. Science is by no means an ideological instrument. Furthermore, science is not an instrument. However, unless science deals with and directs its object of research towards the social and political questions set by society itself, and unless it reconsiders which questions (set by whom?) it seeks to address, it *shall* become an instrument in the hands of political ideology.

Although notably involved with articulating a certain thesis on the scientific subject and object, Horkheimer, as well as Adorno and Marcuse, dealt more with eliminating the idea of a singular scientific subject and focused on dealing with three basic queries:

1. What is science?
2. What social and political meaning does science bear?
3. How is science accomplished?

The rest of the book will attempt to answer these questions, not only in line with critical theory's epistemology, but also in comparison with major trends in modern epistemology.

Critical theory placed epistemological questions at the centre of its research concerns, particularly relating them to their impact on politics and society. However, when science sought truth, critical theory did not view it as a panacea, nor was science said to have an exclusive claim on progress and innovation. Science is another way for society to pursue truth, rationality and progress, but it should never serve as a *deus ex machina* in defence of social instrumentality, in order to establish any scientific or political authority by means of scientific works and words. Science, for critical theorists, is rarely neutral or value-free.

For critical theory, even when the objectivistic illusion prevails that everything can be assessed according to measurable facts, the knowing subject always mediates between facts and knowledge. For the epistemology of critical theory, the emphasis is placed on the conscious agent who enlightens facts by means of knowledge. Moreover, 'the empiricist "fetishism of facts" ignored that facts were, after all, products of collectively developed modes of perception; that we only know "mediated" facts; and that (even unconscious) theories and methods are the mediators'.[6] In addition, the knowing subject is not a meritorious individual; it is, rather, the collective subject of a scientific field, or of a whole society searching for truth by means of scientific dialogue that takes place within society, and which is also influenced by it. Disclosing truth, for critical theory of the first generation, is a social accomplishment, achieved intersubjectively through dialectics. Science cannot afford to abandon either the social field, for the sake of some vague notion of scientific autonomy, or the dialectical process for the sake of dogmatism.

From another point of view, for critical theory from the early twentieth century until the early twenty-first, science is not the docile offspring of any political ideology, nor is it the generating factor of ideological constructions or the theologian of a society eager to impose scientific authority. Authoritarianism develops in different forms. For Adorno, Horkheimer and Marcuse, science avoids reproducing authoritarianism by declining the messianic role of social redemption,[7] and by being diametrically opposed to political ideology and invariably in contradiction with the dogmatism of common-sense knowledge. It never loses sight of the concern that part of science's substantive content is to be or to become political, where the rudimentary elements of concepts, methods and methodology are not merely the coincidental products of historical periods.

By denying the objectification of knowledge and science in a form of political ideology that establishes itself as social mythology, the critical theorists formulated an epistemological argument on the human potential for criticism and reason. They suggested that the knowing subject bearing the inherent capacity to apply dialectics in the scientific field innovates in science by extricating its social and political irresponsibility or immaturity. It was a moment of sheer Kantianism for the Frankfurt School because it maintained the *a priori* potential and the aim of overcoming immaturity, as well as a bold statement of surmounting the Kantian *Entwurf* for science by means of the dynamics of dialectics towards rational praxis. In Arato's words:

> Passive (non-interfering) contemplation belongs to a 'naive' stage where humans confront the world as something 'other': they have not recognized their share in its shaping, nor that the terms in which they relate to it are of their own making, nor that they are dealing with a conceptually or materially appropriated (inner or outer) nature whose terms they can change. When the idea of reason was conceived, it was to do more than regulate the relation between means and ends; it was intended to determine the ends.[8]

For critical theory – whether of the first or second generation, and even today – a commitment to think, particularly for knowing and conscious subjects, and to formulate normative theory may potentially result in a commitment to act and generate rational praxis. This aim was bequeathed to the second generation by the first, and it remains Habermas' priority without ever ignoring the Kantian origins of critical theory and the *a priori* properties of all commitments to normativity.

The second generation: Habermas

In his epistemological concerns (if not throughout his work as a whole) Habermas bears essential Kantian influences, which oppose positivism. Although I will analyse Habermas' work in the first chapter of the book, it is worth noting here that Habermas follows Kant's line of thought and successively that of Husserl in their critique of objectivism.

Habermas perceives the synthetic activity of knowledge neither as being purely based on historical processes, nor as being the result of *a priori* capacities of the human consciousness as in phenomenology. However, though critical of Husserl, Habermas attributes to the sciences themselves the responsibility for self-reflection on their transcendental capacities. He raises questions as to the methodology they follow, the sort of logical inquiry they adopt, and the criteria they base their scientific objectives on. Moreover, doing justice to the substance of historical processes, Habermas attempts to innovate on the Kantian epistemological tradition, not by rejecting the meaning of transcendental consciousness for knowledge, but by combining it with the 'objective life-context'.

One of Habermas' most notable arguments concerning the sciences is his view that the scientization of politics and social life in general is the other side of the technological control of the sciences over society. The latter takes place by means of ideologizing science, which is rendered autonomous and thus delegitimized by the public sphere of society. There is the question of how the colonization of the social becomes feasible by the scientific, rendering the social mute and influenced by ideologies, while the scientific is operational.

Habermas perceives the mode of scientific research and analysis as producing not contradiction but the inter-influence of research and analysis. However, precisely because of the mode they opt for, sciences facilitate and promote or discourage dialogue and argumentative exchange. In not being socially isolated by means of dialectics, they become major forces that shape social dialogue and rationality. Where the opposite is the case – and that is the abandonment of dialectics – they predominate by supporting and maintaining the scientization of politics.

In the same way that sciences become the authoritarian force in society by attempting to offer operational approaches to social and political problems, they also become authoritarian for their own field of research. Thus, Habermas associates science with politics by providing a concise guide to instrumental scientific methodology and the social impact of the scientific sphere as well. The scientific method, then, along with the concept of truth are established as criteria for knowledge 'only from the objective life-context in which the process of inquiry fulfils specifiable functions: the settlement of opinions, the elimination of uncertainties, and the acquisition of unproblematic beliefs'.[9]

In *Knowledge and Human Interests*, Habermas' epistemological concerns as a critique of the sciences converge to a certain extent with Schütz's idea (analysed in the first chapter) that knowledge is not a process of 'in order to', but rather 'because'. That means that people are participants within knowledge, not for reasons of success, namely of an 'in order to', but for reasons that relate to happiness and the good life, namely of an understanding that includes 'because'.

In the preface to *Knowledge and Human Interests,* Habermas, in the same manner as Adorno's 'Subject and Object', maintains that 'a radical critique of knowledge is possible only as social theory'.[10] Moreover, it is essential for the clarification of the subject matter of the book, as well as for Habermas' work itself, to note the latter's explanation of what science is, and how sciences can be considered as a unified whole composed of different fields maintaining a certain method of research.

For Habermas, science is neither the grand narrative of philosophy, nor the eccentric attitude towards the 'actual business of research';[11] moreover, it is neither the retreat to a philosophy of science, nor the methodology of the sciences. Science is rational thought, deriving from critical consciousness, and directed towards setting dialogue into use, questioning fields of research and exploring normative concepts and social rationality. Epistemology, on the other hand, being, to an extent, the self-reflection of science, is also governed by dialectical thought, and questions the social function of the scientific and the socially rational.

With his views being based upon the previous arguments of Horkheimer and Adorno on common-sense knowledge, Habermas opposes the dogmatism of common-sense knowledge, which appears as the outcome of ideology, and reconstructs the 'self-formative process of consciousness', as he states in *Knowledge and Human Interests*. The critique of knowledge – an aim shared by the Frankfurt School of all generations – arises when transcendental consciousness meets the socially perceived demands of science, which are then channelled into a dialectical, self-formative process.

Habermas departs from the latter notion of a dialectical self-formative process of science, and introduces the notion of communicative action. He relates and designates not only social relations of uncoerced dialogue, but also public communication of scientific subjects against scientific as well as social ideologies. Science is a process and aim, created by scientific dialectics and self-reflection, not the corroboration and absolute result of a socially autonomous prejudgement where science loses its social legitimacy. Science is not the empirically or methodically obligatory end; rather, it concerns itself with the dialectical means of achieving knowledge.

The problem and criticism of deduction reappears in critical theory with Habermas' work on epistemological interests and methodological critique. Deduction is associated with purposive-rational action, and because of its claim to methodological certainty, anticipated rules and decisions, it entails scientific dogmatism and thus prejudice. In a wider critique of the symbolic processes of inference, namely induction, deduction and abduction, Habermas correlates the threefold schema with the instrumental approaches of pragmatism to describe the learning process by way of cumulative and quantifying criteria.

Knowledge, for Habermas, is distinct neither from life nor social process. It is not a quantifying procedure, nor is it a simplifying practice in gathering and integrating universal assumptions. Knowledge and science are not the instruments of technical control over an object of the social. They bear the potential of intersubjective dialogue, which attempts to bridge the gaps between scientific fields, social forces and research dynamics that endeavour to form social and scientific rationality.

Dialectics and intersubjectivity acquire a concrete form, which combines empirical research with the 'intelligible character of a community that constitutes the world from transcendental perspectives … in a self-formative process until the point in time at which a definitive and complete knowledge of reality is attained'.[12] Where purposive-rational action represents scientific monism and instrumental aims towards technical control of the sciences and society, intersubjectivity represents a potential but not necessary consensus and, most importantly, it represents the idea of a scientific dialogue that science facilitates and elaborates socially. The idea of communicative action in science becomes the first significant step towards the awareness of ignorance and then of self-formation for knowledge and social claims.

Habermas never ignores the concept of interdisciplinarity and intersubjectivity of the first generation of critical theory, and aims at expanding upon its modern understanding by relating it through communicative action, either in the sciences or in society. It was one of the very rare occasions in modern epistemology that the social role of science was manifested in such a direct affiliation with its power over modern politics. Though certainly not for the first time, with Habermas' work one sees how epistemology took a political turn, avoiding the aporetic considerations of the first generation of the Frankfurt School.

Habermas maintained the political position that knowledge acquires through the elaboration of social claims and the legitimacy attributed to it within the lifeworld and the scientific public sphere. Communicative action among the sciences generated within the lifeworld and the dialogical processes in the public sphere of the sciences commit the scientific realm to redefine rational praxis through normative theory.

The lasting impact of critical theory on epistemology

Opposing relativism as reproducing some form of subjectivist characteristics, Horkheimer, in his seminal 'On the Problem of Truth', argues that perception and truth are shaped by individual consciousness that is bound up with a social standpoint. Subject and object are two simultaneous instances of human understanding, which contradict the metaphysical dimension of human knowledge. Although, in the first place, Horkheimer criticizes Kant for attributing to transcendental subjectivity the sole responsibility for knowledge, he remains inclined towards Kant's work, and questions the possibility of embracing both the mechanistic concepts of empiricism along with a theory isolated from practice.

The domination that the sciences exerted over nature produced in turn domination over human beings, and although domination over nature, for Horkheimer, lacked a unified plan, it was still domination that reproduced suppression, passivity in the social realm and metaphysics in the field of knowledge and scientific advance. Most of all, regression in the social and political sphere, because of the domineering character of human knowledge and the turn of the sciences towards metaphysics, '[does] not emerge into clear consciousness and [is] put up with something necessary and eternal, rather than as an object of effective change'.[13]

For the Frankfurt School, science is a process of cognition, which contains integrity in its aim and method, as well as in its methodology. Science aspires to maintain strong bonds with social reality, but it also claims to articulate social criticism and put this into practice. On a second level of understanding, science is the process of dealing with contradictions and elaborating on them by means of dialectics. Dialectics is critical because it involves opposing positions and arguments, and producing a framework for dialogue and for discussing what is scientifically, as well as socially, rational.

First-generation critical theory dealt with the distinction between subject and object, and regarded the subject either as a collective or as an individual actor of science and society. Nevertheless, for Habermas, the object is replaced by another subject, namely the 'co-participant', in a dialogue between scientific fields within the process of communicative action. The first generation of the Frankfurt School largely fought against deduction and, in general, a particularistic understanding of knowledge and its methodology. The main point of focus was the idea that transcendental subjectivity, in Kant's formulation of it, never gave a sufficient explanation of the quandary regarding cognition and knowledge, and the fact that knowledge is drawn towards transcendentalism from both social reality and experience. Habermas attempted to find a resolution to the intricacies of the acquisition of knowledge by means of communicative action, the latter being exercised by the scientific subject that produces scientific thought through dialectics, which aims at realizing emancipatory interests. In marked contrast to the latter, when dialectical communication is muted, scientific and social elites are never far away and knowledge for the degraded 'masses' also results from the silencing of dialogue.

According to the Frankfurt School, controlling science by means of technological rationality meant directing extensive parts of the 'thought' process of a society by eradicating all dialectical approaches to social problems. For Adorno, the totalizing process of extricating dialectical contradictions paved the way for scientific as well as social elites to rule over an undetermined mass by means of so-called common-sense knowledge. The latter replaces dialectical understanding in social, political and scientific cognition.

The main argument of the book concerns the undiminished significance of dialectics not only as a method, but also as a process and mode of understanding for the sciences. It is an inherent characteristic of the sciences to generate and deal with contradictions and hence any epistemological understanding of the scientific includes the scientific dialogue on theses and antitheses, as equally important for the evolution of any scientific argument.

For Marcuse, dialectics is the scientific stance towards what remains contentious for the sciences; or, in other words, no scientific neutrality can be accomplished as long as dialectics itself does not claim neutrality. Science is either dialectical or it is nothing. The moment in which critical theory embodies dialectics is, for Marcuse, the moment of negation of the given thesis and principles. In many references, in his work and interviews, Marcuse recognizes that the scientific constructions of modernity in the twentieth century are deprived of such an embodiment of a dialectical advance and are thus subject to a scientific deficit that is concealed by means of technological progression. The latter holds the position of scientific innovation in terms of operative modes of knowledge use. Scientific dialectics, including both the subject and the object of knowledge simultaneously, is almost extinct, thus changing the character of scientific revolutions. The latter is replaced by technology and the establishment of a technological civilization that stifles the sciences and society alike.

Although, in many critical theorists' work, the scientific thesis represents the first advance of scientific development, namely that there has to be an articulate and coherent position regarding scientific issues, what in essence constructs a moment of scientific reflection is the acceptance of critique and probable negation; this is encompassed either in the negation or the synthesis of the two. Critical theory then brings criticism to bear on the sciences, not from the position of the grand inquisitor, but rather from the point of view that allows for science to take an expressive position and simultaneously include the negation of a thesis and the potential synthesis, serving a self-reflective attitude towards science and its objectives.

Dialectics is a form of scientific entirety, including a certain position, its negation and its alternative. However, the negation is not a reactionary moment within the scientific stance. It is the articulation of a critical argument that opposes a given thesis. For Adorno,[14] critical theory is not a scientific field itself; rather, it constitutes the moment of self-reflexivity for the sciences. It can indicate that science is not a field of totality and homogeneity; on the contrary, it is a site of disagreement, negation and opposition to the given and taken for granted.

In my understanding, science constitutes simultaneously the formation of questions and the potentiality for answers. The culture of scientific discourse that Habermas introduces and analyses throughout his work extends from the notion of a critical theory (as originally understood by Horkheimer) to a critical science. The positivist dispute of the twentieth century, between mainly the positivists and the critical theorists, revealed that positivism was simplistic and, therefore, manipulative of the social role of the sciences.

The first two generations of the Frankfurt School provided concrete retorts to positivism and defended the perception that positivism is rationalistic, by claiming to identify absolute causes and effects, which are neither rational, nor realistic, nor critical. Positivism's causal explanations represent scientific prejudices and superstitious scientism, and definitely not the free exchange of scientific explanations and arguments; instead they entail dogmatic approaches towards contrived scientific problems. In order to formulate a rational scientific answer, science has first to designate a concrete scientific question and a dialectical problematic.

During the late modernity of the twentieth and twenty-first centuries, critical science has maintained that its aim is dialectical, in terms of producing social criticism, whereas epistemology has acquired a political character. A rational reconstruction of the sciences will not become the scientific concern of modernity because philosophy occupies the position of the scientific consciousness for modern science. Rather, a rational progression of the sciences will take place when epistemology becomes political and, therefore, socially influential. The main points raised above will be explored further in the following chapters, with reference to particular epistemological trends of late modernity, with the intention of raising claims that reinforce the potential accountability of science in its relationship with society. Through the formation of a normative theory, the task of political epistemology is to initiate and maintain the promise and potential of conscious subjects towards a rational praxis.

Notes

1. 'The enlightenment which follows from radical understanding is always political.' Jürgen Habermas *et al.* (eds), *Hermeneutik und Ideologiekritik* (Frankfurt am Main: Suhrkamp Verlag, 1971), 158.
2. Norman Stockman, *Antipositivist Theories of the Sciences* (Dordrecht: D. Reidel, 1983), vii.
3. Kafka's original phrase was that 'Ein Buch muss die Axt sein für das gefrorene Meer in uns', meaning that a book must be the axe for the frozen sea within us.
4. Max Horkheimer, 'Die Philosophie I. Kants und die Aufklärung', www.youtube.com/watch?v=KyP6li6AnE0, accessed 29 September 2012.
5. Herbert Marcuse, 'Im Gespräch', www.youtube.com/watch?v=C5PU0EASi_Q, accessed 22 October 2012.
6. Andrew Arato and Eike Gebhardt (eds), *The Essential Frankfurt School Reader* (New York: Continuum, 1998), 6.
7. For Horkheimer the state of knowledge of a society defines what each society considers or recognizes as ideological and, moreover, converts it into a supposedly common sense knowledge, which, because of its ideological character, is dogmatic and unwavering.
8. Arato and Gebhardt (eds), *The Essential Frankfurt School Reader*, 392.
9. Stockman, *Antipositivist Theories of the Sciences*, 67.
10. Jürgen Habermas, *Knowledge and Human Interests* (Boston, MA: Beacon Press, 1971), vii.
11. Habermas, *Knowledge and Human Interests*, 4.
12. Habermas, *Knowledge and Human Interests*, 135.
13. Max Horkheimer, 'On the Problem of Truth', in Arato and Gebhardt (eds), *The Essential Frankfurt School Reader*, 412.
14. Cited in Alex Demirovic, 'Was ist kritische Theorie – Ein Vortrag von Pr Dr Alex Demirovic', www.youtube.com/watch?v=alQpJNxGa90, accessed 17 January 2013.

1

Phenomenology and hermeneutics

Alas, there are no absolute certainties and there are no definitive resolutions of fundamental 'crises'.
> 'Phenomenology and Sociology' by Thomas Luckmann in Maurice Natanson, *Phenomenology and the Social Sciences*, vol. I[1]

The means selected become intermediate goals.
> Mary F. Rogers, *Sociology, Ethnomethodology, and Experience*[2]

Introduction

Phenomenology and hermeneutics: the modern passage to epistemology

It always appears very fruitful, scientifically, to consider arguments in relation, rather than in opposition. Such a view does not necessarily imply that differences should be ignored or eliminated, or that relativism ought to prevail as a sign of good faith within a scientific field of thought. Contrary to relativism, criticism and disagreement are said to promote better research. Unless a continuity of problematics is identified, we would probably be unable to trace related arguments adequately and understand fully their wider implications.

Whereas sciences set their questions in advance, epistemology deals with the questions that need to be answered by both science and society. On a conceptual level, I maintain that sciences question their own relations to society or, to put it more distinctively, they question what is social in their scientific oeuvres. Throughout the chapter, I present the argument that epistemology shapes such questions by way of a reminder of the social impact of the sciences on both their own object and subject of research, namely society itself.

On a methodological level, science never becomes socially obsolete or redundant. We never know which alternatives science can demonstrate when society allows science to flourish without the formation of prevailing theories or authoritarian priorities. If scientific dialogue is to thrive and produce research, then it has to be uncoerced and equal without references to scientific criteria of obviousness or social criteria of common sense. The main tasks of science and epistemology are to identify ideological influences and to articulate critique, in a wide social and scientific context, by means of scientific dialectics.

The aim of this chapter is to trace to what extent dialectics is an epistemological concern in Dilthey, Husserl, Simmel and Weber. I enquire into their conception of dialectics as a method, as well as an epistemological process. Throughout the course of these thinkers' work, it becomes clear that dialectics is not a concrete innovative element for the sciences but a peripheral *method*; dialectics is not the pivotal process that serves as the royal scientific path to normativity for the sciences and society. Such concerns limit science to (a) a deficit in normative theory and rational praxis, and, moreover, (b) a lack of accountability criteria for science. The reductionist function of the sciences thus attained may articulate some theoretical arguments, but it remains at a loss when considering the accountability of praxis.

The line of thought that begins with thinkers such as Dilthey, Husserl, Simmel and Weber, at the end of the nineteenth century and towards the beginning of the twentieth,[3] extends to the ethnomethodology of the mid-twentieth century, and reveals itself as having had a major influence on Gadamer's work on hermeneutics. The following sections of this chapter trace the course of arguments that begin with Dilthey's philosophy of a rigorous science, develop with Husserl's phenomenology, Simmel's and Weber's interest in the scientific element within the social, and conclude with the ethnomethodological concerns on the everyday as a method of scientific advance.

Phenomenology: Husserl, his predecessors and the epigones

The pivotal consideration of the chapter can be mostly inferred from the implications of the German language that were so meticulously presented by Immanuel Kant in his renowned essay on the Enlightenment. The German word 'Mündigkeit', namely responsibility, derives from the word 'Mund', namely mouth. The irresponsible personality can be easily associated with the lack of communication. The absence of either dialectical or dialogical concerns, which to a large extent coincide, signifies the epistemological negligence of the thinkers included in this chapter towards theory and practice and their disregard for normative theory that derives from dialectics.

Dilthey prepared the way for Husserl with a series of arguments, some of which Husserl would agree with, whereas from others he would diverge. Both thinkers attempted to establish philosophy as a rigorous science with a specific methodology, significantly different from that of the natural sciences. Dilthey differentiates philosophy from epistemology, and attempts to designate the particular significance, lucid and dissimilar, of both branches of knowledge. From a study of methodology, Dilthey proceeds to the philosophical contribution of epistemology and the epistemological contribution of philosophy to science. Philosophy and epistemology are pivotal parts of his theoretical concerns, without ever losing their conceptual equality in his work.

Dilthey's notion of scientific understanding (*das Verstehen*) clarifies on an epistemological level the form of scientific interface among different scientific scopes. Nevertheless, the method of *Verstehen* reaches essential levels of profundity when it is linked to societies and sciences, and is based within their interrelation.

The pursuit of knowledge – insofar as the *Geisteswissenschaften* in particular, namely the humanities, are concerned – aims at producing a critique of the sciences, human beings and their interrelation. Dilthey lived in an era during which the popularity of humanities' studies was receding, and the brave new world of technology and industrialization were advancing to the detriment of critical thought, rational argumentation and social dialectics. In this respect, his epistemological concerns can be compared to Kant's attempts to redefine criticism and rationality. Positivism started to take shape, as the safeguard of scientific theory and method. The distinctive character of human studies, for which all the aforementioned philosophers argued fervently, underwent a negative critique; it was seen as superfluous and detrimental to real knowledge (represented by the natural sciences and technology).

For Dilthey, scientific methodology was not the central issue. That was bequeathed to Husserl to elaborate upon. Dilthey's thought creates an argumentative platform on which the structure of the humanities can be based. For all the above-mentioned philosophers, dialectics, as a distinguished method and process of the human sciences, does not appear in the foreground. But, as I shall argue, it was not a fear of dialectics that prevented these thinkers from defending such scientific modus operandi; it was the conviction that there remains much to be done – especially with regard to the understanding of a concrete scientific process on which the humanities can base their existence – before we can proceed to dialectics.

Dilthey's work paves the way for Husserl's phenomenology to the extent that the former makes the important phenomenological distinction between phenomena, namely appearances, and noumena, namely real realities (*reale Realitäten*). Although Husserl later transforms Dilthey's distinction, it is noteworthy to see that phenomena, for Dilthey, are the products of appearance, after the human mind has mediated them, to understand physical objects or the objects of knowledge. Noumena occupy the position of real knowledge, the inherent knowledge that the human mind bears, the motives behind human action, and the meaning that people attribute to human action.

The means by which people understand noumena, and particularly their existence which urges them towards the acquisition of knowledge, is provided by language itself. For Hodges, a meticulous scholar of Dilthey's work, 'The way to self-knowledge would be blocked if it were not for the inherent tendency of experience to find expression … what I think and feel is revealed to me first by what I say or do.'[4] For Dilthey himself, the dialectical process of knowledge, although never mentioned in the same words, takes place in rediscovering something in something else or someone in someone else. Only when knowledge of something or someone is transposed into something else or someone else is the complete process of knowing fulfilled; otherwise it remains elliptical and, therefore, insufficient.[5]

Knowledge is the interactive process between at least two knowing subjects. It is not a steady, unchanged product of intellectual solipsism, nor is it a secluded activity in some unknown realm. Although Dilthey sets the bases for the understanding of the knowing subject, that is induced into intersubjectivity, he never centralizes human knowledge as being formed within social processes of intersubjectivity. He neither claims that knowledge is a product of only knowing individuals, nor does he transpose it within society. His understanding of human knowledge never includes the 'but also' perception that Husserl introduces in an attempt to avoid the *aporetic* theoretical conclusions of the exclusivity of the individual, as a potential knowing subject.

Horkheimer's comment, on Dilthey's avoidance of a socially based understanding of knowledge, demonstrates that it was less Dilthey's ignorance or neglect towards knowledge formation processes, than that 'the professorial disdain for the masses in the Wilhelmine era consisted not in enmity towards the system that produces the masses, but in hatred for the forces that could overcome it'.[6]

Considering knowledge as situated within and arising from socially multifarious processes, Horkheimer sees that the claim that human consciousness attempts solely to create cognitive constructs, and consequently gains knowledge, becomes an idealist and fruitless hypothesis, which contradicts itself. A *Weltanschauung*, that is, a worldview, cannot be perceived unless human consciousness exists *within* and reflects *on* the world. For Horkheimer, intellectual accomplishments are either associated with a certain social theory and political praxis or with fruitless hypotheses of ambiguous scientific, social and political content.

With Weber, writing almost at the same time as Dilthey but still thirty years his junior, the foundation of social theory and the methodology of the social sciences enter a new phase. As a result, their understanding becomes more socially focused. Weber opposed the idea of a subject as socially or even collectively understood. Moreover, he denied the possibility of holistic approaches towards the sciences, where the collective rules the scientific. However, his research into individual consciousness, as a source of knowledge, and into the methodology of the sciences marks a clear epistemological concern that relates to the whole current of epistemology in nineteenth-century German academia.

It is essential, in Weber's case, to trace the development of the epistemological function of the category of concepts, which runs as a parallel, chronological line of thought, with his understanding of society. I mention that it is chronologically parallel because, in his work, the evolution of concepts, as epistemological pivots, meets sociological demands and a better understanding and influence of the sciences upon society. Concepts themselves, either true or false, according to Weber, or particular conceptualizations (such as 'rationalization' or 'disenchantment' or 'iron cage'), are attributed to the effort of the individual to perceive concrete observations, which, in turn, result from human consciousness. In Weber, understanding by means of consciousness finds itself in constant tension with understanding by means of evidence, because the former has to be tested against the latter.

If consciousness is the critical and fundamental aspect of human knowledge, then a question arises as to the extent of evidence's indispensability, in respect of the accomplishment of knowledge, and, to a certain extent, with regard to the attainment of rational certainty. If, for Weber, the aim for sciences remains rationality itself and the maintenance thereof, then the means to accomplish such a rational mode of thinking and acting is attributed to consciousness, and not to evidence or experience of reality.

Weber ascribes the potentiality for meaning to slightly different sources than Dilthey. In Weber, the methodological foundation of meaning lies not only in human consciousness, on a general basis, but also in the intention of specialists to follow the correct or valid meaning, which is incorporated into their subject matter. In order to achieve certainty of knowledge, one has to analyse the intellectual processes taking place within the self. The performance of an action remains in constant tension with the intellectual understanding, whereas consciousness, being distant from reality, becomes the source of clarity and rationality for the intellect realizing knowledge. In Weber's work, it is consciousness, not action, which mediates knowledge. Weber considers action as the consequence of the mediating function of consciousness.

The methodology of Weber concerning the forming processes of human knowledge, and, therefore, of the sciences, evolves in his work as a basis for his argumentation on rationality and rationalization procedures within the social. Weber views knowledge as the indicator of action, and collectively reached knowledge as the way to understand collective action: to the degree that the formation of knowledge can serve as a guiding force to analyse human action, the sciences, as a form of collective knowledge – namely a form of knowledge achieved through and transmitted to collective action – can also be a leading force in understanding collective social action.

Probably the most important contribution that Weber provided is the justification of the social character of the sciences. For Weber, the social character is defined by means of two methodological negations and one affirmation: the social mark of the sciences is as follows:

(a) *not quantitative* – this entails that many sciences do not influence the societal because of their number, which addresses many social fields;
(b) *not solipsistic* – according to Weber, one field of knowledge per se does not influence society, as sciences intervene within society as a whole; and
(c) *conditioned* – this is due to society acting in a meaningful and rational way, in order to realize social values, by means of the sciences.

As with all social actions of conscious subjects, the sciences for Weber function in a rational way not only because they reflect upon their own means and ends, but mostly because they also bear the infinite potential to reveal the *consequences* of their social character, addressing themselves as well as society itself.

The triangle of means, ends and consequences, embracing the sciences in Weber's work, establishes a solid social ontology for the sciences, and attributes to society an instigative role with regard to the scientific oeuvre. For there to be any form of reciprocity between the sciences and society, there has to be (a) a bilateral condition constituting 'the probability that an action corresponding to the meaning will take place',[7] and (b) a consciousness of *we*, namely that 'a possibility exists … that particular men, in the context of a relationship organized in a particular way, will perform certain actions in a way which is specifiable in terms of the *meaning* which on average *they intend*'.[8]

Weber laid the foundations for an understanding of the sciences as an institutional system of thought, and prioritizes philosophy as an administrative construction of thought, within the sciences themselves. The fourth chapter traces Luhmann's scientific and epistemological concerns in the twentieth century that were not so far from Weber's epistemology. In the present chapter, as well as in the fourth one, I argue that an administrative system constitutes a source of functional regulations that guides scientific enterprises, but also works on the level of social administration of scientific production. The sciences comprise a system because they refer to an established set of regulations; therefore, they are also institutionally confirmed 'within a specifiable sphere of application on all activities satisfying certain definite criteria'[9] that are socially produced and consummated.

Weber used the notion of the approach of consciousness to cognition that Dilthey had analysed. However, Weber did not attach his concept of scientific knowledge to any Diltheyan notion. On the contrary, he assigned a far more extended character of knowledge than what Dilthey had designated. Weber's contribution towards the role of the sciences was the realization of the social turn, namely the understanding of the sciences as bearing an inherent purposive rationality, without which they cannot be designated as sciences. Under such an understanding, they cannot be ontologized as subjects of concrete social action that take into consideration means and ends and mainly the consequences of their scientific intentions. Moreover, sciences cannot be substantiated as objects lest they lose their social intentions and dynamics.

Apart from his perceptive social comprehension of the scientific, Weber inaugurates social theory and epistemology by contextualizing both the sciences and politics. It is probably for the first time in the twentieth century that political theory and epistemology converge into an argument that gives shape to political epistemology. In his own words,

> The sciences, *both normative and empirical*, can perform only one invaluable service for the politicians and the opposing parties, and that is to say to them: i) there are such and such conceivable 'ultimate' positions to be taken on this practical problem; ii) such and such are the facts which you must take account of in choosing between these positions.[10]

The tension between the cognitive and the empirical, with both being structural procedures for the production of knowledge, continued in the work of Georg Simmel. The distinction between contents and forms attempted to ease the tension that Kant signified as *a priori* categories of cognition and empirical forms of knowledge.

At some point in his work, particularly with the *Lebensanschauung* in 1918, Simmel provides a total view of contents and experience in a uniform schema called 'world'. Simmel discriminated that worlds of knowledge presuppose the functional existence of the human spirit, which nevertheless create a diversity of an organic whole that includes both the *a priori* as well as the *a posteriori* of cognition. Such an argument is fruitfully elaborated on much later in the twentieth century in Luhmann's understanding of the totality of systems theory (which is analysed in the fourth chapter of this book).

The merging of both forms of cognition allows Simmel to assign to philosophy the role of mediator and of the field that incorporates the totality of knowledge. Philosophy is the bearer of epistemological concerns, which, in Simmel, come to form two main philosophical problematics: (a) the elaboration of basic concepts, which, in turn, comprise the expression of questions; and (b) the generation of possible answers to the previous questions, respectively relating them to verifiable knowledge.

Although Simmel's methodology is to an extent a sturdy and solid expression of his sociological understanding, it also contains a firm centralization of the human factor in order to understand cultural, scientific or, in general, social evolution. Even though Simmel indicated a form of social and scientific dialectics between the individual and the social environment, he adopted a methodological singularity that obstructed the possibility of approaching the question which focused on the process of scientific perception. His methodology reduces itself to the disclosure of cognitive forms that become the mental prerequisite for all knowledge and comprehension of the external, the cognitive 'other'. Nevertheless, the intrinsic meaning that he perceives to exist in every social thing or event is not the outcome of individual, but intersubjective understanding of the examined object of thought.

Interaction among humans or sciences is prioritized on account of its being essential for the sciences in accomplishing a total, a whole and, therefore, a valid understanding of the social environment. Thus, the sciences constitute a systematic formation of what exists socially in multiple relations of inter-influence and reciprocal interaction. Because of the latter synthesis of *all* interactive participants within the social, Simmel applied a productive critique that was based on methodological dialectics. Deriving his problematics from the etymology of dialectics, which presupposes at least two arguing parts, Simmel emphasized that scientific, as well as social, understanding incorporates the coexistence of all opposed views, opinions or positions and not just the conflicting ones. A form of knowledge, for Simmel, is a synthesis or a system of cognitive variations, including many opposed ones, that draw from an initial unity and develop into a unified whole of scientific or social (co) existence.

For Simmel, dialectics is a sort of methodological fragmentation, in the manner of the individual and society. The understanding of forms and contents signifies, in a much more enhanced way than the previous segmentation, how we can render objects of knowledge into a knowable totality, whereby tracing interaction among participants paves the way for the understanding of empirical reality. In the same way that 'society exists, where a number of individuals enter into interaction',[11] science also exists where sciences function intersubjectively and where the interaction of particular constituents of the system takes place.

By evaluating (implicitly) dialectics and (explicitly) scientific intersubjectivity, Simmel assesses the essence of his dual schema of forms and concepts, where both constitute the scientific criteria of the humanities. Since the scientist is participating in the social process among other individuals, the evaluative function in reaching decisions on a social scale is not the sole responsibility of the scientist but of society as a whole. For Simmel, scientific understanding 'involves the opportunity for the sponsors of research to experience that not scholarship but *politics* must take full responsibility for the decision making and cannot pin that on the scholar'.[12]

In other words, Simmel recognizes the schematization of knowledge in relation to questions on the methodology of the sciences and, furthermore, according to social systems that develop in relation to other systems, possibly those of knowledge, politics, religion or culture. Unlike Weber, in Simmel we can trace the first implicit identification and critique of dialectical processes of knowledge formation. The concept of the whole world that comprises a multiple totality, although much dissimilar to Adorno's thought later in the century, namely a social environment that includes the inter-influence of the individual with the social constitution, connotes the institutionalized structures of society. The latter claim the formation of social praxis, which emanates from the realization of forms themselves, as primal appearances of human cognition. A similar argument – explaining that social structures produce praxis – evolves in Bourdieu's structuralism. I analyse this argument in the second chapter of the book.

Quite a long time after Dilthey, Husserl's phenomenology returned to the epistemological foreground the notion of intentionality of consciousness, which, by being aware of noumena, holds a position of phenomenological *epoché* in order to approach knowledge of *something*. Before proceeding into some basic arguments in phenomenological understanding, it is illuminating to trace the conceptual basis of *epoché* in the ancient world. For the ancient Greeks, the noun *epoché* [ἐποχή] derives from the verb *epécho* [ἐπέχω], which implies that the subject holds a firm position neither of participation [*metécho, metoché*] nor of abstinence [*apécho, apoché*] regarding social things. The subject maintains the position and attitude of a critical stance over and above things, which allows human consciousness to express the intentionality of cognition.

Husserl argues that *epoché* constitutes the manifestation of human cognition and that it is only because of consciousness that the individual acquires knowledge of an object. For Husserl conscious intentionality signifies the potential for a rigorous understanding of human knowledge processes and, therefore, of the sciences. In phenomenological terms, the meaning of things, namely the *noema* becomes understandable by means of human *noesis*, defined as human conscious intentionality to comprehend and give noematic, meaningful shape to *eidos*. The latter constitutes the aim of phenomenological *epoché*, which, as a method of phenomenological research, approaches the conscious understanding of eidetic appearances. Phenomenology sought to clarify how we acquire knowledge through cognitive processes that derive from consciousness and intend to render objects of knowledge in the external world understandable and familiar.

The critique of the Frankfurt School, shortly after the articulation of essential phenomenological argumentation, came as a poignant response to the idea of cognitive manifestations of phenomenological intentionality. The Frankfurt School, particularly through Marcuse, expressed a solid epistemological interest that was not reducible to any negative critique, but mainly resorted to reason and dialectics in order to redefine the theory of knowledge. Critical theory acknowledged the privileged position of human consciousness, but related it to reason (notably reformulating the Kantian indispensability of the theory of knowledge). Unless the knowing subject undergoes a process of *methexis* (that is, inter-influence with reality and the dialectics that evolves between knowledge and critical reason within social reality), any cognitive processes remain incapable of perceiving how knowledge appears.

Furthermore, Adorno becomes far more critical than Marcuse and attributes to Husserl the intent to understand knowledge as idealism, withdrawn into a world of absolute ideals that only consciousness can reach. Husserl's idea of science lacks the conjunction with reason and, therefore, becomes uncritical and elitist. Regardless of which stance the modern epistemologist takes, Husserl did, however, attempt to bridge the gap between consciousness and reality. In this sense, Adorno formulated a significant and poignant, if perhaps unfair, critique of Husserl's oeuvre.

The concept of the lifeworld was Husserl's self-reflective understanding of phenomenology. Were his work to become idealist and isolated into a phenomenological approach towards knowledge, it would not have been extensively used and applied by the second generation of the Frankfurt School, namely Habermas. The *aporia* of Husserl's work did not consist, on the theoretical level, of a phenomenological understanding towards knowledge, and, on the practical level, of ignoring the function and the dialecticity of consciousness with and within social reality. Husserl most probably focused on the methodological level of prioritizing *epoché*, and persistently omitted dialectics from the methodological agenda, on account of the fact that *epoché* is a methodological *aporia* itself when compared to the rational, epistemological and social potential of dialectics.

Epoché, for Husserl, is the path of consciousness regarding the approach of the lifeworld. It is mainly a negation of participation within (*metoché*), or of abstinence from (*apoché*) the condition of the lifeworld and of reality itself. Although *epoché* takes place within the lifeworld, it presupposes not an indispensable existence of reality as such, but rather that of human consciousness aiming towards the human world. Therefore, it is the method of phenomenological understanding, but it is also the form of individual existence within actuality in a closed system of human cognition where intersubjective forms of knowledge are rendered an unlikely possibility. It appears that while Husserl eagerly attempted to situate knowledge and its processes within reality itself, on the methodological level he avoided the means to understanding reality: namely dialectics. He replaced dialectics with *epoché* and as a result his attempt remained epistemologically unfinished.

Husserl does not appear to exclude the first two stages of *metoché* and *apoché* in order to reach *epoché*. It seems more probable that, in order to ground the proposed method on a more solid methodological platform, he perceived that the first two stages are significant so as to introduce the lifeworld by its acceptance or denial on the part of the individual. Subsequently, *epoché* appeared in Husserl as the unavoidable route to knowledge, where the lifeworld is a preconception and simultaneously the phenomenological aim of cognition. Nevertheless, in *Cartesian Meditations,* Husserl considers synthesis not as the inner potentiality of dialectics, but rather as the coherent sequence of subjective processes. In other words, any changing modes of consciousness (though it is never fully clarified which ones) that compose a whole structure of noetic and noematic intentionality, are perceived as a synthesis of diverse and transcendental approaches to knowledge.

Although not in contradiction, dialectics presents a more complex advance in methodology as well as the attainment of knowledge. Particularly for the critical theory of the Frankfurt School, which overtly contradicts all the latter approaches of Husserl's phenomenology, dialectics is a three-stage process. The methodological emphasis of dialectics is placed on the second phase of antithesis/negation, and the third stage of synthesis is a potentiality but not an indispensable or absolute end. Dialectics is considered by critical theory to be

Table 1.1 Basic characteristics of phenomenological and dialectical approaches to knowledge

Phenomenological *Epoché*	Dialectics of critical theory
1. *Metoché*: constant participation of the individual within the lifeworld.	(a) Thesis: the position of an argument.
2. *Apoché*: conscious denial on the part of the individual to participate in the lifeworld by means of cognition.	(b) Antithesis: the negation of the initial position by means of exchange of argumentation.
3. *Epoché* – intentionality – synthesis: human consciousness acquires knowledge owing to its intentionality towards reality.	(c) Synthesis: the potentiality of dialectics to reach a new position of a twofold optional character, namely either consensus or agreement through the acceptance of diversity.

a rational epistemological and social concern, for it utilizes its inner dynamic to exert criticism, by means of negation, and to address the social by means of its intersubjective function. It is not an encircled process of self-generation from the thesis to synthesis through antithesis, where everything is socially included and epistemologically permitted, or vice versa. It is a linear process where the crucial moment is the negation and the expression of the antithetical. The element of antithesis potentially entails a synthesis, or rather the opposition between thesis and antithesis is already enough to attain knowledge. Table 1.1 stresses some basic characteristics of both the phenomenological as well as the dialectical approaches to knowledge.

Phenomenology, ethnomethodology and beyond

In condensing Husserl's epistemological arguments, I outline three basic points:

(a) knowledge, for Husserl, is subjective because it is consciousness-centred, which in Husserl's understanding implicates and involves a reflective experience of knowledge;
(b) knowledge is an *a priori* perception of modes of appearance; and
(c) knowledge is *life-worldly*, that is to say, it tends to be articulated within the field of the lifeworld, which is also perceived *a priori*.

The *Encyclopaedia Britannica Article* that Husserl wrote in 1927 gives a concise description of the above-mentioned positions: 'Thus every such pursuit has its "object" [Thema]. But at any given time we can effect a change of focus that shifts our thematic gaze away from the current matters ... and directs our gaze instead towards the manifoldly changing "subjective ways" in which they "appear", the ways they are consciously known.'[13]

The problem that the concept of the lifeworld in Husserl's work attempts to solve is the question of the possibility of a universal understanding of phenomena or, in other words, of modes of appearance of reality in human consciousness. The lifeworld does not merely mean to become the object, as well as the presupposition, of knowledge; it also becomes the intersubjective-interactive moment that allows knowledge to be the common-universal property of many conscious subjects. In the *Encyclopaedia Britannica Article*, Husserl clarifies again that 'Without an original intuitive example there is no original universalizing, no concept-formation ... Such intuition has two levels: self-experience and intersubjective experience.'[14]

In his later work (which the *Encyclopaedia Britannica Article* clearly represents), Husserl occupied his thought with the methodological and epistemological differences between the theoretical sciences and the natural ones. Husserl maintained the following theses:

(a) theoretical sciences maintain a scientific autonomy;
(b) they retain a distinct epistemological character marked by the features of rationality, *a priori* intentional objectivities and eidetic reduction; and
(c) owing to the presence of the previous two qualities, they form a rigorous empirical science 'without which it is not possible to think the I (or the we), consciousness, the objects of consciousness, and hence any psychic life at all along with all the distinctions and essentially possible forms of syntheses that are inseparable from the idea of an individual and communal psychic whole ... [T]he method of phenomenological reduction is connected with the method of psychological inquiry into essence, as eidetic inquiry'.[15]

Husserl moves between two diametrical poles, and although they do not appear notably oppositional, they remain in dispute. On the one hand, he considers intersubjective understanding of conscious individuals to be the indispensable condition of knowledge in order to reach interactive communality. However, he firmly supports the position that transcendental reduction can lead to transcendental experience, which signifies the process of knowledge for conscious intentionality.

When knowledge is attained, then the concrete formation it acquires denotes that science is also a transcendental accomplishment 'because it encompasses within itself all transcendental or rational-theoretical inquiries'.[16] The latter consideration marks the bone of contention between phenomenological epistemology and critical theory. While the former proceeds from a transcendental methodology and subjectivity to a transcendental and *a priori* science, the latter situates knowledge within the social and the political, thus defining science's interdisciplinary and political character.

The pivotal conception of Husserl's phenomenology was the unity in knowledge and the methodology of knowledge, both of which, he claims, form a *mathesis universalis*. The ideas that science and, before this, knowledge are transcendental and *a priori* and that scientific method of every possible subjectivity towards every possible objectivity consists in the capacity of human consciousness to approach a universal ontology are key themes in Husserl's epistemology. For Husserl, transcendentalism and eidetic experience by means of *epoché* become the panacea of cognition. In his words:

> As the work of phenomenology advances systematically from intuitive data to abstract heights, the old traditional ambiguous antitheses of philosophical standpoints get resolved by themselves without the tricks of argumentative dialectics or feeble efforts at compromise – antitheses such as those between rationalism (Platonism) and empiricism … [become] half-truths and inadmissible absolutizations of partial positions that are only relatively and abstractly justified.[17]

The self-contradictory character of the abstract is the first thing that strikes the reader. In the first lines, Husserl refers to 'abstract heights' as attainments of phenomenological *epoché*, whereas, in the last line, he rejects dialectical antitheses as only abstractly justified. He maintains that dialectics is a phase of attempted compromise between hypothetical antitheses before scientific conclusions of truth are reached; although he never appears to clarify how they can be reached by means of a solipsistic eidetic reduction.

The antithesis to phenomenology can be drawn from critical theory's negation of the phenomenological scientific totality and methodology. Phenomenology intends, according to Adorno and Marcuse, to leave both the scientific and the social world unchanged and, therefore, it becomes a pre-scientific mode of thought because of its lack of not only dialectics but mainly of the argumentative character that the latter encapsulates. Critical theory, being opposed to the previous tradition, considers science to have a multifarious scope, bearing a method, which, in its essence, generates, among other things, diversity and dialectics. Although Husserl intended to provide a synthetic totality of the modes of consciousness within the lifeworld, critical theorists prioritize both theory and practice, opposing Husserl's absolute subjectivity that runs the risk of creating an idealized version of thought and thus of cognition. In contrast, theory and practice derive from the argumentative character of intersubjectivity.

Husserl appears to avoid focusing on reason and the attainment of scientific rationality because he avoids tackling dialectics. He reaches the *aporia* of situating reason only within a self-evident self-understanding of eidetic intentionality. By contrast, for critical theory, there is no other way to reach and perceive reason if dialectics is excluded. Subsequently, the aporetic turn of phenomenology appears to exclude truth and validity, which, because of the queries that science articulates, become the aims of scientific work through reason. The phenomenological universe, for the sake of the sciences and the rigour to which they aspire, appears consummated but insufficient for positioning scientific aims within a human universe of diverse approaches, which might potentially reach a human understanding of truth and method for the sciences.

Phenomenology idealized a pre-scientific situation of cognition. Eidetic reduction was not an ideal scientific situation, as Husserl claimed it to be, that excludes dialectics. If science is not socially perceived and theorized, then what does it mean for the scientist to bid farewell to social-scientific theorizing, and what is the social impact of understanding or perceiving knowledge through *epoché*? In other words, the question for *epoché* is not so much *what* it means, but rather for *whom* does it mean something?

Is knowledge a solipsistic invention, or a socially realized process with political implications and impact? And if the first is valid and plausible, how does it communicate with the social in order to become objective, as Schütz attempted to establish later in the twentieth century? Are solipsism and *epoché* forms of epistemological authoritarianism, in terms of knowledge, cognition and method? If they are not, then on what grounds do they eliminate what is understood collectively by means of scientific dialectics? These remain open questions for phenomenology or, for a worst-case scenario, the *aporias* of phenomenology that remain timely and unanswered.

On the other hand, the Frankfurt School positions science amid the social and the political. Critical theory considers that science becomes scientific when it introduces a philosophy of the social and when the political aims of science and epistemology bear the continuous need to disclose the social and political manifestations of the scientific realm. The previous critique of phenomenology does not intend to formulate a negative or dismissive attitude, or even an argument against the phenomenological approach to science and knowledge. It aims at arguing that phenomenological *epoché* can serve as the transitory phase *from* individualistic processes of acquiring knowledge *to* socially and politically grounded cognition by means of dialectics. The latter is not *only* an accidental activity of the transcendental ego; it is *also* an aim potentially accomplished through arguments of an antithetical nature, where the indispensable condition of reaching reason is accomplished because of the negation of the initial thesis and *not* because of '*an all-embracing essentially necessary structural form belonging to all transcendental subjectivity*'.[18]

With Alfred Schütz, the phenomenological perception of knowledge is occupied with the social reality and more precisely with the signification of the common-sense world for the sciences. Alfred Schütz attempted to reconcile Husserl's phenomenological *epoché* of transcendental consciousness with the notion of a common-sense knowledge that derives from the lifeworld and becomes a *sine qua non* for the perception of social reality. Therefore, Schütz acknowledges the common-sense world of daily life as the field of social action.

However, the argument on the metabasis from eidetic reduction which is conditioned *a priori* to a common-sense perception of the everyday world seems incoherent in Schütz's work. Schütz follows the reverse process in comparison to Husserl. In Natanson's analysis, 'common-sense reality is given to us all in historical and cultural forms of universal validity, but the way in which these forms are translated in an individual life depends on the totality of the experience a person builds up in the course of his concrete existence'.[19] According to Schütz, universal validity is presupposed as reaching individual life through a 'stockpiling' of typifications that are endogenous to common-sense life, but the questions remain: how is universal validity possible or 'given' as cited above? Is it only a matter of quantitative 'stockpiling'?

Validity is a qualitative property, whereas stockpiling is a quantitative one, and they do not appear to combine in order to achieve knowledge in Schütz's first volume of the complete works. Schütz positions common-sense knowledge somewhere other than in the common-sense world of intersubjectivity. Again, it seems vague and ambiguous: on the one hand, he turns to individual intentionality in order to define knowledge; whereas, on the other, he considers intersubjective communication as indispensable for the grounding of common-sense knowledge. It is again in phenomenology and its epigones that dialectics *is* implied, described in detail and considered significant for the foundation of knowledge, but is still not named.

On a second level of understanding of the Schützian phenomenology, it appears that common-sense knowledge and dialectics contradict one another. How is it possible to consider the intersubjective function within the social community as the presupposition of the validity of knowledge? How can we regard knowledge produced as a total whole of unified content as becoming a common-sense property for all members of society? Knowledge bears either a dialectical character of intersubjective nature and entails a diversity of opinions, or a transcendental character that originates from the intentionality of individual consciousness. The amalgamation of dialectical and common-sense knowledge does not appear plausible, either in the field of epistemology or in that of society.

Purposive subjectivity preconditions the intentionality of consciousness when people, for example, individually or collectively intend to know meanings, and simultaneously form their mode of cognition. The interpretation of meaning that consciousness reaches is facilitated by means of the method called *Verstehen* through which people acquire meaning and interpret knowledge. It is mainly presented as the form of common-sense knowledge with an epistemological as well as a methodological interest. *Verstehen* is situated within the lifeworld, and is realized as a concrete experience of the individual. Nonetheless, it literally opposes, in the Schützian work, the method of the natural sciences; it covers the deficit of the social science with a methodological suggestion, and differentiates the object as well as the subject of the social sciences from the overwhelming prevalence of the natural sciences over the scientific sphere. In this sense, Schütz reclaims the lost honour of the social sciences, and attempts to render the latter the rigorous objects of cognition and knowledge that Husserl presupposed.

In a challenge to the contradiction between natural and social sciences in Schütz's work, Natanson writes as follows:

> The social scientist ... must face a qualitatively different situation. His objects are not only objects for his observation, they are beings who have their own pre-interpreted world, who do their own observing; they are fellow-men caught up in social reality. These 'objects', then, are second-order constructs, and the method of *Verstehen* is employed in the social sciences in order to come to terms with the full subjective reality of the human beings they seek to comprehend.[20]

Therefore, Schütz reaches a point where he admits in essence the potentialities of his proposed method, as well as its scientific efficiency to grasp the reality of the world. He acknowledges that such a method opens up only to those aspects of the world that we are able to perceive and does not provide a whole picture of the world. It is only a set of rules, which means a set of common-sense rules in science that we adopt in order to interpret facts and come to terms with thinking and scientific ideas. It is precisely because of a whole construction of common-sense rules that people adopt the results that are easy to predict and formulate.

Individual intention, knowledge and action construct a system of rationality that derives from a designated set of common-sense rules and entails a rational choice, where the individual acts according to a plan of *Verstehen* at hand, which 'has nothing to do with introspection'.[21] However, the guarantee of mutuality and commonality of the set of rules is never explained in Schütz's attempt to ground knowledge on conscious intentionality that combine with intersubjective perspectives. Schütz's attempt at the socialization of knowledge becomes a vacillation between two opposing extremes, where the methodology proves limited in interpreting either the accomplishment of knowledge or its socialization.

The latter, much sought-after scientific result of socialization constitutes a *mathesis universalis* and a form of eternal truth, which initiates from contributive intentionalities that still seem unable to give a sufficient explanation of what Schütz considers as scientifically indispensable. Schütz falls short of giving his readers a plausible explanation of how mutual understanding and communication among knowing subjects can be realized. The independence of the spirit and consciousness within transcendental spheres is not rescued by seeking the Other's or Others' intentionality, where language expresses intentionality.

The resort to linguistic intercommunication was an admission that, in order to reach knowledge, the human subject is involved not only in dialogical processes of reaching understanding within the sphere of the lifeworld, but also in the sphere of the scientific concerns for cognition. The anxiety that prevailed in probably all phenomenological analyses in order to ground the social, the intersubjective and, moreover, the socialization of knowledge appears to reveal an avoidance of dialectics as the core point of scientific and epistemological concerns. Nevertheless, phenomenological explanations highlight the potential of dialectics to promote knowledge intersubjectively and communicatively. With the advent of ethnomethodology after Schütz, the focus of phenomenological epistemology is turned towards action. Action is regarded by ethnomethodology as a means of determining the socialization of knowledge and the sciences through mundane or everyday processes of cognition.

Ethnomethodology and particularly its main representative, Simon Garfinkel, attempted to trace, but also to ease, the tension between the subjective world of consciousness, on which perceptions of experiences are imprinted, and the objective world of the social, which the knowing subjects form and participate in. The epistemological trend was the neo-positivistic attack of the unity in scientific method and the isolation of observable social facts, both in social life and the sciences. Towards neo-positivism, ethnomethodology traced the potentiality of socializing knowledge by stressing the significance of social action, as a methodological, as well as interpretive compass for the social sciences.

Garfinkel's ethnomethodology can be identified as a further step in modern epistemology to consolidate knowledge under a twofold schema, which presupposes for the knowing subject the symmetry between

(a) individual reflexivity, and
(b) social accountability.

Unless knowledge is socially questioned, it becomes an empty construction appealing to ambiguous modes of cognitive procedures, an analysis of a hypothetical method, and does not suffice to address the *social accountability* of every human creation. The self-reflexive interpretation of social action becomes, for Garfinkel, the essential framework for interpreting human knowledge, which is the yardstick for understanding social action. Throughout Schütz's work, ethnomethodology, and Garfinkel's writings, it becomes obvious to me that their concern was to place knowledge within reality itself and to test cognition and the realization of knowledge against reality and everyday life, or in other words against the common sense of everyday knowledge.

Garfinkel reverts to the Schützian writings, where everyday knowledge was the criterion of knowledge, in its intersubjective and therefore most fruitful form, where intersubjective knowledge was 'the instance of the same thing'.[22] It is, I think, at this specific point that the problematic argumentation in ethnomethodology becomes lucid because of its particular persistence on sameness, homogenization and the coincidental character that human knowledge acquires and reproduces for the sake of interpreting social action. The fluctuation of Garfinkel's argument from knowledge to society poses the problem of its mediation, which, in turn, implies that the issue of cognitive conflict remains unresolved, and renders the social appeal of knowledge questionable because of the omission of conflict in intersubjective understanding. Garfinkel overlooks the possibility that knowledge might not solely produce consensus among people, societies and knowing subjects in general, but that it might also generate disagreements and conflicts where the so-called and so-considered commonsensical knowledge is not as evident as its commonality would suggest.

Common-sense knowledge for Garfinkel is the easy-to-reach aftermath of a process of intersubjective consensus and sameness of opinions, where the object of cognition is produced and most importantly reproduced, thus becoming a moral activity with a consensual character. Nevertheless, under such an assumption the practice of dissensus within the social remains cognitively unaccepted if it does not cause the disruption of the formation of moral constructions, and the social actions they entail. The main dissonance in ethnomethodology remains the claim that knowledge cannot be otherwise than the acknowledgement of an objective reality that is marked by the coincidence of intersubjective opinions and not by the allowance of disagreement.

Subsequently, when issues of moral acknowledgement arise, there follow political questions and doubts. In Heritage's brilliant analysis, 'Under these circumstances, a contest over experienced reality may emerge which is "political", in the sense that a version of reality is adhered to and used as a basis for further activity, despite the recognition that it is contested and rendered equivocal by the counter-claims of the other'.[23] For ethnomethodology, knowledge is perceived as the area of common-sense competence, which, because of its common-sense character, facilitates the accomplishment of consensual recognition of social actions. The socialization of knowing subjects through the antitheses that they practice by means of dialogue becomes superfluous. For ethnomethodology, normativity through dialogue is considered disposable too. The point probably missed in the concept of common-sense knowledge is the query concerning the feasibility of intersubjective dialogue without the elaboration of either scientific or social controversies considered under a wider spectrum.

If intersubjectivity questions its own effectiveness, how then is it possible without reaching decisions? The criterion of social action becomes the presupposition of reaching decisions that are realized according to discursively produced normative criteria. The lapse in ethnomethodology appears to be the foundation both of normativity and of a discourse ethics that produce decisions and, therefore, social actions. If the knowing subject has to decide about the 'is', that subject has simultaneously decided about the 'ought'; otherwise, he or she can undertake neither decision nor action.

The constant concern in Garfinkel's ethnomethodology is to avoid the usage or application of dialectics in social research, although it is suggested in his intersubjective understanding of cognition. The fact that Garfinkel ignored dialectics reveals not only a methodological avoidance, but also an attempt to overcome both consensus and conflict theories in equal measure.

The stable social world that Garfinkel attempts to theorize is not just methodologically but cognitively restricted between perception and action, and consequently it is reflexively accountable. Although it seems that Garfinkel challenged and rejected the dialectical interpretation, he did not avoid implying that the scientific stability he pursued can be consolidated when we take into consideration the multifaceted approach of dialectics, and not when we designate cognitive processes within a dual schema of scientific determinism in order to justify knowledge. The essential lapse in ethnomethodology was not that it grounded knowledge on a common-sense understanding of social consensus and action, which is reflexively accountable; it was that ethnomethodology ignored the fact that knowledge and dialecticity within intersubjective processes render cognition morally accountable to every knowing subject, whether individual or collective.

From the first pages of *Studies in Ethnomethodology*, Garfinkel appears occupied with the explication of the rational, either in science or in social reality. In his own words:

> As process and attainment the produced rationality of indexical expressions consists of practical tasks subject to every exigency of organizationally situated conduct.
>
> I use the term 'ethnomethodology' to refer to the investigation of the rational properties of indexical expressions and other practical actions as contingent ongoing accomplishments of organized artful practices of everyday life.[24]

Garfinkel apologizes somehow for using the term 'rational', but what most strikes the modern epistemologist is the fact that the rational character of indexical expressions and actions, which he intends to justify, does not derive from organizationally situated processes and understanding. It rather signifies that unless dialectics is used as a means but also as an end to social and scientific theorizing, its absence allows space for instrumental observations. The latter instrumentality renders scientific arguments vulnerable to producing and reproducing a manipulation of social action where, although 'For Kant the moral order "within" was an awesome mystery; for the sociologists the moral order "without" is a technical mystery'.[25]

The question of truth: a hermeneutical understanding?

Phenomenology's hermeneutic turn was inaugurated by Heidegger. Although he remained faithful to the phenomenological tradition, Heidegger distanced his work from Husserlian phenomenology. To be more precise, the hermeneutic turn that Heidegger introduced was an ontological turn of phenomenology, probably against Husserl's epistemological transcendentalism of the eidetic reduction. With Heidegger, truth lies in the ontology of the phenomenological perception and not (as in classic Husserlian phenomenology) in *epoché*.

Later scholars in Husserl's phenomenology, such as Merleau-Ponty, emphasized dialectics, with the intention of restoring its validity in the Husserlian works. Merleau-Ponty based his arguments on Husserl's intention not to analyse but not to reject the potential conjunction of the methodological combination of induction and deduction. In Husserl's words 'every empirical discovery as well as every eidetic discovery made on the one side must correspond to parallel discovery on the other'.[26] In this region of Husserlian thought, Merleau-Ponty identified the potential formation of dialectical interests that would enlarge the phenomenological problematic, which had been to a great degree confined to examining the eidetic intention of consciousness. The potentiality for truth arose as a direct consequence of phenomenological reduction.

While, for Heidegger, scientific truth is not a matter of reflexive processes of consciousness through *epoché* but an intrepid method of understanding the being of things, the bone of contention for both him and Husserl becomes the concept of truth, around which the divergences of their epistemological concerns revolve. The schema in Table 1.2 illuminates their points of dispute.

The attainment of truth is not, as in Husserl, the emergence of transcendental knowledge through eidetic reduction in a world which consists of the totality of objects. For Heidegger, it is the accomplishment of the essence of the pure ego, of the intentionality of pure subjectivity, which endeavours to approach the *Dasein* of things. For both thinkers, philosophy, either rigorous or ontological, is the *a priori* science but both philosophers silenced the issue of dialectics, either as defining the sciences, or as designating the method and the methodology of the sciences. It was not an omission that articulated

Table 1.2 The concept of truth in Husserl and Heidegger

Husserl	Heidegger
1. Phenomenology as **rendering philosophy** a rigorous science, with the **intention** of a **firm epistemological foundation.**	1. Phenomenology through the **being of things.** Philosophy as a **fundamental science.**
2. *Einstellungsänderung* (**change of epistemological attitude**), indispensable for a **theory of knowledge.**	2. **Transcendental subjectivity,** interpreted as subjectivity, and **not as necessarily transcendental.**
3. Eidetic reduction **orientated towards** the **unity of consciousness.**	3. *Verhaltungen* of *Dasein*, namely the **ontology of the subject towards the realization of knowledge.**
4. Meaning **over truth.**	4. Truth **over meaning.**

a concrete negative critique; it was probably the association of dialectics with relativism and, to a greater extent, with scepticism, on account of its inherent process of negation.

Because of their persistence in identifying philosophy as a rigorous science and then, in Heidegger's work, as the ontology of being, there is the constant course of reasoning that considers the thesis and the antithesis as a schema that is only successful for its own abolition (*Aufhebung*). The reasoning of a rigorous science has to be concrete, bold, and must avoid the potential maze of a dialectical discussion. It is not only dialectics that has to be avoided; it is the process of discussion as a whole that should be averted by means of either eidetic reduction, in Husserl, or the ontology of being, in Heidegger. Both thinkers converge in the view that it is rigour and boldness that lead to scientific truth, while, on the contrary, argumentative exchange incorporates both the thesis and the negation of the presupposed affirmation of an argument. Dialectics is epistemologically fruitless because it is contradictory; it annuls its own object of cognition and, therefore, for both Husserl and Heidegger, it is initially challenged and subsequently rejected for its inability to articulate rigorous and doubtless arguments, and reinforce philosophy itself as a rigorous science.

On a further level of methodological understanding, there is also the slight but not unimportant differentiation of Heidegger's work that stresses the ontology of being beyond the intentionality of consciousness. For Husserl, intentionality revealed a level of intention where consciousness intends to approach the object of knowledge because of the sheer interest of the knowing subject. Conscious intention is directly interrelated with and mediated by the interests of the knowing subject for the objects of knowledge. The latter Husserlian understanding of cognitive processes reveals, for Heidegger, a crack in the construction of philosophical knowledge.

Such a crack allows dialectics to intervene and, therefore, a formalistic argumentation to develop ('formalistic' in the sense that it is governed by a dual schema and not by the untainted knowledge of the essence of the being, namely the *Dasein*). Moreover, for Heidegger, dialectics is reduced to mere scepticism due to its negation which yields no tangible results for the sciences. The intentionality of the related interest permits conceptual doubt and cognitive hesitation to maintain a dialectical approach, where the latter is insufficient, if not inadequate, to approach the ontology of the *Dasein*.

The Husserlian intention to situate knowledge within the lifeworld and, moreover, to encourage the *elenchus* of knowledge through intersubjectivity is eliminated in Heidegger's work. Whereas phenomenology brought with it an aura of scientific dialogue to lay the foundations for a rigorous science, Heidegger inaugurated the interpretation of meaning of the essence of things according to a sheer line of thought.

The scientific world of Heidegger is one of cognitive and methodological totality. It consists of the sciences seeking truth, and philosophy is consolidated as the fundamental scientific domain of and for all sciences that indicates the ontological approach of the essence of things to other scientific fields. Dialectics is too diverse to be included in the scientific universe of Heidegger's argumentation; it is judged more as a political construction of ambiguous and, therefore, unstable intentions, and is seen to have an ideological character that is not allowed within the sciences.[27]

The crucial thing with Heidegger's epistemological interests is not that he rejects dialectics, and constructs a rigid sphere of epistemological and methodological ontology of being. It is mainly that he renounces and excludes anything dissimilar to his interests with the accusation of its being political and therefore ideological in nature. Although blaming dialectics for following the course of generalization and the formalism of duality and scepticism, it appears that the totality of Heidegger's ontology follows, in itself, the formalizations of absolutism and methodological exclusion. Heidegger himself very rarely, if at all, utilized the term 'phenomenology'. For him, it bore the implication that it was a hypothesis on the essence of the things and, simultaneously, was of a methodological character, because it intended to reveal the intentionality of the *a priori,* where the latter functioned as the conceptual axis of phenomenological analysis.

In Heidegger's work, there is hardly any concern for theory. Theory involves praxis, too, and that reveals their dialectical interrelation, which is considered outdated in Heidegger's epistemological construction. For Heidegger, dialectics is out of the question, epistemologically speaking, and the same is valid for theory too. The quest for truth, which is attained when seeking to identify the thing in itself, is the sole epistemological concern, which is at the same time restricted by his ontology. Truth lies in *Dasein*. For the Heideggerian analysis, truth does not hide in the intentionality of the *a priori*.

For Heideggerian epistemology, truth lies in the interpretation of the meaning of the absolute being, not in the phenomenological intentionality of the consciousness through *epoché*. With Heidegger, epistemology transfers from a phenomenological understanding to an ontological concern of the *Dasein* in order to formulate true and valid statements. However, it appears that both the intentionality of consciousness as well as the *a priori* cognitive process can be, to a great extent, more diverse and, therefore, more prolific in our understanding of knowledge than the perception of the thing in itself (*Ding an sich*).

Although it seemed, according to Heidegger, that dialectics is marked by a dual formalism effortlessly surpassed by his ontology, his rigid and impenetrable epistemological totality of the absolute being was destined to follow a circularity of repetitive perceptions. Dialectics appeared unstable but still prolific and open to a self-reflexive mode of cognitive perception, whereas the ontology of the absolute being appeared as an epistemological statement devoid of pluralistic creativity and the interpretative mode of thought of the essence of things. Heidegger's ontology did not create any concrete epistemological questions and, hence, was unlikely to produce answers that were open to the creativity of scientific discussions. According to Heidegger, philosophy is the venture that starts from existence and reaches essence.

Nevertheless, I understand philosophy as bearing the potential to be much more than what the Heideggerian explanation attributes to philosophical work, which Heidegger presents as significant but nevertheless insufficient. From the opposite point of view, there is the sudden realization that philosophy, apart from identifying the essence of things, can be or become the missing link between the knowing subject and the object of knowledge. Philosophy can become the mediator of knowledge that takes a particular form and formulation, when it turns into the simultaneous comprehension of the object of knowledge by at least two subjects willing to co-comprehend.

Luckmann has provided a convincing approach to the epistemological concerns of phenomenology and its unfolding into hermeneutics by arguing that the aim of science is the search for a *mathesis universalis*, and that abandoning this aim hastened the crisis of modern science. In his words,

> One side stopped looking because it thought it had found it already, and was content to let the concrete problems and the recalcitrant 'facts' ... look for themselves. The other side never started looking because it was convinced there was nothing to find ... The crisis is not to be confused with the 'reactionary' and 'revolutionary' attacks on the limited but, within this limitation, necessary and legitimate autonomy of science.[28]

In this sense, cognition and especially comprehension are developing into a coexistence within knowledge, and comprise not a consensual or tautological view but rather the willingness to understand through the other, where the latter is either an individual or a scientific field. The *other* represents the opposition as well and becomes the potential to render science accountable to society for the moment of negation it provides. Through the acknowledgement of every *other* that becomes oppositional to our stable and dogmatic acceptances, science renews itself and, consequently, society.

Philosophy and in general every form of scientific knowledge appear to evolve and expand their limits of definability in our interest in everything *other* or, moreover, *opposing other*, which can also be sharable and jointly elaborated. For Thomas Luckmann, 'In an age when science – which, after all, is a human activity – is either deified or satanized, it is also an eminent political question.'[29] The important contribution of Luckmann's phenomenological approach to the science is not the claim that science is political, but rather that science raises a question that can only be answered plausibly or convincingly by means of the political.

In hermeneutics, Gadamer tried to save and redefine the aforementioned dialogical tradition. His work is situated in a continuum with Heidegger's, but remains nevertheless equally distant from the Heideggerian hermeneutics. What marks out Gadamer's work is, first and foremost, his philosophical hermeneutics comprising, first, the understanding of political issues, and second, the prioritization of dialogue in his theoretical as well as methodological thinking. For Gadamer, if the sciences are to achieve any understanding, then this would not arise out of some method or dictum, but rather from within the dialogical understanding that sciences promote and produce in order to direct their aims towards practical and, most of all, political concerns.

In order for the sciences to reach a meaningful whole of anticipatory structures of understanding, Gadamer indicates the importance of asking questions. In order to reach answers, sciences have to locate their problematics within fore-structures of subjective understanding of the objects of knowledge that give expression to questions over the latter and produce hermeneutical answers of a dialogical character. While owing much to the Platonic and the Aristotelian tradition of preconceived notions that the subject tends to approach cognitively, Gadamer defines dialogue as a process between the cognitive subject and the object of knowledge.

Once again, dialectics is regarded (implicitly or explicitly) as a cognitively rewarding process, which is nevertheless limited through the negation that the intersubjective dialogue inherently bears. Philosophy is rendered the object of hermeneutic consciousness that attempts to achieve dialogue with the philosophical object and to perceive a meaningful understanding. In such a process, the object of philosophical knowledge, constituting a cognitive horizon in itself, calls for the merging of horizons of other knowing subjects that can thus attain the expression of a hermeneutical understanding as a whole.

For Gadamer, the reaching of truth, through the merging of philosophical horizons, is not a method, tactic or technique; it is an ongoing procedure of the sciences. Truth, in Gadamer, is a potentiality, accomplished through hermeneutical understanding with no deterministic end. The dualistic and therefore methodological distinction between the *Geisteswissenschaften* and the *Naturwissenschaften* is not only a reductionist approach; it is also a scientifically fruitless position that limits the horizon of the sciences to non-understanding.

To the extent that sciences designate their aims according to a hermeneutical understanding that formulates scientific theory, they also turn their problematics to the application of the theoretical framework previously established. The gap between philosophy and politics is, for Gadamer, merged into the scientific whole of theory and practice. At this point, two major disputes with Habermas' critical hermeneutics have already occurred: first, that hermeneutical dialogue is an intersubjective process bearing the potential for meaningful understanding; therefore, Habermas stresses the importance of communicative action among knowing subjects. Second, apart from the conjunction of theory with practice, and of philosophy with politics, which appear cognitively plausible schemata, what designates practical knowledge is also the grounding of both dualities on the basis of reason as the latter facilitates communicative action and critical understanding.

Habermas did not only innovate critical theory with the conceptual input of communicative action for the sciences and society. His innovative contribution not only attributed to critical theory a hermeneutical turn (among many significant innovations he elaborated), but also redefined hermeneutics as a critical capacity, which can show that the sciences and society are neither self-evident nor reciprocal. He distanced dialectics from the thesis–antithesis representation, which in all likelihood had reached its limit with Adorno's negative dialectics, and drew the outline of dialectics according to its *dia-lectic* dynamic, that is to say, according to the prospect of intersubjectivity.

In ancient Greek, the dialectic meant the speech among many where the preposition *dia-* implicated the *inter-* process. Habermas abandoned the indication of the German tradition, which considers the dialectic as comprising the thesis and the *anti*thesis (which in its turn indicates the *wider-* in the German language; e.g. *Widerstand* is the exact translation of antithesis, namely the part that stands opposite). Habermas' critical theory focuses on the connotation of the intersubjective that dialectics bears and of the communicative dialogue of all participants within the scientific or the social sphere.

Habermas' linguistic turn towards communicative action owes much to Gadamer's linguistic understanding of hermeneutics, where both understanding and hermeneutics are defined as 'dialogical' processes. Although incorporating many Heideggerian concerns in relation to the interpretation of the being, Gadamer defines hermeneutics not as the ontology of being, but as the attempt to initiate dialogue, namely to consider language as the primary reaction of knowing subjects. Gadamer reframes the closed and circular system of Heideggerian ontology as a fusion of horizons that leaves behind the subject–object understanding of knowledge and instead situates knowledge in relation to human reaction with words. Gadamer's cognitive world is a linguistic world, a world with words that facilitate the intersubjective understanding of a certain object.

The linguistic turn in Gadamer has two main points. First, it signifies language as the source of truth – whether scientific, cultural or social. Second, it denotes language as the source of scientific method. In terms of the sciences, language is both the bearer of truth as well as the bearer of method, namely the method of intersubjective understanding through language. For Gadamer, the language sphere is a form of scientific and social belongingness, where truth, method and intersubjective relations are merged into a horizon of hermeneutic truth.

So far so good, if Gadamer himself had not doubted his own argumentation on hermeneutics by attempting to provide more precise means for attaining scientific knowledge. Hermeneutics is a process that includes the linguistic turn, but the latter appeared insufficient in terms of accuracy, particularly when compared to the potential of dialectics, where the essence and aims appeared more lucid. Therefore, Gadamer employed a precise explanation of dialogical processes taking place within the scientific. He argued for the importance of realizing particular questions in order to attempt to formulate specific answers. In an analysis of hermeneutics, Bleicher writes:

> Science follows the laws of its subject-matter and can only be judged in relation to that. When it transgresses its legitimate sphere of activity – that of objectifiable objects – and when it usurps the role of purveyor of all truth, hermeneutic consciousness will assert the legitimacy of a discipline of questioning and inquiry in which the methods of science cannot take hold; and it will re-affirm the fact that method cannot guarantee truth, but only secure degrees of certainty about controllable processes.[30]

Gadamer elaborates on dialogue, not dialectics. Taking into consideration all epistemological tendencies in this chapter, it is essential to note that although the grounding of philosophical and epistemological concerns is orientated towards the lifeworld or the intersubjective, dialectics is the unspoken word and undervalued epistemological approach. It appears that, for some reason, the *avoidance of dialectics* was a common thread connecting the thinkers discussed above.

For Husserl's phenomenology and Heidegger's ontology, the plurality of dialogue appears indispensable for epistemology, but the antithetical schema of dialectics probably entails epistemological and particular methodological misunderstandings. Husserl and Heidegger, and to a lesser extent Gadamer also, considered dialectics as an epistemological method that necessitates or incorporates the mistaken, the error. If thesis is to be contradicted by an antithesis, it is manifestly inferred, then, that one of them is wrong and unstable in its reasoning. What all three thinkers sought after was the methodological and systematic rigour and conceptual stability or certainty of a theory for the sciences.

Nonetheless, for critical theory, dialectics appears to evade the risk of comprising or even generating the erroneous. The epistemological, social or political consideration of dialectics is not a mere identification of opposing sides. Such a mode of thought neglects the pivotal deliberation of dialectics, namely the intention to proceed and advance reason. When the discourse on the epistemological fruitfulness of dialectics focuses on the question 'How can philosophy or epistemology obliterate the possibility that some part of dialectics can be compatible with the untrue?', the central focus of the answer should probably be the shift towards reason and the perspective of rationality.

The idea that reason is the consequence of social dialectics bringing opposing parts into dialogue, and that reason promotes social rationality in the spheres of science, culture or politics, prioritizes the indispensability of reason for the formulation of epistemological critique in the scientific sphere. It brings social rationality to a position where it can influence or designate the social function of the sciences, by means of social and political dialectics. Dialectics is not a frugal means of advancing science; rather, it is the potential to ground science in reason and on social rationality, which appear crucial and a condition *sine qua non* for innovation in science and simultaneously the social condition of the scientific.

Conclusions

If communication is the issue dealt with not only by the sciences, but also by theorizing the *Lebenswelt,* then how can modern epistemology ignore both dialectics and dialogue? If *mathesis universalis* is not the intention of reason to reveal all sides (not just the antithetical ones) of the intersubjective intentionality within the sciences as well as within the social, then what task must reason and rationality fulfil? A reciprocal process between reason and science can be a valid issue to be epistemologically examined. The plausible way to approach such an issue appears to be the examination of social and scientific dialectics in mutuality.

Communicative mutuality, cannot be perceived unless rational criteria are also defined socially and politically in their concrete application. Science is neither a mere hypothesis nor an abstract creation of the mind tested within the social. It is, to a great extent, a social and political decision over certain issues that become the object of systematic examination and elaboration. The scientific truth that can become the *telos* of science can be formed not only under *a priori* cognitive conditions, but also in conjunction with social and political normativity formulated and theorized by the rationality of dialectics.

In Habermas' fifth thesis on knowledge and human interests, 'the unity of knowledge and interest proves itself in a dialectic that takes the historical traces of suppressed dialogue and reconstructs what has been suppressed'.[31] The process of knowledge is sustained by the process of doubt, which produces questions about human interests, which can only generate dialogue in its uncoerced form of dialectics. Phenomenology, or the ontology of being, considers that 'every object in the world, whether natural or social, and every item of knowledge [is] viewed only as a correlate of a particular experience of an individual, [thus] reflecting [a] person'.[32] The realm of pure individual reflection paves the way for the positivistic modus operandi of trial and error that becomes stifling for the sciences and fruitless for the mediation of social interests within the scientific sphere. How can we measure or assess error in science and particularly in the social sciences? What criteria should be used? Far from relativism, societies are not so easily measured, and assessment of results should probably follow rational criteria that appeal to human interests and the realization of more humanistic and progressive societies that prosper because of dialogical procedures.

The crises of the sciences that were expounded and criticized by all tendencies in phenomenology revealed 'an intellectual myopia which, while insisting on the complete purity of scientific enterprise ... [render] both the scientist's inventiveness and ... social and political purposes served by this work ... outside the range of his professional concern'.[33] If phenomenology stresses the importance of discourse for the understanding of a theory of knowledge, then it has also to ask questions and attempt to give an answer to 'discourse by whom?' and 'appealing to whom?'

The cunning of dialectics is revealed when the focus of cognitive attention is shifted from 'knowing that' to 'knowing how and by whom? Or with whom?' Even if knowing is a personal commitment of the individual, understanding knowledge also involves appealing to the 'others', while mediating and applying knowledge to the social involves realizing it through discourse and through a constructive exchange of arguments. The latter mediation of knowledge, within the social, appropriates the potentiality of knowledge and science to recognize social dynamics. In this sense epistemology reveals and consolidates its character of political understanding of society through science.

The intersubjective understanding of knowledge is the common property of many individuals or scientific subjects in general, not just the outcome of opposing or rival attitudes potentially reaching consensus. Therefore, intersubjectivity for science is rooted in social practice that engenders political epistemology. The avoidance of scientific crises incorporates both the acceptance of an *ongoing* process towards dialectical critique and towards a political understanding of science. The latter appears to become the object of research for political epistemology, namely to formulate arguments on the socialization of the sciences and on their political communication with the social. Political communication of the sciences would replace the mythical and the authoritarian, either in the multiple spheres of the scientific, or in social theorizing and action.

The negative element in the dialectical process within the sciences involves not necessarily a step of further 'learning' or 'knowing' but mostly the progression towards 'unlearning' of the alienating turn of phenomenology from the social and the political. The unlearning process that dialectics maintains indicates knowledge as a form of truth that bears the inner potential of leading the knowing subject towards decisions within the social. Both knowing and 'unknowing' steps do not consider knowledge as a neutral object of thought and cognition, but rather as a sphere that involves decisions and, therefore, politics as well. If philosophy is focusing on criticizing the scientific, then it is defined (among other things too) as a political epistemology because it includes a critique of the sciences under a political prism of understanding.

It is through the loss of such a social and political orientation that science is plunged into crisis. What provides science with coherence and continuity is its communication with the social sphere by means of dialectics. Dialectics is not only a scientific trait, but also the communicative mediator between society and science that allows the expression of rational negation, and allows successively for a synthesis of the ideas or for a transcendence of the existing theses and antitheses.

With such an understanding, knowledge and transcendental subjectivity are not the prerequisites of cognition and scientific productivity. Knowledge realizes the potential alternatives to an individual intentionality that is ameliorated by the communicative rationality of dialogical procedures. To the extent that the scientist participates in a communicative scientific rationality, she avoids falling into scientific silence and social irresponsibility.

Notes

1. Maurice Natanson (ed.), *Phenomenology and the Social Sciences*, vol. I (Evanston, IL: Northwestern University Press, 1973), 182.
2. Mary F. Rogers, *Sociology, Ethnomethodology, and Experience* (Cambridge: Cambridge University Press, 1983), 153.
3. It might be worth noting their respective lifespans: W. Dilthey (1833–1911), E. Husserl (1859–1938), M. Weber (1864–1920) and G. Simmel (1858–1918). Historical data do not illuminate a scientific period to the full, but can provide some very interesting indications as to the scientific tendencies in epistemology of the previous two centuries.
4. H. A. Hodges, *Wilhelm Dilthey: An Introduction* (London: Kegan Paul, 1944), 14.
5. In Dilthey's own words, 'das Verstehen ist ein Wiederfindung des Ich im Du', Hodges, *Wilhelm Dilthey*, 15.
6. Max Horkheimer, *Between Philosophy and Social Science* (Cambridge, MA: The MIT Press, 1995), 304.
7. W. R. Runciman (ed.), *Max Weber, Selections in Translation* (Cambridge: Cambridge University Press, 1993), 31.
8. Runciman, *Max Weber*, 31, my emphasis.
9. Runciman, *Max Weber*, 37.
10. Runciman, *Max Weber*, 77.
11. Georg Simmel, *On Individuality and Social Forms* (Chicago, IL: The University of Chicago Press, 1971), 23.
12. Horst-Jürgen Helle, *Georg Simmel: Introduction to his Theory and Method* (Munich: Oldenbourg Wissenschaftsverlag, 2001), 6, my emphasis.
13. Edmund Husserl, 'Phenomenology', *The Encyclopaedia Britannica Article*, Draft A, 1–2, accessed 13 September 2012.
14. Husserl, 'Phenomenology', 7.
15. Husserl, 'Phenomenology', 11.
16. Husserl, 'Phenomenology', 18.
17. Husserl, 'Phenomenology', 22.
18. Edmund Husserl, *Cartesian Meditations* (The Hague: Martinus Nijhoff, 1988), 57.
19. Alfred Schütz, *Collected Papers*, I (The Hague: Martinus Nijhoff, 1962), xxviii.
20. Schütz, *Collected Papers*, xxxvi.
21. Schütz, *Collected Papers*, 56.
22. John Heritage, *Garfinkel and Ethnomethodology* (Cambridge: Polity Press, 2010), 212.
23. Heritage, *Garfinkel*, 218.
24. Harold Garfinkel, *Studies in Ethnomethodology* (Cambridge: Polity Press, 2011), 11.
25. Garfinkel, *Studies*, 35.
26. Cited in Maurice Merleau-Ponty, 'Phenomenology and Anthropology', in Natanson (ed.), *Phenomenology and the Social Sciences*, vol. I, 81. In my opinion, it is not unimportant to note that the particular citation belongs to one of the latest Husserlian texts in which Husserl attempted the dialectical as well as the social turn by centralizing the concept of the lifeworld. For the student of Husserlian phenomenology, such a turn might appear as a form of epistemological apology for earlier *aporias*.
27. It is certainly not by mere coincidence that Heidegger's political stance in the 1930s and 1940s followed the same line of thought, namely of a rigorous and puritan, if not reactionary, understanding that supported, within and outside academia, the

Nazi regime. In this regard, Darrow Schecter's book *The Critique of Instrumental Reason from Weber to Habermas* and research on Heideggerian philosophy proved to be very helpful to me.
28 Thomas Luckman, 'Phenomenology and Sociology', in Natanson (ed.), *Phenomenology and the Social Sciences*, vol. I, 161.
29 Luckmann, 'Phenomenology', 150.
30 Josef Bleicher, *Contemporary Hermeneutics* (London: Routledge, 1980), 120.
31 Jürgen Habermas, *Knowledge and Human Interests* (Boston, MA: Beacon Press, 1971), 315.
32 Marvin Farber, *The Aims of Phenomenology* (New York: Harper Torchbooks, 1966), 67.
33 Fred R. Dallmayr, 'Phenomenology and Social Science', in David Carr and Edward S. Casey (eds), *Explorations in Phenomenology* (The Hague: Martinus Nijhoff, 1973), 166.

2

Structuralism and poststructuralism

One of the pulsions that led me to launch this study is the naively ethical feeling that we cannot let state technocrats continue like that, in a state of total civic irresponsibility, and that it would be intolerable and unconscionable for social scientists *not* to intervene, with all due awareness of the limitations of their discipline.

If, as Bachelard says, 'every chemist must fight the alchemist within', every sociologist must fight the social prophet within that his public asks him to incarnate.

Pierre Bourdieu and Loïc J. D. Wacquant, *An Invitation to Reflexive Sociology*[1]

Introduction

Structuralism and poststructuralism: The understanding of science that dares not speak its name

In structuralism, the fear of dialogue prevails. The dialogical thesis and its negation are deemed to be limited, partial and therefore misleading. For structuralists and poststructuralists, the study of social and scientific structures can offer much more than what dialectics can reveal. This chapter focuses mostly on the epistemological thought of Pierre Bourdieu and Gilles Deleuze in terms of their persistence in constructing an epistemological understanding of social practice that is free from the burdens of dialectics, reason and rationality.

The main bone of contention for structuralism, and soon afterwards, if not concurrently, for poststructuralism, remains the understanding of theory *as* the bearer of practice *or* the prioritization of practice *instead of* theory.

In this chapter, I argue that no matter how hard the structuralists and poststructuralists try to avoid dealing with scientific dialectics, or as much as they merely reject it, their thinking still remains within the confines of dialectics. This is especially the case with regard to theory and practice, or the potential of the sciences to realize truth and adopt a certain methodology that relates scientific work to truth. Both tendencies, though differentiated, find themselves trying to prove the following:

(a) that dialectics is obsolete and methodologically fruitless; and
(b) that the core scientific and social concern, as the path to truth, shifts its focus from the individual to the collective, and this time dares speak its name in order to reveal itself, and is called 'structure'.

Simultaneously, structure represents practice and thus leads us towards understanding the social in real, practical and not theoretical terms. If truth is revealed through social practice, then theory is associated with dialectics. For structuralists and poststructuralists, dialectics seems inadequate and incapable of representing the complexities of social and scientific practice through a bipolar thesis–antithesis schema.

Following parallel lines of evolution, structuralism and poststructuralism relate to a phenomenological perspective on the sciences that intends to reveal a more rigorous science, which is achieved either *a priori*, as in Husserl, or *a posteriori*, as in ethnomethodology. Furthermore, structuralism emphasizes the relations of structural elements within a systemic formation, be that of a social, political or scientific nature. Such systemic structures, which remind us of the Luhmannian systems' analysis, are achieved either empirically (according to structuralism), or cognitively (according to poststructuralism). But such structures are certainly not achieved dialectically and are by no means consummated through practice. What relates both epistemological tendencies is their intention to devalue dialectics and render it, either as a scientific process or a methodology, parochial and epistemologically fruitless when compared to the structural approaches to science and society, and the political benefits they can draw. The main benefit that structuralism highlights is the understanding of practice within structures. However, the questions arise almost effortlessly: who creates structures and who practises practice?

The present chapter will show that even if structures help the reader of epistemology to understand the scientific edifice, there can be no performative structure with dysfunctional or non-existent subjects of action. Even if structures influence subjective action, subjects maintain the capacity to realize structures and exert criticism or negate the existent and coercive function of structures. Subjects create rationality by means of dialectics that is transformed into conscious action and the realization of reason within the social and through the political. As for science, subjects become the bearers of dialectics and critique, which become socially existent and potentially applicable through their political accountability to society itself.

The main argument of the chapter develops a critique of the structural model for the perception of the sciences as a pre-scientific understanding, through which social and scientific structures function as prejudices for society or the sciences, respectively. I argue that, particularly for the formulation of scientific truth, dialectics is an indispensable method and process in realizing both theory and practice. Practice is conceived *a priori,* and undergoes the *elenchus* of social and political accountability through the dialectical normativity formulated in theory. If practice is so closely related to theory, as I maintain, because it undergoes the accountability control of the question 'what ought to be done?', then the dialectics of theory and practice becomes an indispensable method and understanding of science.

The chapter addresses the epistemological and scientific deficit that lies *ante portas*, unless science realizes that practice *needs* theory; otherwise, it seems like an empty exercise of merely sociological interest that bears dubious scientific and political import given the marginalization of normative rationality (namely of the above-mentioned question regarding the *ought*) that is generated through theory and practice.

Furthermore, the chapter addresses the implicit but remarkable 'anxiety' of structuralism and poststructuralism as far as the void of scientific *elenchus* is concerned. Poststructuralism attempts to address the previous deficit by prioritizing scientific reflexivity that produces accountability criteria for the sciences. It appears that the preceding concern was not sufficient to replace or even relegate dialectics to the level of a methodology that bears the neutral scientific impact of reductionism, or that has no particular significance for society and politics. The more structuralism and poststructuralism attempted to downgrade and suppress dialectics, the more they reverted to its merits and implicitly acknowledged that it bears an inherent cunning in order to render itself epistemologically and politically indispensable for its capacity to articulate critique.

A science of practices?

From the beginning (since the *Outline of a Theory of Practice*), Bourdieu develops theoretical phases through which dialectical strategies produce the science of practices. Bourdieu's purpose is to formulate a theory of theories that entails a threefold schema of approaching knowledge that is grasped from the outside, namely from practice. The three phases that he considers are as follows: first, phenomenology in close association with ethnomethodology; second, the break with the primary knowledge of phenomenology, which is objectivist knowledge; and third, the science of practices, which constitutes the most evolved part of Bourdieu's scientific chain of developing phases. The following sections of this chapter present the three phases as they develop throughout his work, but also as they produce inner contradictions, which Bourdieu attempted to alleviate through the notions of structure, habitus and practice, so as to avoid elaborating on dialectics and dialogical processes in science and the political sphere.

Rather than being considered or rejected individually, all phases are included in a chain that produces scientific reactions that go towards founding science on practice, not just on primary experience, but on the explicit knowledge of structures. The theory encompassing the previous theories turns science towards a social practice that renders possible a new, *other* version of dialectic – one based on the interrelation between the objective knowledge and structural dispositions of the social. For Bourdieu, such a science of practices is not only an alternative dialectic; it is also a rigorous form of science, sought after by phenomenology in the epistemological past.

The advance is twofold: 'The structuralist movement ... expresses a very general and distinctive orientation to scientific inquiry in any field, as well as a particular approach to the study of social systems.'[2]

Bourdieu's structuralism gave form to a question that reformed modern epistemology and opened the way for a series of arguments and attempted answers: Which scientific condition allows both a theory of practice to flourish and a theory of scientific practice to focus on social practice? His answer was complicated and scientifically consistent. He examined the structures that systemic totalities produce and coined the term *habitus* in order to explain the transcendence of dialectics for understanding structural relations and practices, as preconditions of a novel interpretation that is both a theory and a methodology of the sciences.

Hence, the dialectic is formed and, in working order, owes its existence not to the functional element it attributes to extremes or contradictions of a twofold nature, but rather develops as a result of the range of relationships among (not between) multiple structural elements of a system. Bourdieu is almost uninterested in defining or tracing the contradictions facilitated by dialectics. He considers extremes or dualisms to offer limited prospects because, in such a way, the epistemologist or social scientist generally misses the range of options *within* the extremes or dualisms. The network of practices evolved is considered a whole or, in Bourdieu's terms, a 'habitus', which allows for multiple practices and owing to which a science of the dialectic develops.

The recognition of structural relations within systemic totalities, such as the sciences, suggests, in Bourdieu's thought, two points: first, that such relations are based on communicative processes of interrelation; and second, that the view of the sciences as a system of functions signifies that the interpretive dualism of the subject and object of knowledge is unable to give a sufficient explanation of scientific representations within the social. In such a sense, dialectics, easily construed but limited in perspective, between the knowing subject and the object of knowledge, appears inadequate in the social world.

Although it is difficult for the student of epistemology to compare physical phenomena with social and political analyses, the chapter examines the epistemological insufficiency of structuralism as a basis for proving that structures are a *sine qua non* for modern epistemology, and that they provide adequate solutions when politically examined. When studying structuralism I realized that it seems like the attempt to blame the earth's gravity for the pollution of the environment, namely that gravity causes pollution to gather and accumulate on earth and not disappear in space. Even if the natural law or structure of gravity were manifested differently, the latter would not deprive the earth's subjects of their intentions generally, nor would it eclipse their more specific intentions to pollute or not to pollute. Even if structures *are* important epistemologically, this does not shift the focus of science or epistemology, as a social and political explanation for the science, from the subjects to the structures themselves. Structures are the outcome of the subjects' conscious or unconscious deliberation and potential action.

It is my intention, however, also to show that the dualism of subject and object appears epistemologically limited. The acceptance of the existence or the potentiality of existence of a knowing subject presupposes the existence of an object of knowledge upon which the subject is self-confirmed. The whole idea of such dualism resides in the coercion that the subject exerts upon the object and, given that in structuralism the subject is collectively understood, the same can be said of the object, too: a collective object is shaped as a result of the existence of a collective subject, and vice versa. Such a dualistic interpretation is reminiscent of dialectics, but more so of a coercive dialectics that signifies hierarchical and, therefore, scientifically and socially limited or partial ways of approaching knowledge.

The challenge for Bourdieu remains on the methodological level, too. He knows that structural relations can be the best way for science to disguise relativism. The risk that structuralism runs is to designate relativism, and a lack of clear epistemological analysis, as 'structures'. When no social or political explanations are reached because of a lack of questions and answers, then we can blame the structures and all is quiet on the epistemological front. There is another gain too: when no dialectical answers are reached, there is no demand for change within the structures. Bourdieu is well aware of all the previous *aporias* and that is why he turns to practice. The notion of practice seems sufficient in order to save structuralism from relativistic and inapplicable hypotheses.

The understanding of practical relations within a certain structure avoids both relativism and realism, which transfer a distorted image of the social or the scientific structure. At this point, it becomes clearer in the *Outline of a Theory of Practice* that systemic structures suggest a network of practical relations, and that 'practical relationships ... comprise ... not only the sum total of the genealogical relationships kept in working order ... but also the sum total of the non-genealogical relationships which can be mobilized for the ordinary needs of existence'.[3] Between relativism and realism stands a whole range of practical relations that form a network functioning in the service of the social or the scientific system. As is the usual epistemological case with dialectics, structuralism falls into the same misunderstanding: structuralists see dialectics as a methodology. Even so, even if epistemological theses of structuralism are pushed and therefore reduced to the sphere of methodology, methodology is hardly innocent or scientifically neutral. Structuralism implies the formation of a frame of reference for the sciences that is separated from any past and future epistemological critique and crystallized into the following positions.

(a) It denies the subject-object dualism and interprets the relational character of whole structures within the social or the scientific in order to disclose general meanings of collective understanding.
(b) It also denies the exclusion of scientific subject matter in favour of some form of apolitical aloofness. For the first time in the twentieth century, in structuralism, epistemological concerns acquired a distinct political affiliation with social practice, and sciences are represented as systemic totalities that are proactive in being regulated by social practice itself.

Moreover, habitus is the focus of Bourdieu's epistemology. In addition to the notions of the science of practices and the structural paradigm, he attempts to transcend the subject–object relation. He also abandons the hierarchical edifice of modern sciences that reproduce relations of coercion and partiality, where the scientifically established order is considered a natural form of the social order. The vicious circle grows even more coercive when the reverse side of the previous mutuality prompts the evolution of science according to the social status quo. Nevertheless, what comes as an immediate reaction to the above argument on habitus and the structural paradigm, referring to relations of intercommunication that articulate a structure, is the question of the bearers or the participants of all the latter interpretations. Bourdieu's reader is inclined at some point to wonder: 'the habitus of whom?' or 'the structure of relations of whom?' or 'the practices of whom and to what purpose?'

Apart from establishing coercive modes of scientific understanding, according to structuralism, the dualism of the subject and object of knowledge provides a sufficient explanation of how and by whom knowledge is produced. The latter cannot be considered a defence of the rather obsolete dualism of subject–object, but a critique of Bourdieu's insufficient attempt to overcome such dualism in favour of a more inclusive view of science and society.

The realization of the habitus from a part of a collective whole, which is either society or the sciences, also entails the realization of the dialectic and intercommunicative relations that constitute such a whole. However, Bourdieu's epistemological notion of habitus comprises a moment of transcendence from objective or existing knowledge. It also innately bears the alternative and the potential, or else the system of practices seems static, deterministic and coercive. The probable and the potential are not this time brought to the fore, as in traditional dialectics, by means of the formation of the negative; rather, it is the learning process of practices that forms an *ethos* of multiple alternatives for the scientific.

The concept of dialectics in Bourdieu is significant but rare. It dares not speak its name, and, when it does, it acquires a character of open discourse devoid of contradictions and in the service of eliminating ideological perceptions of science. Bourdieu attempts to eradicate ideological misunderstandings by means of a dialectics that has aborted its power of negation. It is based on a *theory* of practice, which in its turn is based on a detailed consideration of structures, and not on a *critique* of practice.

In an attempt to redefine the dialectic element within the sciences, Bourdieu identifies the old and the new, namely the traditional and the structural understanding of the dialectic. The supposedly traditional dialectics comprises dualisms of subject and object, and reductionisms of thesis and antithesis or thesis and its negation. In structural dialectics, Bourdieu suggests the rejection of the previous separations. He maintains that the new dialectics bears

(a) the multiplicity provided by the scientific habitus;
(b) the methodological alternative that the consideration of practices facilitates; and
(c) the scientific *other* that the potential of intercommunicative practices forms.

Habitus does not produce intercommunication of perception, conception or action. Rather, the reverse is the case: all the latter forces function alongside internalized structures of subjective systems to produce a habitus, namely a network of functions that is fallible but mostly coherent and therefore functional.

Bourdieu takes practice for granted and applies it to whole systemic structures without ever defining practice, unless he attempts to accomplish such a definition by means of the interpretation of habitus, which is pivotal in his understanding of scientific as well as social structures. In Bourdieu's epistemological argument, neither discourse nor a theoretical model per se, nor the examination of individual or collective consciousness provides sufficient explanation of the scientific construction. The intrinsic aim is to trace the *scheme* that underlies all scientific constructions and which is immanent in practice.

The crucial point in the schema 'instruments of knowledge – reproduction – classification – hierarchy' that Bourdieu criticizes is not the steady progression and establishment of such an evolutionary process, but mostly the link that renders the latter chain coherent and functional. The bondage among the four phases is the formation and generation of a certain *doxa*. In Bourdieu, *doxa* spreads and acquires the function of instrumental knowledge. It is instrumental knowledge itself and leads to a self-evident and natural unanimity as far as the sciences or the social and the political order are concerned. It appears that at this level of understanding social and scientific structures, the notion of habitus becomes problematic, for it bears a Janus face of function as well as a distortion of the network of practices.

Although Bourdieu does not question the idea of practice as, in any case, scientifically fruitful, it remains unclear as to whether knowledge produced by the realization of practices can simultaneously be critical knowledge. The critical stance innately bears the dialogical questioning of all participants, either individual or collective, and exchange of argumentation towards the end of realizing rational scientific and social aims. Nevertheless, the overview of a theory of practice finds itself at a loss when it comes to representing dialogue, argumentation and rationality, simply because practice does not self-evidently involve these three elements. Bourdieu, on the contrary, was not directly concerned with them; rather, he presented another form of dialectics, whereby the *structures* of social and scientific domination are indeed perceived, but the foundation for their overcoming remains vague.

The distinction between a theory of practice and critical knowledge is particularly acute because for the latter the subject and object of knowledge are not conceived as being separated. The same is valid for the theory and practice relation. Both elements are interpreted not as one being alienated from the other or reducible to the other, but rather as producing critical activity in their interrelation within political praxis. Otherwise, the epistemological deficit created by a theory of practice becomes a political deficit concealed by the attempt to define social and scientific structures at a general level.

The blurring of the subject and object of knowledge insinuates an additional risk: the interchange of their scientific positions. My persistence to define the subject and object in terms of what structuralism presents does not act in favour of methodological dualisms and the easily reached exclusion of functions that thereby reproduces domination. Instead it intends to clarify that unless differentiations are comprehensible and scientifically realized, they run the risk of reproducing the coercion and distortion of social and political dynamics potentially fostered by the sciences. My inquiry into which is the subject and which is the object of the sciences in structuralism derives from the perspective of critical theory, which prioritizes the subject in order not to eliminate it. It is again the same old methodological and epistemological concern: before getting rid of some object of knowledge, I have to first define and understand it.

So far, Bourdieu's epistemological arguments appear to converge with Habermas' idea of knowledge-constitutive interests. For both thinkers, networks of intercommunication create networks or systems of assessing the empirical validity or the practical acceptance of knowledge and scientific theories by working groups or societal collectivities. Although, as will be discussed in the next section of this chapter, later in his work Bourdieu moves towards the critique of positivism that the first and second generations of the Frankfurt School articulated, at the point in which he identifies criteria of scientific and social validity, he appears to be closer to Habermasian territory. Bourdieu diverges from Habermas in two main respects: first, he does not acknowledge, as Habermas does, a pre-scientific formation of knowledge interests in the realm of 'the communicative self-understanding of the subjects involved in a research process as an unavoidable presupposition of the sciences';[4] second, Bourdieu distances his epistemological argument from a subject-centred research process. He interprets the scientific structure as ontologically valid and devoid of cognitive interests of which individual or collective subjects are the bearers. Thus, the issue of interdisciplinarity arises simply because it cannot be as bereft of subjectivity as Bourdieu wishes. Just as Habermas' epistemology is driven towards interdisciplinarity based on intersubjectivity, so too in Bourdieu interdisciplinarity is either deprived of any epistemological concern or is merely incorporated into the scientific structural whole.

Nevertheless, as already stated from the outset, Bourdieu's contribution to epistemology is crystallized not in itself but in its affiliation with the political. Bourdieu distances his epistemological concern from an idealized version of the systemic organization of the sciences, and formulates *a self-referential critique* of his arguments. Far from presenting the dialectic of the sciences as an ongoing process within the habitus network of relations of the sciences, he identifies that the instruments of knowledge reproduce systems of arbitrary classification, namely systems of ambiguous dualisms between the social and the mental or the objective and the internalized. Such classifications of a much disputed nature either politically, socially or scientifically are considered by means of constant reproduction as reality itself, which in turn establishes forms of social, political or scientific hierarchies. For Bourdieu, 'The theory of knowledge is a dimension of political theory because the specifically symbolic power to impose the principles of the construction of reality – in particular, social reality – is a major dimension of political power.'[5]

If the dialectics of thesis and antithesis, which was previously abandoned if not rejected by Bourdieu, is so thoroughly obsolete and scientifically fruitless, why then does it seem to Bourdieu, in the last part of the *Outline of a Theory of Practice*, as the only way in which instrumentality might be suspended practically and through which *doxa* is socially and scientifically marginalized? *Doxa* reigns within the sphere of opinion, where discourse and argumentation also prevail. What is undisputedly valid socially or scientifically remains so, because *it was established undisputedly*. Where discourse produces validity, it also produces and reproduces itself. The sphere of discourse (unavoidably for Bourdieu) creates the wishful contradiction *between* the heterodoxy and the orthodoxy. Even if Bourdieu's argument – namely that the habitus implies a nexus of relations – is based on practice, the question of what happens when contradictions are reached remains unanswered. The nexus interpretation appears insufficient when 'the locus of confrontation ... [or] the competing possibles'[6] remain the steady social and scientific problematics. In order to reach alternatives, science has first to face its environment, namely the fields of confrontation where scientific truth 'happens' and gives way to political truth and social innovation.

It appears that Bourdieu dares not speak the name of the notion he employs in order to analyse and interpret how political and scientific truth is reached. Bourdieu's much sought-after concept of truth may entail excluding *doxa* and preventing the successive myths it produces from holding sway within the scientific or social condition. Notwithstanding, the discourse condition is not self-evident or deterministic in character as structuralism would wish it to be. It does not follow as the natural alternative to myths and hierarchies. It produces alternatives for science and society, but it does not just flow out of the distortion of the scientific or the social sphere as a predictable reaction that produces scientific and political truth. Moreover, the idea of an instrumental knowledge presented by Bourdieu, which influences the social and political sphere, functions initially on the level of symbolic capital. It produces mechanisms of knowledge reproduction, but it also generates ideological functions of knowledge, which, at the social level, predetermine objective mechanisms and establish a widely and passively accepted political order. For Bourdieu, 'The most successful ideological effects are those which have no need of words, and ask no more than complicitous silence.'[7]

The major effect of the previous process on the sciences concerns the founding of determinism in scientific perceptions of the social and the political. The reproductive mechanisms of the social take for granted and consider legitimate the sphere of politics in which a preconceived notion of its function is applied and consequently remains unchallenged. In the case of political science, for instance, Bourdieu identifies a major distortion of science's perception of the social in the first place and, furthermore, the silencing of social and political alternatives, which entails the silencing of scientific alternatives as well. Coercion and systemic domination prevail in all spheres of structural reproduction, be they social, political or scientific. In Bourdieu's words:

> Once a system of mechanisms has been constituted capable of objectively ensuring the reproduction of the established order by its own motion ... the dominant class have only to *let the system they dominate take its own course* in order to exercise their domination; but until such a system exists, they have to work directly ... to produce and reproduce conditions of domination which are even then never entirely trustworthy.[8]

The way to scientific truth

In his comparison of Husserl's phenomenology, Schütz's ethnomethodology, and structuralism, Bourdieu recognizes knowledge as the outcome of practical theory in conjunction with scientific theory, or as the construction of practical logic in combination with theoretical logic. However, his main point of differentiation remains Kant. He charges Kant with scholasticism for trying to situate reason within an unexamined social condition called rational action. As such, Kant 'projects into practice ... an unexamined social relation which is none other than the scholastic relation to the world'.[9] Bourdieu disagrees with the social condition of reason in every respect, namely in its potential to define every action as consciously aimed. Against reason and rationality Bourdieu counterposes the habitus, which he considers epistemologically a far safer basis than reason and rational theory. In his words, 'habitus has the primordial function of stressing that the principle of our actions is more often practical sense than rational calculation'.[10]

An innate negative criticism underlies Bourdieu's intention to relate reason with a rational predisposition towards choice and scientific or social intentionality. In structuralism, reason is affiliated with a strict calculability that acquires the form of a scientific and social prejudice as something predestined and presupposed. Notwithstanding, reason remains external to or alienated from practice and the networks created by practice in the form of a habitus. But that is exactly the methodological lapse in Bourdieu's epistemological argument. Reason – either in the Kantian or post-Kantian sense – is not affiliated with the rational choice theory that Bourdieu intends to avoid, if not deconstruct, methodologically. Scientific reason is defined by the Frankfurt School as the 'ought to be' or as the normative potential.

For Bourdieu, the task of scientific truth carries a particular implication. It entails that the scientists should, among others, mostly 'stir themselves out of their dogmatic slumber and ... put into action ... put to the test, in a scientific practice, theories and concepts which ... are assured of ... false eternity'.[11] For Bourdieu, the struggle for truth is not merely a theoretical quest, but primarily a struggle for the formation of a science of practice that has developed through the rejection of myths, prejudices and scientific fallacies, which became social fallacies. Bourdieu's claim is straightforward: the sciences have not simply contributed to the realization or interpretation of myths and prejudices, but have also contributed towards their consummation and domination within the social.

The scientific struggle for truth entails a methodological test for revealing social truth, and it can also have political implications and can allow scientific and social discourse to qualify or disqualify existing scientific and social beliefs. In the last parts of *In Other Words*, Bourdieu attempts to formulate a concrete threefold argument on the sciences as follows:

(a) the sciences create a construction, which, according to rules, regularities, mechanisms and interests, allow the scientist to play the scientific game as a game;

(b) although structures are clear, they are never impersonal but always formed by the scientists themselves, who in their 'effort to find reasons ... [risk] ... justifying, even of excusing the existing order';[12] and
(c) the scientific game is not a frame for objective argumentation and symbolic strategies, which aim at, first, 'imposing the partial truth of a group as the truth of the objective relations between groups',[13] and second, objective knowledge as well.

Following Bourdieu's line of thought, it is clear that he acknowledges the scientific edifice as undergoing specific practices, conditions and rules of development. In such a structure, Bourdieu distances himself from his initial impersonal approach in the *Outline of a Theory of Practice,* and criticizes the responsibility that the scientist bears towards the scientific struggle for truth. For the scientist, tracing truth unavoidably becomes a struggle for social truth, denying myths, domination and the dogmatism of absolute knowledge. Such a scientific struggle owes its existence to the scientific capital based on criticism, divergence from the existing social order and objective confrontation with what is a reductionist objectification of a partial approach on the part of the sciences.

For Bourdieu, the anti-authoritarian and autonomous nature of science collides, unavoidably, with the scientific imperative, dictated by social coercion. Nevertheless, in a form of agonistic pluralism, Bourdieu's notion of science also confronts political denunciation, although the latter shapes scientific criticism as such. Bourdieu's realization of the sciences suggests autonomy from what is socially and politically established, but avoids negative political critique, which places the sciences in their objective position to practise negative reason and tackle opposing arguments. I consider Bourdieu's epistemological position a form of denial of scientific responsibility. The negative critique, which Bourdieu denounces, places the sciences outside of the comforting position of 'neutrality'. In such a case, social intervention becomes superfluous for the sciences simply because there is a political side to its critique that bears the responsibility of arguments. Thus, a rigorous science for Bourdieu maintains three significant characteristics: it is (1) anti-authoritarian; (2) autonomous from the commonsensical perceptions of society; and (3) agonistic among the oppositions and conflicts of a scientific or social and political nature.

It is at this point, when elaborating on symbolic violence of science in the *Pascalian Meditations*, that Bourdieu makes a slight turn to relativism, claiming that truth 'like any other kind of disposition, necessarily owes something to the conditions in which it was formed, in other words a social position and trajectory'.[14] Truth for Bourdieu acquires a situational form. It is neither subjective nor objective. It cannot be external to the subject or the object, nor can it be sought after by the scientist herself. It is rather the object of activism, namely the aim of science acquired through practice or activism. In his later text of 2001, 'History and Truth',[15] Bourdieu extends his relativistic argument and emphasizes that the recognition of truth, either individually or collectively, is mainly a matter of consensus deriving from the following:

1. the existence of a community of agents or seekers of truth;
2. the common principles of confirmation; and
3. the common identification of methods that are followed.

Truth, for Bourdieu, appears to be weak and dependent on recognition. It is quantitative in nature. If many subjects consent as to its validity through the above phases, truth then acquires a concrete form and is therefore situationally valid. However, the distinction in such an argument rests precisely on the conceptual differentiation between truth and social or scientific validity.

My argument is more critical and less consensual than Bourdieu's. Truth exists without the formal corroboration of some collectivity and even without social corroboration, which is apparently, situationally or historically applicable. Validity is subject to relativistic criteria; truth is not. Particularly when truth appeals to collective phenomena regarding society or science, it is not collective validation that ratifies truth. Rather, it is the rationality of dialectics that allows truth to become socially and scientifically recognized. Nevertheless, there is no need for consent, or *homologein* in Bourdieu's terms in *Science of Science and Reflexivity*. Consent is an option but not a presupposition in relation to truth. Between validity and truth lies the legitimacy of truth arguments, namely that truth does not take for granted social or scientific validity. On the contrary, it endogenously bears the potentiality for social and scientific legitimacy, accomplished through the dialectics that argumentative reason adopts and promotes within the intercommunication of individual or collective subjects.

I assume that truth exists irrespective of people, societies or sciences recognizing it. However, truth allows for social validity or scientific legitimacy by means of people exercising dialogue and exchange of arguments. It allows for theses, but it can also appear in the form of negations or consent to what occurs in society or in science. Critical theory for the twenty-first century should probably raise objections against the situational character of truth that structuralism claimed, and argue for criteria of truth that validate what is rational and how rationality applies to science and society.

Instead of producing a total knowledge, as Bourdieu intends, by means of the structural interpretation of networks of practices, critical theory opposes a systemic conception of knowledge and instead formulates a negative critique on the systemic realization of knowledge. The critical aim of the Frankfurt School becomes precisely the conceptualization of critique through the recognition of contradictions in science, thereby revealing its dialectical character. In Adorno's *Minima Moralia* and *Negative Dialectics* in particular, the outcome is that 'theory does not take the form of long and systematic arguments but rather of short paradoxical pieces that emphasise ambiguity and contradiction'.[16]

Nevertheless, an additional observation against Bourdieu's systemic networks of knowledge deriving from practice refers to the structural perception of knowledge being also a presupposition in itself and, therefore, a form of scientific prejudice. Apart from a dialectical understanding of knowledge-forming procedures, there is also human rationality expressed potentially either in the sciences or in society. Both dialectics and rationality are not determined or presupposed conditions within the social or the scientific, and as such they cannot be blamed for undergoing or producing 'rational calculation' in disguise. Scientific discussions, being articulated by conscious subjects, express reason and the intention to reach scientific rationality, which 'in the course of an inter-subjective dialogue, gradually liberates self-incurred but as yet unrecognized deceptions'.[17]

By revealing and realizing deceptions, scientific truth becomes the potential *not self-evidently* but more easily reached through scientific discourse on contradictions. By contrast, the structural perception of the sciences, not being in itself or denoting any process, appears to be a presupposed condition that produces calculative rationalism as a prerequisite for the interpretation of the sciences. In structuralism truth is the self-evident result of the nexus of structures, while in critical theory it is the potential of critique and dialogue exerted by conscious subjects, either individuals or collectivities.

Instead of realizing what science is, critical theory – from Horkheimer to Habermas and their epigones – insists that we do not perceive science as it is and then dispense with it by attempting to transcend or even reject it, and form a new one. On the contrary, scientists or every involved part of an individual or collective endeavour raise claims as to the different, the alternative to the existing order, the 'ought to be' as far as scientific aims are concerned, and through such a process perceive the scientific and social status quo under a far more precise and valid perspective. The value judgement that reason instigates serves as the best path to perceiving, understanding and criticizing the already experienced and practiced.

For Habermas, truth is measured against three criteria: first, the objective conditions in science and society; second, the social normativity representing reason; and third, the conscious intentionality of the individual towards the object of knowledge. What joins the three elements in a coherent manner that aims at the formation of truth is the communicative process occurring between them. This safeguards the progression of uncoerced dialogue. In this way, truth emerges as the outcome of coordination among individuals, society and objective conditions governing the sciences. There is no purposive-rationalizing intention in the coordination of these elements of science; rather, the primary intention is to set criteria of truthfulness for the sciences and to coordinate any subsequent action.

Therefore, the major difference between the epistemological understanding of Bourdieu and that of critical theory lies in the origin of scientific theory and its relation to practice. For the former, science and theory derive from the examination of social practice and, accordingly, truth emerges from such an evolutionary course of action. For the latter, practice is part of a process based on social and scientific normativity and individual consciousness, which constitute a whole owing to their interaction. Hence, for Habermas practice is not the necessary presupposition or outcome, but the part and potentiality of a scientific process aiming to encompass knowledge and rationality.

The second differentiation between structuralism and critical theory is located in the field of terminology and signification. Both approaches address the question of where scientific problematics occur, and each adopts a similar but ultimately divergent answer. For Bourdieu, the crucial focus within the functional argument of the sciences becomes not the sciences themselves but the structure of the scientific edifice and the relative network of associations that develops among them. For critical theory of the second generation, science 'occurs' when the lifeworld allows processes of intercommunication to follow their own course and, therefore, generate social and scientific rationality that aims at truth. In both cases, knowledge and the derivation of truth is a collective process, but as in epistemology, it is not the result but the process adopted that allows truth to emerge and to be consummated as the outcome of scientific endeavour. In Bourdieu, science and truth are the unintended mark of the functional, whereas for critical theory both science and knowledge are the conscious objectives of dialectics and communicative action.

The particular comparison between systems of action and the lifeworld indicates that the two factors are socially unrelated. The former function according to the purposive-rational action of the agents involved, whereas the latter is coordinated in the process of scientific and social integration through communicative processes of uncoerced dialogue. In structuralism, the reproduction of domination within social and scientific systems appears unavoidable, as it is predetermined by the totality of social and scientific structures, while in critical theory it is communicative action promoting dialectics that enables a questioning of the potential of knowledge as well as the potential to formulate truth.

Following the previous comparison, the third differentiation emerges when both approaches attempt to examine the contested field of politics in relation to the sciences. For Bourdieu, politics derives from practice and more precisely from the autonomy of the science of practice towards the social. In such an understanding, politics is the natural outcome presupposed by a theory of practice elaborated by the sciences. For Habermas, politics emanates from the potential of the social and the scientific spheres to form rationality under the auspices of dialectical processes that allow all participants to exchange arguments. For critical theory, either of the first or the second generation, the political sphere is not an autonomous field determined by social and scientific normativity.

To return to Bourdieu's thought that structuralism is about *intervention*, it appears that he has created the iron cage of scientific systems and structures which promote domination, although he initially intended to set science at the forefront of social and political intervention. By contrast, a comparison between critical theorists, namely between Horkheimer and Habermas, would signify that 'the forging of moral solidarity between the intelligentsia and actual social movements – while maintaining distance from the immediacy of the latter's empirical forms of consciousness – is questionable to the extent that the communicative horizon between the theoretical addressee fades away'.[18] As far as structuralism is concerned, it appears that the concept of structure and its realization within the sciences allows for an unfavourable development: it goes hand in hand with hierarchical and rigid formations and procedural rules that stifle any essential form of dialogue and uncoerced communication.

The dialectical turn by Bourdieu, in which science and particularly the scientists bear the potential to tackle the structural mode of the scientific game, which entails facing contradictions and conflicts, implies that social relations are deemed the path to understanding the habitus as a network of dialectical relations, too. The method for such dialectical understanding in Bourdieu becomes the comparison of opposing or conflicting parts, where the social or scientific structure stands not for a static apparatus, but as a *process* that allows and reinforces negative criticism and transformation through the agonistic pluralism of social and scientific agents.

In order to trace scientific truth, the scientists have to make an inquiry into the questions set by philosophy and, through discourse, legitimate them scientifically and socially. However, the problematic thing with Bourdieu's adoption of dialectical relations in the habitus is that discourse does not necessarily legitimate questions and answers. I maintain that the course of dialectics, and the intercommunication it effects, does not predetermine the framework for discursive validity, either in scientific or in social terms. Apart from the risk of naming 'discursive' any authoritative process of coercive negotiation and artificial consensus among social and scientific participants, which represent collectivities, science also runs the risk of attributing validity to social interests dictated by a minority of social or political elites by means of symbolic violence.

In his 2001 book *Science of Science and Reflexivity*, Bourdieu elaborates the notions of self-reflexivity and habitus as transcendental perceptions, thereby relating his whole work to poststructuralism. Habitus is not considered an *a priori* notion, but instead offers the path to overcoming and even contradicting the insufficiencies of empiricism. Before outlining the continuities and discontinuities between structuralism and poststructuralism, Bourdieu's notion of reflexivity, developed in his structural thinking on the sciences, resolves the tension between the dialectical deficit in structuralism and the normativity of social and scientific reason. With reflexivity conceptualized as self-referential reason, Bourdieu does not intend to enter the field of rational theory or the normative considerations of a practice based on dialectics. Rather he manages to avoid the epistemological and methodological *aporia* by oscillating between structuralism and poststructuralism, and granting the latter a major role in his epistemological arguments. He emphasizes reflexivity as the opportunity of the sciences for self-referential reason that remains *excluded in itself* and necessitates practice in order to reach social applicability and enhance the political import of the sciences.

Bourdieu challenges the theoretical context of dialectics by means of reflexivity in the social sciences. He identifies the asymmetry between the legitimacy of science towards the social and society itself. In his words 'what is called epistemology is always in danger of being no more than a form of *justificatory discourse serving to justify science* or a particular position in the scientific field, or a spuriously neutralized reproduction of the dominant discourse of science about itself'.[19] Society appears to prevail over science in its ability to produce practice through which the scientist realizes the perspective of the social itself. Reflexivity is the potential of the social or scientific structure to realize practice *because* the structural edifice is based on the homogeneity that practice predetermines. Therefore, in my understanding of structuralism, structure is the model of accumulation that overcomes, or merely absorbs, differentiations by accumulation, creating a functional edifice of a rigorous science.

But can contradictions simply be absorbed in a structure? The problematic part of the above citation is the omission of dialectics. Such oversight entails the exclusion of arguments for the sake of justificatory discourse or spuriously neutralized positions. Here we find the essence of scientific dialectics: it is neither justificatory and reconciliatory among contradictions, nor does it intend to neutralize them. When interdisciplinary communication takes place, reason constitutes the dialectical force on the part of the sciences that facilitates differentiations not simply to accumulate, as in structuralism, but to convey the alternative – namely that of dealing effectively with justificatory rationalizations of a coercive character and the social and scientific neutralization of arguments that form hierarchical orders. Scientific dialectics cannot demonstrate apparent results, but it does attempt to negate the model of structural hierarchies in science, which colonize and corrode the potential for scientific rationality.

Truth based on self-referential reason

The Deleuzean, poststructuralist views of the sciences both follow and challenge Bourdieu's structuralism in two main respects: first, in relation to truth, and second, with regard to the dual schemata of dialectical critique. If I wish to be more precise, I would say that the reader might actually note two and a half points, as the second point can create an inner point of dispute here. The inner point which I consider a 'half' is that of critique related to reason and attributed to philosophy.

According to the poststructuralist, reversed mode that starts from the end, I start with the last poststructuralist point where philosophy's main task is to overcome critique based on dialectical reason. Philosophy differs from science in that it deals with the formation of concepts, while science deals with the function of concepts and the prospective creation of whole structures of concepts based on their relations. Furthermore, philosophy is not a discursive formation and, certainly, according to Deleuze, it is not concerned with questions and answers. It is the task of science to define discursiveness among structures of conceptions. Therefore, philosophy refers to static formulations, while science refers to the prospects of such formulations. The whole edifice of the Deleuzean poststructuralist approach on science appears static and strictly defined compared to the dialectical mode of scientific endeavour, which defines science in terms of the process of dialogue between opposing agents. While for poststructuralism, philosophy turns to concepts and the immanence that mediates them, 'Reason is only a concept, and a very impoverished concept for defining the plane and the movements that pass through it.'[20]

Although in *What Is Philosophy?*, Deleuze concurs with Primo Levi in demanding that no one shall make us confuse the executed with the executioners, thus, apparently criticizing Adorno for his influential aphorism on Auschwitz, he nevertheless appears to succumb to the relativism he attempts to avoid. For Adorno, truth is Auschwitz itself, no one can deny it. It is there, no matter how we perceive it as citizens, scientists or collectivities, regardless of what group or community we belong to. By contrast, for Deleuze, although truth is not relativistic, relativity is truth itself in the form of perspectivism 'or scientific relativism, [that] is never relative to a subject: it constitutes not a relativity of truth but, on the contrary, a truth of the relative, that is to say, of variables whose cases it orders according to the values it extracts from them in its system of coordinates'.[21]

Reason is drained into the dualism of thesis and antithesis, and the subsequent critique is a partial accomplishment that should have transcended both empiricism and abstractions. As with dialectics, Deleuze makes a distinction that is very similar to Bourdieu's. In essence, he distinguishes between 'old-fashioned' or traditional and modern or structural dialectics. Initially in *Difference and Repetition*, Deleuze heavily criticizes what dialectics denotes before structuralism or poststructuralism. He twice calls it 'a calculus' of scientific implementation that acts as the perverted criterion of a dogma that diverges into truth and falsehood. For Deleuze's poststructuralism, such a dialectics can achieve only a propositional character. Therefore, dialectics constitutes a dogmatic function for philosophy, which imitates the theological modus operandi, and is reduced to the solvability of problems.

The latter is the mere intention of knowledge based on the generality of concepts. Nevertheless, learning, which is a subjective act, cannot be decoded unless we shift our focus to the symbolic fields of scientific solvability that constitute mainly (along with the realization of the transcendental moment) the ideal synthesis for the solution to a problem. In his attempt to eliminate a dialectical understanding of the process of knowledge, Deleuze resorts to apparent positivism in *Difference and Repetition,* which comprises three basic points:

(a) repetition, which demands a superior, overarching positive principle in order to be scientifically applicable and eternally returning as a totality of action;
(b) since repetition incorporates singularities, it is characterized either by steady and unchangeable processes or by dynamic ones; and
(c) such stable processes in the form of certain structures, which increasingly replace any form of process, are constituted by signs that communicate with one another. However, intercommunication of signs entails causal relations and the application of the causality principle that mediates positivity itself.

The association of dialectics with an instrumental solvability is rather arbitrary and questionable. I do not consider dialectics as the plain criterion of knowledge that produces plausible solutions of a calculable nature. It is not even the product of calculation for the appeasement of differences. On the contrary, dialectics derives from setting questions and offering answers on the potentiality of reason. It is not of a calculative (how can questions and negations actually be calculated?) but rather a dialogical character, which reveals the truth as it exists socially and particularly scientifically. It is not external to the scientific, but is the bearer of the scientific potential based on the social condition. The main characteristic of dialectics is that it cannot lose sight of what occurs within society because it derives from subjects interrelating by means of dialogue. The opposite potential that Deleuze attributes to dialectics, the criterion of 'trial and error', is hardly attached to the dialectical processes related to science and remains dissimilar to the notion of critique that dialectics pursues in the process.

Nevertheless, Deleuze's dialectics (such as it exists) is not structural but relativistic in form. In his words, 'Consider the great negative notions such as the many in relation to the One, disorder in relation to order, nothingness in relation to being: *it makes no difference* whether they are interpreted as the limit of a process of degeneration or as the antithesis of a thesis.'[22] Although Deleuze recognizes the oppositions that define the problem, he firmly denies recognizing the problem, which is opposition itself. He acknowledges that opposition '*makes no difference*', but the retort to such dogmatic acceptance could have been the following question: 'how does it make no difference when it is *there*, within the scientific?' Opposition and negation are not hypothetical schemata or constructions of some individual or collective imaginative agent. They form the process within the scientific and the social based on dialogue and on dealing by their own nature with the limit as well as the potential of transcending themselves.

There are, however, also two apparent points of divergence from Bourdieu's structuralism in Deleuze's work: first, habitus is substituted by repetition; and second, the subject is reconceptualized as a constituent part of the knowledge process that is also divided into the following:

(a) the conceptualization of generality, which deals with what can be replaced in terms of knowledge and ideas;
(b) the elaboration of repetition that deals with non-exchangeable singularities; and
(c) the representation that restores the subject as the knowing agent.

Starting from the last point again, we find that concepts have been represented by memory and self-consciousness on the part of the subject. But what remains unclear in poststructuralism is the retort to the questions 'self-consciousness of *what*? And *how*?' The first question is partly answered when Deleuze explains that what is achieved by representation is the manifestation of a concept to its object, without yet explaining what happens when a concept is blocked by its antithesis. He defines the comprehension of the idea as infinite and inalienable, but the knowledge process and its representation is virtually hampered, according to Deleuze, when reason negates an exchangeable idea. The second question on the mode of advancement through self-consciousness remains totally vague because advancement in Deleuze suggests an *a priori* intentionality of consciousness, but firmly remains attributed to actuality. This becomes problematic if we consider that what is suggested previously by Deleuze is that a subject comprehends the object of a utilized idea as exogenous to the subject.

Deleuze attributes to the knowing subject the potential of thought, of action, and most significantly, of philosophy. Therefore, he draws a circular argument from the subject to cognition itself, and opposes it to the potential of negation mediated through dialectics. Although he persistently attempts to avoid dualities, he distinguishes between the *Eudoxus* as the bearer of philosophy and *Epistemon* as the bearer of science. The first is the subject of the unconditional and unhampered thought of philosophy, whereas the second is 'perverted by the generalities of his time'[23] and by the excess of exhibition to what is supposed to be public. As such, his mode of understanding thought and philosophy has something of a theological angle. The commonsensical recognition of the *Eudoxus* is not simply an *a priori* comprehension of the subject and the object of thought, but a predefined deterministic attitude towards knowledge.

The process of knowledge according to consideration (c) is schematically represented in Figure 2.1.

The object of consciousness is mediated between representation and actuality. Deleuzean poststructuralism reminds us of the Husserlian approach of situating consciousness within reality. In other words, the intentionality of

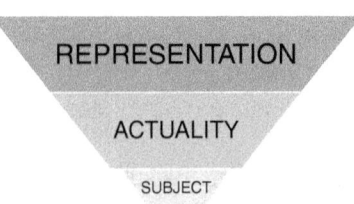

Figure 2.1 The process of knowledge according to consideration (c) on p. 71.

consciousness is manifested in the representation of its object that is thus attributed to the intentionality of the knowing subject.

For points (a) and (b), their function becomes obvious through the controversy of both with difference, which refers to indefinite concepts that become indistinct on account of the plurality of notions to which they refer. Difference becomes the royal path for Deleuze in order to alleviate the dialectical deficit regarding contradictions and negations of concepts. In order to avoid the emerging critique that is condensed in the question 'how does science deal with conceptual contradictions?', Deleuze articulates the solution of *conceptual differences* of ideas and, thus, renders dialectics and negation epistemologically useless. Within the conceptual schema of difference, he acknowledges the multiplicity of ideas and not the limited recognition of an antithetical construction. While *difference* finds itself external to the concept and to the object it mediated, and yet internal to the ideas, *repetition* addresses an object of cognition. Nevertheless, repetition does not necessarily refer to the concept of cognition.

Reason itself is considered not as forming dialectics but as the medium of conceptual representation. It remains a constant concern for Deleuze to show that difference represents *all* forms of opposition but does not bear a *particular* form of opposition with some other element or concept. Difference exists in itself and, therefore, becomes a cause that is also *a priori*. The mind mediates, recognizes and renders it a reflexive concept. In Deleuze's words, 'As a concept of reflection, difference testifies to its full submission to all the requirements of representation, which becomes thereby "organic representation".'[24] Difference itself functions in defence of a consensual model of scientific structure. It avoids dialectical oppositions in every respect, and constructs a totality of reason that diverges into two functions: first, the reciprocal determination of veritable reason that allows the intercommunication of notions to take place; and second, the complete determination of the object of cognition as a phenomenon as such.

For example, Deleuze sees Hegelian dialectics as a logical monster. The object denies what it is not and therefore succumbs to 'the infinite circulation of the identical by means of negativity'.[25] In essence, for Deleuze, negativity is the surface of the difference, which implies that knowing the negation does not necessarily entail knowing the depth of the negation. Deleuze finds dialectics unable to cope with the multiplicity of the object and its mediation. In his own words: 'It is not difference which presupposes opposition but opposition which presupposes difference, and far from resolving difference by tracing it back to a foundation, opposition betrays and distorts it.'[26] For Deleuze, scientific structure presupposes difference, *not* contradiction or opposition. There cannot be a structure that bears inherent contradictions.

More precisely, Deleuze considers that science includes multiple oppositions, thus forming a systemic network of functional performativity, but not a *particular form* of opposition to some existing element of the structure. However, even his intention to refute Hegelian dialectics itself constitutes a negation, which produces methodological dialectics. It appears that Deleuze lapsed into his own structural argument.

In essence, he never negates negation or he cannot simply do without it. In his words:

> difference is primary: it affirms difference and distance. Difference is light, aerial and affirmative. To affirm is not to bear but, on the contrary, to discharge and to lighten. It is no longer the negative which produces a phantom of affirmation like an ersatz, but rather a No which results from affirmation. This is also in turn a shadow ... A *Nachfolge*. The negative is an epiphenomenon. Negation, like the ripples in a pond, is the effect of an affirmation which is too strong or too different.[27]

As with the structuralist edifice (as noted before, Deleuze's poststructuralism both converges with and distances itself from Bourdieu), the whole structure of Deleuze's argument on knowledge and cognition remains valid for Deleuze himself on the basis of one simple thing: the power and critique of new politics. In his critique of Kant's notion of critique, Deleuze rather unfairly accuses Kant of comprising everything but a potential for new politics, which should have prompted a change in the comprehension of thought. Both Bourdieu and Deleuze set the critical ability of the sciences at the spearhead of the overturn of thought and, thus, of the potential for politics. Therefore, an *a priori* power of politics is formed: it is not politics that produces or even influences the thinking subject, but rather vice versa – the potential for thought and critique (for new critique, for Deleuze) gives a concrete form to politics. In Deleuze's words:

> The conditions of a true critique and a true creation are the same: the destruction of an image of thought which presupposes itself and the genesis of the act of thinking in thought itself. Something in the world forces us to think. This something is an object not of recognition but of a fundamental *encounter* ... In recognition, the sensible is not at all that which can only be sensed, but that which bears directly upon the senses in an object which can be recalled, imagined or conceived ... the object of encounter ... gives rise to sensibility with regard to a given sense. It is not an *aistheton* but an *aistheteon*. It is not a quality but a sign.[28]

Structuralism and poststructuralism attempt to trace the social legitimation of science by the concept of social practice. They seek to render their scientific concerns socially legitimate and valid by their affiliation to what society produces in practice. It was probably obvious for both structuralists and poststructuralists that a lack of social grounding has a dual effect. On the one hand, it renders their argument on scientific systems autonomous from the social sphere, while on the other, it bases science on an unstable social deficit. By contrast, for the dialectics of critical theory, science does not exist in order to exert critique on the social sphere; on the contrary, it forms part of the latter and is legitimated by society itself.

Critical theory acknowledges that the scientific sphere is socially legitimized and, therefore, changeable in relation to social process. Social dialectics influences both the methodology and objectives of science. Dialectics induces the subject (either individual or collective) to think according to social contradictions, to 'think the opposite', and not according to hierarchical systems or structures of thought and what is identical in structural multiplicity. The aim of social and scientific dialectics is to 'think' and not to 'converge'.[29]

In the dialectical process, which is a learning process for the subject, the subject succeeds in learning to construct a critique of opposites and to reject conceptions of the totality of the identical. Scientific dialectics becomes the norm, which indicates that the purpose of science is not to become asocial or apolitical, but to hold a critical stance of the 'negation' of the authoritarian system of relations where, for Brunkhorst, 'Knowledge is not power, but the medium for the critique of it.'[30]

The crucial difference between critical theory's dialectics and structuralism/poststructuralism lies, first, in the former's potential to exert critique within, as well as outside, the existing scientific structure or system. It maintains equal distance from both dogmatism and relativism, and applies critique not only to the existing scientific rationality, but also as a way of forming potential through the negation of the coercive scientific status quo. This is the inalienable character of modern dialectics: the trait of potentiality that paves the way for the responsibility of the subject for another politics. Even if all conditions and relations of elements or signs of a structure are recognized and studied to the full (but who can actually testify to that, and how?), as structuralism and poststructuralism suggest, the existing condition of science nevertheless remains the same, unalterably consummated and unchallenged within the networks of structures.

Thought and critique would promote the formation of a new politics, encouraged if not substantiated through science itself. However, even if the conditions of a true critique are based on signs, this does not in the least safeguard the creation of a plausible political alternative. In both structuralism and poststructuralism, reason, rationality and communication are often accused of aiming at an instrumental consensus, that is, a consensus in which instrumentality is inherent. What both epistemological explanations overlook is the potentiality of dialogical *elenchus* brought to the fore of epistemological concerns through dialectics and the negation of the existing conditions either in science or society.

For dialectics of the oppositional and critical kind, science is not simply a matter of recognizing systemic structures and of eliminating oppositions by ignoring them through self-referential reason; rather, it is a matter of criticizing – namely *elenchein through social reason* – what form of science is produced by society and to what political ends. It is just such a politics, either old or new, towards which dialectics strives.

Conclusions

As far as the duality of philosophy and science is concerned, for both structuralists and poststructuralists, science undergoes a strict causality, which is also verifiable and controllable. Particularly for Deleuze, philosophy hovers between two contradictory positions: on the one hand, it '*merges with ontology and ontology merges with the univocity of the Being*',[31] and on the other, 'Philosophy is indissociable from a theory of intensive multiplicities insofar as intuition as method is an anti-dialectical method of research and affirmation of difference.'[32] Deleuze reaches the aporetic point in his epistemological analysis when he first regards philosophy as associated with the ontology of the being which is monadological. Philosophy for Deleuze is also *a priori* on account of the use of intuition as method, while the *multiplicity* in philosophy safeguards not only its undialectical but also its anti-dialectical function.

Deleuze intends to dispose of dialectics as a method for knowledge, but in realizing that denying dialectics is the self-confirmation of dialectics itself, he replaces it with difference and redeems the lost honour of poststructuralism. Furthermore, philosophy as a construction allows scientific functionalism to 'happen' but not necessarily to flourish socially, because this is precisely what it tries to avoid, particularly in poststructuralism, namely the idea of social necessity as a form of presupposition.

For critical theory, philosophy produces critique and, in communication with science, infuses the latter with the potential for recognizing rationality and formulating critique.

Adorno's negation of the totality of the scientific sphere as an inclusion of identical considerations paves the way for a critique of the social totality and the coercion it generates by denying the oppositional. According to the structuralist and poststructuralist account, dialectics and scientific reason become endangered when tackling negation.

But it is precisely the moment of uncoerced scientific rationality in critical theory that relates to social critique endorsing oppositions and conflicts. For Horkheimer, science and philosophy are understood as forming an inextricably intercommunicative relation that creates dialectical critique. Achieving social and scientific rationality is the task of both philosophy and science, which aims at political rationality through multiple forms of dialectics. There is no question of the subordination of philosophy to science or vice versa; they both coexist or else both are distorted in coercive and hierarchical relations.

Structuralist and poststructuralist epistemology, relating to similar Heideggerian arguments, is subjectless (or almost so), aims at a mediative intentionality in order to intervene into science to some extent (mainly through Deleuzean representation), and relates science to politics through a hierarchical perception of the autonomy of science as a structural edifice per se. Even if a new politics *is* perceptible from a structuralist perspective, it appears to reproduce the existing scientific hierarchy and social or political status quo.

The query then arises as to how a sphere, which claims its autonomy from society, can influence or wield a critique of the latter, particularly when it is reproduced through rigid structures. The original idea of a rigorous science, initially in Dilthey (although partly on account of its reference to the humanities) and successively in Husserl and the ethnomethodologists (which also runs through the work of Bourdieu and Deleuze) does not merely intend to set out a lucid definition of science with clear-cut aims and intentions. It has two implications: first, that the autonomy of science frees it from the coercion of social and political normativity; and second, that a rigorous and sovereign science can even come to replace politics itself.

For the above approaches, dialectics is seen as the obnoxious brat that keeps asking questions, challenging existing structures and practices, to which structuralism persistently replies: 'For what? The existing order is good enough, it is reproducible and negotiable.' However, the challenge for scientific dialectics is not to reproduce or negotiate, but to negate, or at least to be realized as the potential for negation. This is the all-too-human scientific world of conflict, doubt and argumentation over what is oppositional and what can be negated.

Even the concept of social practice, which seems to save structuralist and poststructuralist epistemology from the clutches of transcendental approaches, does not appear a plausible explanation that relates the scientific to the social. For Deleuzean poststructuralism, experience is 'the collection of distinct perceptions'.[33] that also facilitates relations to construct different associations and thus form a different subject beyond experience. The crucial point in such an argument is not that experience produces networks of associations that transcend experience, implying that experience incorporates a moment of self-transcendence, but rather that networks of empirical associations form a different subject, one that is depersonalized and refers to abstract constructions of systemic structures. It mainly appears to ground science within the empirical and less within the grand perspective of the social.

By contrast, in Horkheimer's epistemological intention towards truth, the latter cannot be achieved unless the social condition for the conjunction of theory and practice is also accomplished. The world of social practice does not necessitate the placing of truth among scientific concerns. Furthermore, abstract formulations of the sciences do not act in defence of truth, but rather serve as ideological constructions of an autonomous and, therefore, rigorous science.

Following Horkheimer's critical remarks on science, I would note that the development of the sciences throughout the twentieth century indicates that the persistent study of empirical data does not produce a socially and politically sufficient theory. Instead it functions in a reductionist manner, even for empiricism itself. Even when all empirical data are thoroughly studied and all structures are fully perceived, *what* produces change and alternatives remains unclear for instrumental apparatuses and untouched by relativistic elaboration. The second point that appears problematic when analysing the notion of social practice is the *aporia* that arises when social practice itself is not socially legitimate or politically plausible. What seems initially to be socially redemptive for Bourdieu appears to be rather problematic when compared with Horkheimer's idea that practice is not necessarily the verification of a theory but many times its distortion. Science is part of the social process that produces both theory and praxis, and not the predetermined outcome or presupposition of social determinism. In his *Eclipse of Reason,* Horkheimer states: 'The neutralization of reason that deprives it of any relation to objective content and of its power of judging the latter, and that degrades it to an executive agency concerned with the how rather than with the what, transforms it to an ever-increasing extent into a mere dull apparatus for registering facts.'[34]

In the other sphere of dialectics, as represented by critical theory, science is equally a productive sphere that deals with contradictions in the same manner as philosophy. They are both socially prolific because they are prepared, first, to recognize oppositions, and second, to elaborate them through dialectics. This is the process – either scientific or social – that produces socially rational critique. The idea that dialogue governs either the mode of scientific advance, as well as the social process, does not merely reside in the notion of a methodology that gives shape to the dualisms of subject–object, thesis–antithesis, affirmation–negation or theory–practice.

Dialectics is not simply a methodology. It is, rather, a scientific as well as social process that allows criticism and rationality to shape the potential of politics. Therefore, it carries a normative charge, which indicates that when we realize and practice dialectics, we essentially find ourselves within the realm of normativity and not merely within empirical data, which emerge unprocessed by the social and scientific subjectivity. Scientific dialectics avoids rendering science a socially and politically neutral realm in which science remains separate or 'autonomous' (!) from social demands and interests even when all empirical data have been functionally processed.

The political moment in the epistemology of critical theory underlines the mutuality of scientific dialectics with social critique that represents theses and antitheses to the existing order. The political solutions that structuralism and poststructuralism wish to provide do not automatically derive from systemic structures and their scientific understanding; nor do they derive from isolating social practices and applying them to imagined structures. It is more likely that they reside in the intercommunication of science and society, where the latter determines the former through dialectics. Solutions derive from practice, but intrinsically they derive from *practising* with problems that originate in social negations of the status quo. Instead of seeking a political outlet in its autonomy from society, which might implicate its political alienation, science should probably shift its focus to reflecting upon itself politically, namely according to a socially grounded rationality generated by dialogue and the recognition of social and political dialectics.

Scientists are not prophets and science is not a self-fulfilled prophecy or a stereotypical construction of ideas, but they can at least attempt to alleviate social and political irrationality through the acknowledgement of dialectical reason, either in society or politics, and participate in the formation of normative rationality. The latter, deprived of its normativity, was one of Foucault's main concerns, which he attempted to present epistemologically. We will turn to his work in the next chapter.

Notes

1 Pierre Bourdieu and Loic J. D. Wacquant, *An Invitation to Reflexive Sociology* (Cambridge: Polity Press, 2007), 202 and 195.
2 Tom Bottomore and Robert Nisbet (eds), *A History of Sociological Analysis* (London: Heinemann, 1978), 593.
3 Pierre Bourdieu, *Outline of a Theory of Practice* (Cambridge: Cambridge University Press, 2013), 39.
4 Axel Honneth, *The Critique of Power* (Cambridge, MA: The MIT Press, 1991), 219.
5 Bourdieu, *Outline of a Theory of Practice,* 165.

6 Bourdieu, *Outline of a Theory of Practice*, 169.
7 Bourdieu, *Outline of a Theory of Practice*, 188.
8 Bourdieu, *Outline of a Theory of Practice*, 190.
9 Pierre Bourdieu, *Pascalian Meditations* (Cambridge: Polity Press, 2006), 53.
10 Bourdieu, *Pascalian Meditations*, 64.
11 Pierre Bourdieu, *In Other Words* (Cambridge: Polity Press, 2007), 179.
12 Bourdieu, *In Other Words*, 182.
13 Bourdieu, *In Other Words*, 184.
14 Bourdieu, *Pascalian Meditations*, 3.
15 Pierre Bourdieu, *Science of Science and Reflexivity* (Cambridge: Polity Press, 2004).
16 Ian Craib, *Modern Social Theory* (London: Harvester, 1992), 215.
17 Honneth, *The Critique of Power*, 231.
18 Helmut Dubiel, 'Domination or Emancipation?', in Axel Honneth et al. (eds), *Cultural-political Interventions in the Unfinished Project of the Enlightenment* (Cambridge, MA: The MIT Press), 12.
19 Bourdieu, *Science of Science and Reflexivity*, 6.
20 Gilles Deleuze and Felix Guattari, *What Is Philosophy?* (London: Verso, 2011), 43.
21 Deleuze and Guattari, *What Is Philosophy?*, 130.
22 Gilles Deleuze, *Difference and Repetition* (New York: Continuum, 2001), 253, my emphasis.
23 Deleuze, *Difference and Repetition*, 165.
24 Deleuze, *Difference and Repetition*, 43.
25 Deleuze, *Difference and Repetition*, 61.
26 Deleuze, *Difference and Repetition*, 62.
27 Deleuze, *Difference and Repetition*, 65.
28 Deleuze, *Difference and Repetition*, 176.
29 For Hauke Brunkhorst, 'Das Neue ist keine subjective Kategorie, sondern von der Sache erzwungen, die anders nicht zu sich selbst, los von der Heteronomie, kommen kann. Aufs Neue drängt die Kraft des Alten, das, um sich zu verwirklichen, des Neuen bedarf ... Das Neue ist immer ein Potential neuer Möglichkeiten', in *Theodor W. Adorno: Dialektik der Moderne* (Munich: Piper, 1990), 33.
30 Brunkhorst, *Theodor W. Adorno*, 145. My translation from the German text.
31 Eric Alliez, *The Signature of the World* (New York: Continuum, 2005), 92.
32 Alliez, *The Signature of the World*, 92–3.
33 Alliez, *The Signature of the World*, 89.
34 Max Horkheimer, *Eclipse of Reason* (New York: Seabury Press, 1974), 55.

3

Modernism and postmodernism

O gentlemen, the time of life is short!
…
If life did ride upon a dial's point,
Still ending at the arrival of an hour.
And if we live, we live to tread on kings.
William Shakespeare, *Henry IV, Part 1* 5.2.82–7.

So we should not expect Foucault to give us a philosophical *theory* that deploys … notions. Still, philosophy is more than theories.
'Foucault and Epistemology' by Richard Rorty in David Couzens Hoy (ed.), *Foucault: A Critical Reader*[1]

Introduction

Foucault: the catcher in the modern rye

When discussing modernity, one has to refer to Kant's theorizing of the Enlightenment, and particularly to the idea that reason professes to give social shape to both politics and science. But how? By the public use of its capacities to transform the social sphere, which includes all forms of power and authority, whether political, scientific or cultural. It was precisely through the attempt to reintroduce reason into scientific criteria that Kant deserves credit for acknowledging the potential for a modern epistemology with a political perspective, which owes its social existence to the method and process of dialectics.

In one of Kant's most explicit writings on what reason emphasizes, his objective gravitates not towards reason, which he considers an indispensable and inalienable social, political and scientific trait of modernity, but towards the *public use* of reason. In his words:

> But now I hear called out on all sides: do not argue! The officer says: do not argue, just drill! The tax collector says: do not argue, just pay! The clergyman says: do not argue, just believe! ... I answer: the public use of one's reason must be free at all times, and this alone can bring about enlightenment among humans.[2]

The significance of what Kant explicated was twofold. First, he affiliated reason with critique. Kant defined reason not as some form of ambiguous vindication by societies or individuals, but as a creation of dialogical processes that form the social and political critique of the public sphere. Second, humans formulate rational critique through dialogue and, therefore, influence the social sphere by means of their rational perspective on what the public sphere should or should *not* include. From Kant to the theorists of the Frankfurt School, dialogue and critique presuppose the expression of agreement *or disagreement* on the part of citizens, scientists or collectivities.

The public use of dialogue that generates reason and rationality gives form to a rational *theory*, not in the form of a hypothetical or imaginary formulation triggered by self-reflection, but one that is shaped and adopted *because* it incorporates practice on all levels of the public sphere. Rational theory, concerning what normativity is and how it is put into practice, internally bears the potential for rational praxis *because* it is formed and exercised within the public sphere. The normative element of both theory and practice is not, according to the Kantian perspective, a reductionist approach that dictates social rules or inapplicable actions. It is the fundamental part that bears the potential for conscious changes within the social sphere indicated by critique and dialectics.

In relation to these Kantian perspectives, Foucault attempted to introduce an approach which essentially rejected the nature of rationality, modernity and dialectics. Foucault argued that if epistemology wishes to get rid of normative theory, which functions as a scientific straitjacket for free thought and uncoerced arguments, it has to discard dialectics. However, the idea explored in this chapter is that by the use of such a course of reflection, science abandons its claims for rational praxis as well. The normativity of theory provides praxis with inner constitution and external accountability criteria because normativity is not a hypothetical construction but is formed according to the social function of dialectics. Science needs dialectics in order to be accountable to society. Structures, experience and systems seem inadequate for science to render itself socially accountable. Therefore, social praxis appears as a partial scientific and social concern where the critique that theory articulates through dialectics is missing, rendering science uncritical and, thus, pre-modern.

Foucault's opposition to modernity's theorizing on the part of his theoretical contemporaries, such as Habermas, lies in two fundamental points: (a) his concept of reason; and (b) his understanding of critique. Notwithstanding this, Habermas' approach to modernity mainly resides in his overall assessment of Kant's work. Consequently, Foucault's divergence from modernism as well as postmodernism deserves credit for contradicting both Kant and Habermas in their main arguments on modernity, and for maintaining that science is the bearer of the discourse ethics of the political.

Foucault's main contribution to the critique of modernity was his array of analyses that interrogated the *public use* of social and scientific reason. Under such a perspective he turned his attention to science as being the sphere where the public use of social and political reason takes place. On the other side of scientific criticism, where Foucault questions and challenges the *aporias* of structuralism, he avoids the impasse of structuralism regarding practice (mentioned in chapter two), by reconsidering the effects of science on political and ethical *practices*. For Foucault, science has literally no practices whatsoever; its *effects* are politics and ethics, or in other but more precise words, science *happens* when we identify scientific, political and ethical effects upon people in the here and now. Foucault compensates for the structuralist bottleneck of practices by considering the latter as experiences of truth, power and forms of relations for the participants of science and/or politics.

The disagreement over whether or not Foucault was a structuralist was intense during the twentieth century and probably remains so. But apart from formalistic categorizations (from which Foucault remained rather aloof), he preferred methodological as well as essential scientific discontinuities to stable structures. He made a similar observation of dialectics, which he juxtaposed to scientific discontinuities, both in terms of methodology as well as in reflections on objects, which constitute the work of philosophy. For both – methodology and reflections on objects – it signalled a confrontation with the structuralism of the twentieth century, and with modern science and society as represented in Kant's work.

Foucault introduced his idea of critique in marked contrast to discourse and, accordingly, dialectics. For Foucault, what is discursive throughout human history can serve as the cloak for suppression, by means of either scientific or social reason. In parallel, the idea of practice, on which structuralism and poststructuralism are based, can be highly discursive or even negotiable, and as such can also serve as equally suppressive axes in human thought.

I recognize that when, for Foucault, modern science or social constructions are charged with contradictions that generate their successive suppression, they both reply 'it's purely dialectical' and revert to organized authoritarian mechanisms and political manipulations largely coordinated by modern science. However, I raise two major objections to Foucault's critique of structuralist practice and modern dialectics:

(a) Practice exists within social structures, but the scientific or social subjects still need *a theory*. They need a certain theorizing, which safeguards that, in times of crises, practice is based on experience, but mostly has roots and is generated by their theoretical concerns and anxieties over what constitutes the rational. Lack of any form of normativity, which results from dialectics being adopted either as a methodology or a scientific and social *modus vivendi*, might be experienced as a cautious rejection of forms and limitations within the here and now. However, the normative deficit can gradually and steadily, often quicker than expected, serve as a path towards relativism and presentism, as Habermas rightly observed in his work on the philosophical discourse of modernity.

(b) Foucault determined that the idea of scientific interdisciplinarity relates to the idea of difference and open discourse. However, as was also the case with the structuralists, he avoided concluding that his idea of discourse might serve as a means of suppression in modernity through its all-encompassing capacity, namely as a means to include everything within dialogue and at the same time to avoid giving concrete answers when urgent questions arise. The problematic point with Foucault's conception of discourse is that it does not give a plausible answer to the question 'what happens to scientific differences when they *have to* answer to certain polarized theses-antitheses schemata?' This question seeks a straightforward answer, as is often the case in social and scientific controversies.

At the level of what is critical, he does not reject but transforms the idea of critique as being accountable to the degree of non-consensus it furthers and incorporates. His idea of critique included something that Kant and the Frankfurt School may have overlooked, namely the view that if critique is to be rewarding, both intellectually and practically, then it must first be accountable to the social and scientific subject. Second, Foucault maintained that critique has to include not just dialogical controversies but the non-consensual and the divergence of the varied theses of the scientific and social system. For Foucault, we are 'doomed' to stand within the present; therefore, there is no other consideration of critique than the critique of the present time, science and humanity, which generates knowledge and not merely scientific discourse.

On the other side of modernism, where Habermas stands and is precisely opposed to pre-scientific anxieties, it is discursive reason that leads to normative rationality. Habermas correctly emphasizes that, from Heidegger to Foucault, the course of epistemological thought focuses on a critique of reason by means of an associated destruction of both metaphysics and dialectics. He attributes relativistic intentions to Foucault's critique of modernity, which is rather situationally orientated, concentrating on the 'here and now'.

Foucault embarks on new enquiries into reason and modernity, and identifies two concepts of reason: one referring to its critical nature, and the other to its instrumental characteristics leading to the creation of an institutional framework governed by the rationale of the panopticon. Foucault's critique of modernity sought to connect knowledge and science to social institutions. He turned his attention to the affiliation of science with particular social and political institutions, and in this sense accomplished a rather compact understanding of modern science after Kant.

The most essential thing to consider with regard to Foucault's epistemological intentions is his redefinition of modernity through notions such as power, science and discourse. He opposed reason in the Kantian sense in a manner that is also found in the work of the structuralists. By opposing to reason, Foucault formulated a redefinition of modernity through the critique against reason and science in and after Kant. Before elaborating on more particular themes that comprise modernism as well as postmodernism in Foucault's work, it is worth dealing with Habermas' defence of modernity, which was concurrent with Foucault's negative critique towards modern science and rationality. Although both thinkers emphasized the discourse produced by modernity, they differ accordingly (see Figure 3.1).

Both Foucault and Habermas acknowledged that the activation of a critical attitude inaugurates modernity's creation of its own normativity. Nevertheless,

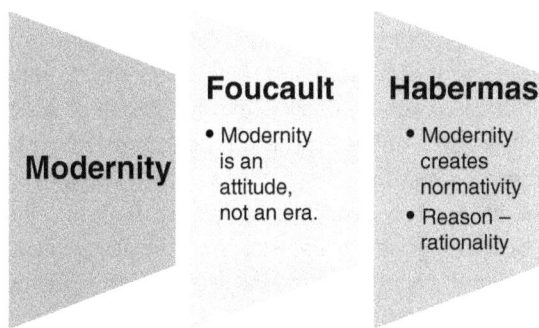

Figure 3.1 Foucault and Habermas on modernity

they developed dissimilar positions on the question of whether the validity of modernity's normativity is as local as the historical context out of which it emerges, and towards which its critical eye is turned. The following sections enquire into issues of normativity and modernity within a comparative perspective on modernism, postmodernism and critical theory.

The politics of science in Foucault

Foucault's position on politics crystallizes when seen through the magnifying glass of science. Far from using science as a tool to criticize politics, he gave clear empirical form to the mediations between science and political decisions that become lucid when critique demystifies and deconstructs them. Being critical, in such a sense, involves the negation or deconstruction of modern scientific and political matters without necessarily providing new theses on what modernity should be. In an attempt to exert negative criticism on modern dialectics, Foucault emphasizes that deconstruction does not entail, either methodologically or historically, the generation of a new scientific or political paradigm.

Such epistemological critique enjoins that science move beyond the thesis-antithesis dialectics, and it differentiates not in terms of traditional and critical epistemology, but rather by giving priority to the following:

(a) an anti-science;
(b) the archaeology of knowledge and its influence upon modern science; and
(c) discourse as a means of avoiding coming to terms with the truth generated by deconstructive critique.

Foucault's anti-science began with the 'archaeological and genealogical study of practices envisaged simultaneously as a technological type of rationality and as strategic games of liberties'.[3] Thus, Foucault moves from a critique of ideology, according to the modern and critical tradition, to a positivist understanding and critique of reason itself within the frame of Kantian epistemology. For Foucault, modern epistemology reproduces existing theses by merely contradicting them with respective antitheses for the sake of their justification. Hence, the status quo, which remains both scientifically and politically unchallenged, overcomes the dialectical impasse, by producing syntheses of supposedly antithetical schemata. He sketches the contours of modern epistemology as being uncoerced thought, where the latter stands in direct opposition to suppressive dialectical critique.

Foucault magnifies the asymmetry between discourse and practice, where what is discursive serves as the disguise for suppression throughout the history of science. In this respect, the notion of 'practice', represented by the structuralists, can be a much more 'discursive' idea, in the sense that dialectics wished it to be, and, therefore, a much more progressive route for epistemological critique. In Foucault's work, the significance lies not in 'rules' or 'practices', but instead gravitates towards the 'system' of rules or practices, which excludes, or at least marginalizes, the discursive nature of dialectics. Foucault's above points of epistemological reference are not extraneous to his criticism of structuralists. His work was innovative in the realm of structuralism by introducing the significance of cognizing subjects within structures and practices. He did not consider the system of structures as producing social interventions or deterministic aims, and applied the potential discourse within structures as the outcome of structural practices, not as the precondition for them. In the case where discourse is regarded as the presupposition of structures, Foucault charged science with the production of non-science or even more impressively, as far as terminology is concerned, with the orientation towards 'a false science'.[4]

In essence, Foucault invalidates, in epistemological terms, both dialectics and structuralist practice. Both appear to reduce the conflictual potential of scientific and political reality. They serve as ideological functions that stand in virtual opposition to scientific truth and political transgression of the established modernity. Foucault radicalizes the scientific and political critique he articulates, and traces the epistemological position of political philosophy at the opposite end of dialectics and structuralism. In his words, 'What we need ... is a political philosophy that isn't erected around the problem of sovereignty, nor therefore around the problems of law and prohibition. We need to cut off the king's head: in political theory that has still to be done.'[5]

The desire for critique can be similarly traced in Adorno and Foucault: it initiates from a similar point, develops into divergent epistemological understanding, and forms a diametrically opposed political perspective. Both thinkers provided the initial impulse for the critique of dialectics by focusing on the negation of the initial thesis proposed by sciences, politics or society. Arguing against the objectification of the subject, Foucault suggests that 'Maybe the target nowadays is not to discover what we are, but to refuse what ... we have to imagine and to build up what we could be to get rid of [a] political "double bind", which is the simultaneous individualization and totalization of modern power structures.'[6] Similarly, both Adorno and Foucault consider critique as the expression of conscious, uncoerced opinion, as well as the process that challenges existing institutions; as such, critique is the expression of the conscious and cognizant subject. The latter consideration, particularly in Foucault, constitutes the moment of separation from structuralism where no conscious subject exists or brings change to the social, scientific or political fore. The social structures suffice to produce practice that governs the social process.

To the extent that the conscious subject criticizes the inadequacies of the predominant forms of science and the objects of science themselves, to an equal extent, the subject in Adorno understands the social and political process that produces irrationality, while in Foucault the cognizing subject remains persistently critical of the here and now, and is embedded within the moments of history and the discontinuities of the sciences. Thus, while Adorno takes up the view that distorted rationality prevails in science and society as a result of the dialectical deficit and the absence of concepts that contribute to the understanding and *criticizing* of the material world, Foucault opts for the explanation of science and society through power relations that govern existing forms of irrational rationality within modernity. For Adorno, reason is the universal claim of science and society, and a universal claim to truth so that the irrational contingency of Auschwitz is eliminated from present and future modernity.

From a different but not necessarily antithetical point of view, Foucault rejects universal claims to scientific reason, and attempts to criticize the scientific and the political by questioning the processual 'how' that lead to Auschwitz, the panopticon and the modern institutional suppression of madness. For Foucault, reason is a social practice exercised by the cognizing subject. Therefore, it is not of universal but of *multiversal* value, and as such it does not necessarily provide guidance for societies in order to avoid instrumental science or irrational politics. It is precisely at this point that a significant moment of relativism is brought to the fore in Foucault's critique of modernity: if reason is thus situationally formed, how can science formulate claims to truth?

Alas, in Foucault, claims to truth appear to be of a presentist nature. If Auschwitz was the manifestation and culmination of distorted claims to truth and rationality, how can the conscious subject avoid the recurrence of claims to irrationality that present themselves as assertions of truth that are actually situationally formed? In defence of the autonomous subject as being historically determined, Foucault opposes necessity to rationality as well as humanism and the values that necessity represents to the reason and rationality of the Enlightenment. The practical, instead of the theoretical, critique that Foucault articulates takes the form of a critique of dialectics and crystallizes at three different moments:

(a) reason is formed by sterile discursive means and supposedly universal claims and values in order to judge modernity;
(b) reason cannot serve as the path to judging the eclipse of reason; and
(c) the duality of rationalism and irrationalism is a rather fruitless epistemological case, for it does not clarify the exact social character and political intentionality of reason.

Nevertheless, the experience of two world wars and the revelation of the concentration camps in modern societies put a rather harsh end to the complacency of the pointlessness of reason and of scientific or social rationality. The idea of imposed scientific rationalization, that reinforced political irrationality on an unprecedented scale, rendered the argument of dialectical ineffectiveness and its rational deficits an issue that could no longer be seriously invoked. Relatedly, Foucault's threefold argument suffers from being, in itself, a dialectical schema that is either epistemologically obsolete or even boring, as he claims of dialectics in general, or sterile in nature.

The problematic side of Foucault's critical assessment of dialectics lies mainly in an overlooked but equally critical position: that dialectics does not necessarily or by coercion lead to a synthesis of contradictions either in science or politics or both simultaneously as being autonomous from each system, which remains interactive with the other. Being critical becomes a theoretical and practical impasse for science and politics when, instead of both the latter generating innovative passages, they continue to be socially immobile and excluded, either within deconstruction and thus barren negation, or within a compelling and coerced synthesis. Dialectics concerns mainly the negation of a thesis, but it is important to note that it also generates theses, which are original in essence and appearance precisely because of the inherently processual character of dialectics itself. Accordingly, dialectics becomes self-innovative, not by rejecting the possibility of a synthesis, but by allowing the thesis–antithesis schema to reflect upon itself and create a novel 'other' thesis.

In his later work, in an interview conducted just before his death, Foucault recognizes that dialectics in the form of questions and answers, elaborated by the knowing subjects, is not unavoidably a coercive procedure of finding answers. It is mainly a process through which conscious subjects have *necessarily* to agree on the questions posed. The same Foucauldian position has both real and apparent consequences when transferred onto politics: the aberrant deviation of political practices lies not in avoiding answers, but in avoiding questions, as well as the critical stance the latter impose when addressed to power (inter)relations within scientific or political systems.

The marginalization of discursive processes, particularly in human sciences, producing thus discursive discontinuities and the incorporation of non-discursive practices that can be traced for their continuity, is a recurrent consideration in Foucault's *The Order of Things* and *The Archaeology of Knowledge* emphasizing the persistence of knowledge–power relations. In both books, Foucault recognizes that discourse is interrupted by lack of coherence towards power, and that practice is also undermined by the steady and unobstructed perseverance of its application. It is never stated normatively in Foucault, but he appears to suggest the rediscovery of coherent discourse that produces a multiplicity of options and a regeneration of practice by means of critique being imposed on practical matters.

Foucault rejected any identification with structuralism, but nevertheless rescued the lost honour of structuralism by reintroducing the autonomy of the subject within systems of thought. He innovated the notion of the archaeology of knowledge, articulated within systems of signs in structuralism, by prioritizing genealogical questions concerning the politics of science and the social role of power relations interlinking politics and discursive regularities coordinated by scientific systems.

Before attempting to clarify critical knowledge, Foucault focused on the archaeology of knowledge that deals with the *objects* of science as acquiring meaning when discursive processes take place within a rule-governed system of thought. He differentiates between two forms of objects of knowledge: (a) those that are neutral in meaning and understanding; and (b) those that are mediated by systems of discourse practices and that raise claims to validity precisely because of discursive formations they facilitate. In such a sense, the latter divergence arises as a moment of dialectical consideration in Foucault's work.

Although he considers dialectics an epistemological straitjacket, Foucault fails to guarantee a methodological and epistemological alternative. He proclaims discursive rules as a methodological passage for tracing unities of disciplines through discursive practices, and thus innovates within structuralism through dialectics. 'But when he comes to propose a principle of unity through discontinuities ... he again passes over the possibility that disciplinary unities might be the result of unreflectively shared practices, and assumes that the unities must be found on the level of rule-governed discourse.'[7]

Despite his intention to disqualify a dialectical thesis–antithesis schema, he clearly differentiates between *mathesis* and *taxinomia*, where the first stands for the unified science of truth and the second for the knowledge of beings, signs and their articulation. Under such an understanding of knowledge, he develops a rather incoherent course of arguments. He acknowledges that science can take the form of a universally accepted truth, which in some cases is marked by the validity societies attribute to it. Nonetheless, he considers science, as stated above, a situationally valid bearer of truth in order 'to intervene in contemporary political struggles in the name of "local" scientific truth'.[8] In the latter quote Foucault defines situational truth as an urgent question on what is socially valid at a *particular* moment in history. In a moment of self-reflection on his epistemology, Foucault identifies that political struggles in the name of scientific truth – despite both being related by their impact within the social process – are hampered by their local character, which deters them from acquiring a more universal perspective. Therefore, panegyrics to situationalism and presentism, which isolate science and its political concerns from being universally valid, give relativism a running start and provide it with an open field for developing an insufficient, if not self-contradictory, epistemology in Foucault's work.

The idea of scientific truth ensures, in Foucault, several deterministic victories: it is associated with power and thus with the politics of truth, as if truth could undergo some form of relativistic social manipulation. In my understanding, it is, rather, the reverse: because Foucault deems truth to be situationally based, he views its validity as being stigmatized by the manipulation of politics. Although he differentiates between the scientific battle for truth and the social status it enjoys, as well as the political role it plays, the cunning of truth is not necessarily linked with 'a system of ordered procedures for the production, regulation, distribution, circulation, and operation of statements',[9] nor is it fatalistically interlinked with a 'regime' of truth coordinated by social and scientific systems. However, Foucault's critique of truth cannot avoid pre-modern regression.

The starting position of pre-modern arguments in Foucault becomes clearer when we reconsider his polemics against theory. Again, as with the idea of the structuralists towards practice, he pluralizes the possibilities of options, and views practices as a constellation of themes that are organized within systems of action. Thus, he allows a multiplicity of practices to prevail within the social 'here and now' and bids against the existence and acceptance of objective truth and rationality. His pre-modern position crystallizes around the multiplicity of theories as options against a teleological impasse of rational truth, whereas the latter hinders the emergence of successive strategies and *actions* for the sake of rational action.

He wins the fusion of the transcendental and the empirical, and the horizon of descriptive and prescriptive rules that govern both regularities and operative forces, but he loses track of rationality, truth through discourse (for the sake of multiple truths?) and modernity, which introduced fundamental changes, both in methodology and the rationale of the science. Foucault's perspective was pre-modern precisely because he excluded the formation of a normative theory that would generate rational praxis.

His method of exclusion entailed the marginalization of dialectics; however, this meant a failure to recognize that by leaving dialectics aside (or downgrading it), the multiplicity of options and practice allows the relativism of both theories and praxes to prevail over any other consideration of rational theory and praxis. It permitted just what he intended to avert, namely both theory and practice to become wholly contingent. Foucault promised the innovation of modernity through *episteme,* but provided the regulation of modernist method, theory and action that derives from the previous two elements through a well-coordinated retreat to the pre-modern.

Within precisely such a pre-modern frame of understanding lies the deterministic and therefore positivist *telos* of sciences: it concerns discursive rule formation, practices and principles of regularities that turn into the regulation and reductionism of science per se.

Despite Foucault's persistence in releasing the multiplicity of options of scientific and social actions, it is exactly these actions that modern sciences take into consideration in order to form their object of research, which forms a theoretical understanding of humanity. The task of modern science is not to identify the criteria of multiplicities or the governing rules of systems' formation that become the timely iron cage, both for knowledge as well as for humanity. The task of science in modernity is the formation of the rational and the *elenchus* (the critical assessment) of devices of political rationalization over which science can potentially claim political jurisdiction.

If science is to have a function, this can be approached by answering the crucial question of what science does with rationality. However, the aim of the following sections in this chapter is to explore the idea that Foucault's thought remained far from critical, and even farther from formulating a concrete argument for the rationality or rationalization that science self-reflexively produces. He remained aloof to the idea of a critique of modernity, in the way that was brought forward by Adorno or Habermas, despite the fact that he acknowledged rationality as the main way in which the genealogy and interrelation of science and politics govern within modern societies.[10]

Towards a redefinition of modernity

Throughout his work, Foucault intended for his arguments on epistemology to be applicable but not necessarily theoretically grounded; for him, 'the "best" theories do not constitute a very effective protection against disastrous political choices'.[11] The main argument of this section emphasizes that they move in the opposite direction. The lack of theories does not eliminate the probability of opting, on the part of societies, for the worst political choices, as we will see with Foucault's political stance. With Foucauldian analyses of knowledge and science, the reader recognizes their timely applicability, but is often unable to trace the theoretical grounds on which criticism is articulated; thus, she is at a loss to justify, not just historically but systematically, the genealogy of his epistemological points. The deficit in theory that Foucault argues for generates an equal deficit in accountability. It is through theories that individual or societies both found and find *accountability*, which frames rational criteria in respect of the social and the scientific.

There arises in Foucauldian epistemology a form of sheer relativism whereby what is empirically rational has to be preceded by the foundation of an empirical truth. The problematic core of such an argument is disclosed when we shift focus from the formation of truth to its empirical manifestation, because what Foucault systematically avoids explicating is *not* what constitutes the truth, but rather what constitutes *the empirical*. The epistemological deficit in such perceptions develops when it begins to challenge its own reflexivity: if the empirical is of an individual character, it is then ignorable but not unimportant (albeit of limited scope). If it owes its validity to widely accepted concerns, it is then produced by the universal exchange of argumentation that indicates the generation of dialectical processes, which introduce and consummate accountability criteria.

In social terms, what the empirical consists of and signifies can be either of individualistic, corporately shared or socially valid intentions and cannot be judged as such until the social subjects that politically prioritize their experiences confirm their validity and urgency. The empirically rationalized often served in social and scientific history as the best path to the transcendentally irrational, or, in other words, as the justification for universal authoritarianism and political totalitarianism because empirical claims were manipulated by sciences or politics as such. Scientific repression and political authoritarianism were never shunned on account of their claims to empirical vindications. What deterred authoritarianism was rather the combination of theory and praxis that derives from the formation of theory on the part of conscious subjects.

In terms of epistemology, Foucault attempted to reorganize the modern scientific game by combining three major elements:

(a) the scientific discourse;
(b) the cognizant subject; and
(c) the rules of practical, and therefore valid, application of what results from discourse, where discourse stands for not the consideration of contradictions, but rather their suppression and orientation towards 'other', alternative modes of identifying modernity.

However, all the above-mentioned points of epistemological reference seem modern in their intentions, but appear pre-modern in their manifestations, particularly when criticized according to the dual differentiation of *mathesis* and *taxinomia*. In conjunction with developing particular points that relate science to truth, Foucault's centre of attention addresses the notion of critique. Foucault's epistemological focus seeks to question how and to what extent criticism of modern science (mainly in Kant) can serve as the royal path to formulating 'another' modern epistemology by transgressing the critique of the sciences after the nineteenth century. Although implicit in the course of Foucauldian arguments, the contours of what constitutes criticism circulate around four forms:

1. Focusing on the reflexivity of words;
2. Analysing the order of construction;
3. Identifying the modes of representation;
4. Revealing the relations of representation.

Moreover, it is philosophy, mainly through its political orientation, which is distinguished form historical and archaeological concerns, and which acts as the subject and bearer of modern critical arguments.

Such a form of critique maintains a contextual as well as methodological discrepancy with regard to what was protracted by the modernism of rational discourse and dialectical rationality. Reflexivity, construction, modal analysis and relations of representation can be essential but nevertheless diametrically opposed stances and methods of scientific development to what was professed by the public use of reason and interdisciplinary rationality in early as well as late modernity. In essence, Foucault questions the unlimited range of scientific representation, while challenging the maxims of Kantian reason as imposing limits upon representation by identifying the normativity of reason.

In relation to the autonomous and cognizant subject, the problematics that I consider to be the main epistemological concern remain unscathed and unanswered: if the autonomy of the subject is feasible and potentially consummated, how can the pre-modern deliberation of the subject that Foucault argues for enable an autonomy that is also facilitated by practical reason? Foucault's epistemology, either for beginners or advanced students, is of performative character in the sense that the idea of social practices – that extends into a variety of scopes from culture to sciences – is affiliated with everyday praxis of a limited capacity and intentions that render the cognizant and free subject an acting subject. Such *epistemology of praxis* instrumentalizes social practices in order to assign the arguments within a practical frame. Foucault's epistemology of praxis takes power as the concept upon which innovation is based in the discourse of modernity, but it shirks from a *theoretical* approach to *what* power is and *why* such a concept is applicable.

Therefore, it allows power to be considered as another form of domination, which, it is to be hoped, would be applied to the dominators and not the dominated. Foucault's approach to power also raises a second point of difficulty: even if power signifies the action taken to overthrow scientific or social authoritarianism, the impasse it creates touches upon the question of accountability or merely the alternative to the existing power relations. If a certain form of power is scientifically and socially established, to whom or to what is it accountable, and how can new forms of innovation overthrow the existing forms of power? What is the safeguard to guarantee that existing forms of power would not suffer their own moment of negative dialectic and stagnate into sheer forms of authoritarianism? In other words, what constitutes the thin line that demarcates power from authoritarianism?

Foucault's approach to modernity provides the reader with a meticulous structuralist differentiation and elaboration of power interrelations and their methodology. Figure 3.2 gives a schematic presentation of power interrelations in squares and points of methodology in circles.

Under such a Foucauldian understanding, power through domination without safeguarding social and political accountability and potential for alteration appears a pre-modern continuation of the scientific and social status quo, or even a puritan and conservative practice which lacks discourse and dialectical processes of innovation and the formation of new theses through negative dialectics. I maintain that power in Foucault incorporates domination. Such

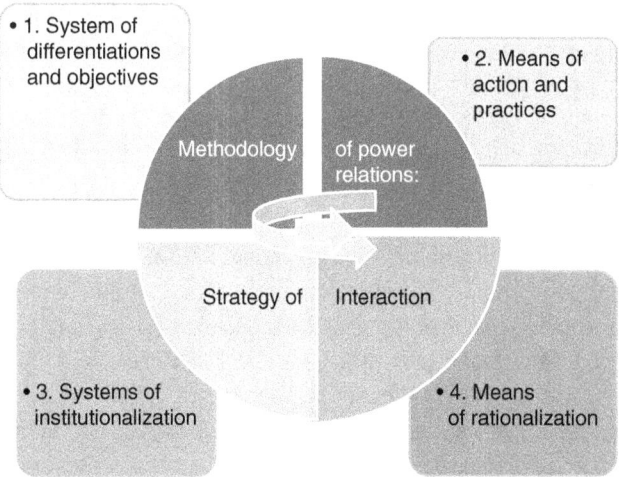

Figure 3.2 Foucault's structuralist account of power relations

authoritarianism needs the rationalization of dominance through power by somehow free subjects, as Foucault claims, which turns radical politics into the negation of its own enlightenment.

No wonder that Foucault's consideration of radical politics was not particularly attractive, but rather dystopian. Despite being of presentist intentions, his concern for political practices and applications was notoriously marred by his defence of the Iranian revolution in the late 1970s. Foucault's position – that power concerns the here and now – was widely accepted in opposition to the allegedly universal suffocation of dialectical reason and rational discourse, but was unfortunately (for Foucauldians) and fortunately (for critical theorists like Habermas) disqualified as applying not to the 'here and now' but to the here and there or not at all.

The examination of systems of power, as areas of scientific and political potentiality of an 'other' modernity, fails to recognize what the potential might be in cases of powerlessness or where there exists a lack of an alternative to the acquisition of power. Although apparently analysing political prospects, Adorno's critique might equally apply to scientific deliberation for the exercise of power: 'the dominant ideology today dictates that the more individuals are delivered over to *objective* constellations, over which they have, or believe they have, no power, the more they subjectivize this powerlessness'.[12]

Foucault's idea of a new modernity resides in his consideration of the innovation of critique and even of the refusal to cope with Kantian arguments for the sake of mobilizing an 'other' critique. He considers the Kantian perspective as potentially modern under social conditions which allow such a modernity to take place, but nevertheless archaeologically produced and genealogically consummated. The modernism that Foucault presented opposed Kant's idea of critique, and in the overall assessment served as a meta-narrative of modernity or as the formative idea of postmodernism. Such critique conforms with modernism when elaborating the significance of scientific *elenchus* that acts as the magnifying glass which emphasizes social and political problematics. Foucault's critique also indicates that self-reflection on the political, in the scientific domain, influences both scientific and social rationality.

However, the new formations of discourse that Foucault professed cannot be explained through a dialectical mode of scientific advance because they are mediated by practices within social and scientific structures and systems. By excluding the theorizing of the social, he ignores the social and scientific subject and prioritizes practices, which generate rules and therefore regulations of the social and scientific process of modernity. Despite his constant structuralist concern – according to Bourdieu's famous phrase – to awake from any dogmatic slumbers, Foucault's contribution to what is represented by social and scientific practices and discourses involves respective interpretations.

The latter embody a particular framework of concepts and criteria of modernity. The Foucauldian power is of transcendental meaning, coming close to the structuralist idea of non-subjectively structured systems of action, while, in Kant, the construction of social and scientific rationality is mediated within modernity through conscious subjects accomplishing meaning within synthetic performances.

Habermas notes that the idea of modernity was signified by the sovereign subject that achieved sovereignty precisely through the exploration of knowledge, and the dialectical modes of advance that either science or society produce. The progress that modernity encouraged and promoted, through science, was geared towards scientific and social relations. Progress 'happens' within the lifeworld, which in turn promotes dialectics through communicative action. The transcendental version of lifeworld in Husserl is given a practical inflection by Habermas. Such a framework is not a barrier to the understanding of modernity; on the contrary, it is integral to it.

With Foucauldian modernity, the barrier is set and represented by the notion of power itself. As well as failing to denote where and how power is practically realized, Foucault neglects to designate *who* or *what* is the object of power, or *over whom* such power is exerted. For Habermas, 'The discourse of the sciences, and, in general, the discourses in which knowledge is shaped and transmitted, lose their privileged status; together with other discursive practices, they form power complexes that offer a domain of objects sui generis.'[13]

Habermas was rather modest in his critique. He correctly recognized that, under such Foucauldian understanding, power derives from the sciences. Although Foucault infers that scientific power influences the consummation of social power with certain mechanisms it produces (e.g. the panopticon), Foucault's modernity intrinsically generates power and domination through a totalizing critique, either of the sciences or of societies. By contrast, the Kantian understanding of modernity generates sovereign subjects of thought and action through dialectics.

My position is that it is precisely dialectics that transforms the pre-modern world into modernity simply by shifting the focus from the sovereignty of domination and the dominant to the sovereignty of the scientific and social subjects. This marks a crucial moment in modernity and critique. In Foucault, the idea of power implicitly bears its negation, namely powerlessness. Critical theory of (the late) Adorno and Habermas (mainly in the 1980s) responds that, far from being an exaggeration, the relations of power and powerlessness designate one of the initial steps towards scientific and political authoritarianism, while the supposedly free or suppressed subject remains unable to react and, therefore, unable to experience, create and exert critique.

The hypothetical security of great collectivities and structures – either for individuals or collective subjects – suggests a tendency towards conformity and passivity, which in social terms tends to marginalize the social and produce a structure of *Gemeinschaft* per se. No matter how hard Foucault's modernism or postmodernism sought consolidation in the idea of power, the very idea of power itself rests upon social or scientific subjects being reliant on a rigid and immovable authority that signifies a renewal of the disaster experienced in authoritarian relations of the social, scientific or political kind.

Despite being postmodernist as such, the idea of power contradicts the principle of divergence and difference that was represented so rigidly by structuralists, poststructuralists and postmodernists. As Habermas correctly identifies, the idea of the distortion of modernity, through irrational reason, instrumentality of the sciences, and the social and political elimination of individual representation constitute the approach that Adorno introduced. Neither poststructuralists nor Foucault dealt with the distortion of modernity.[14] There is a concrete form of asymmetry built into Foucault's understanding of modernity: his conception of modernity is realized by means of practices that construct systems of discourse and, thus, give themselves over to postmodernist arguments in order to conceptualize meta-modernity. Even so, Foucault's idea of modernity is not post- but *pre*-modern for its negation of the social despite the concern for the political. Moreover, it does not constitute a 'new' modernity through power. Foucault's modernity appears insufficient, even in its stance towards the modern. Power is not a modern but a pre-modern moment 'of the coercive, asymmetric influence over the freedom of movement of other participants in interaction'.[15]

Even though Foucault attempted to keep epistemological prejudices under a tight rein, and precisely for the sake of modernity that had to be renewed under a postmodernist perspective, his epistemology reproduced not only the mechanism but the essential concern of pre-modern sciences and societies, namely domination. When modernity is attached to an unchallenged power, it simultaneously entails the experience of powerlessness on the part of any scientific, political or social subject of individual or collective existence. The modern concern of dialectical relations of intercommunication does not merely (although we probably have to question whether it is just 'merely') safeguard the exchange of argumentation of all participants, despite valid criticism for its distortions and deviations; it also places cognizant subjects in a position of *equality* within a dialogical situation. Last but not least, such dialogue acts as a learning process for participating subjects where they publicly express reason, and attempt to form rationality – sometimes individually while other times throwing themselves 'into the melting pot of the collective ego'.[16]

Foucault to postmodernism: Poor fool! No wiser than before![17]

Just as Foucault denounced the idea of being a structuralist, so too he rejected any form of categorization of his work as modernist or postmodernist. However, even if the wishful thinking of postmodernists would like to see Foucault's work being referred to as postmodernist, his perseverance in innovating the concept of modernity according to 'another' form of modern demands continued unabated. Hence, one of the most appealing exchange of arguments in the twentieth century took place between Habermas and Foucault, with both parties arguing for or against the content of modernity, and both being motivated by the same interest: what marks modernity as modern, and how the modern evolves into being an 'other' self-reflective modern, thus acquiring a politically practical and socially realizable form.

Although seeming to converge, both thinkers followed a different course of argument. Habermas was accused of following the Weberian path of rationalization, and Foucault was seen as redefining the modern according to the postmodern. The aim of the present section is to indicate that both critiques of Habermas and Foucault were rather inaccurate. Especially for Foucault, the *aporia* of his arguments lies in not being modern and definitely not postmodern. He abandons structuralism, but he reverts to pre-modern conceptions of science, critique and the political.

I consider as a common myth the conception that words cannot influence or shape reality, but the Kantian motto '*sapere aude!*' served as an answer to the question 'what is Enlightenment?', and attempted to determine what modernity signified: the audacity to think that which would (whether implicitly or explicitly) encourage people to act. As stated in the initial lines of this chapter, Foucault's understanding of modernity performed a reversal: practices generate modernity – practices that produce processual discourses lead to social development.

The postmodernist critique of modernity, proposed by the likes of Lyotard, stood in marked contrast to both Kantian and Foucauldian positions. Since it is theory that leads to praxis, this conjunction is of great importance. Postmodernist thought identified an absence of this conjunction explicitly in Kant and implicitly in Foucault. The legitimation provided by means of praxis is annihilated when distinguishing between intellectual oeuvres and the practical consequences of knowledge. In terms of knowledge and science, things become complicated by the addition of the fundamental demand of truth. The postmodern condition identifies that even if a scientific statement is considered true, this does not necessitate that it might also be considered just.

The problematic nature of this postmodern view produces a position on knowledge that is correct in its implicit assumption, but wrong in its interpretation and questionable in its political appeal. Although the divergence between theory and practice is of a methodological nature, facilitating epistemological research and explicating procedures of knowledge acquisition within the realm of science, it does not tally with abstract or monistic reflections of an 'either ... or ...' nature. Rather, it brings to the fore an epistemological mentality of 'both ... and ...'. The latter does not deterministically demand the totalizing inclusion of all potentials. On the contrary, it focuses on the validity of the social legitimation of science by means of realizing what *is* true and just.

There is a cogent distinction to be made between critical theory and postmodernist or Foucauldian epistemology, namely that scientific or political reason, formed through the public use of dialectics, and transformed into communicative action, provides the criteria for the realization of *both* truth *and* justice within the social. The procedural and critical nature of the dialectic allows for the social consummation not of what *is considered* true and just, but of what *is* true and just. Otherwise, a methodological and epistemological dead end is unavoidable, as the Heideggerian case bitterly indicated – a judgement also shared by postmodernist criticism.[18] Hence, the legitimation that science seeks is safeguarded not by an approach of either theory or practice that signifies an attack on both legitimate fundamentals of the scientific domain, but rather by both theory and praxis together, inextricably.

The complex intermingling of the descriptive and the normative, in the scientific area, is the line of thought that relates the Kantian critique of reason with the critical theorists' epistemology and interdisciplinarity. On the other hand, the postmodernists, in their general hostility towards modern science, presented a performative idea of science that produces 'results' by mastering reality through technology. Despite it being too premature to consider in full, the latter postmodernist claim on the practical value of science being technology per se might have found several historical confirmations during the early twentieth-first century when the global expansion of communication through computers has sustained the demand for social and political changes across the globe. There was no authoritarian or tyrannical political regime, in the late twentieth or early twenty-first century, that neglected to withhold the functioning of the Internet within its domain for the sake of instrumental political and social stability.

Nevertheless, there is no such instrumentality or performativity, and that constitutes the problematic side of postmodernist interpretation. Performativity is limited in terms of its political implementation. After a short while it achieves fewer instrumental ends than the postmodernists' deterministic predictions. The performative character of technology, which modern science generates, does not represent the moment of fulfilment and completion of the scientific process towards its political realization. It constitutes the mediating process that reaches uncoerced decisions of political change, where it is not technology that consummates political innovation, but the *potential* for both theory and praxis generated through technology. The postmodernist misconception of such a process is further elaborated when political change is affiliated with power and 'decision-making authority'. The position throughout Lyotard's argument is crystal clear, and to a great extent it is influenced by similar Foucauldian views, while also opposing them to some extent: power is authority and its performance, 'not only good performativity, but also effective verification and good verdicts'.[19] Thus, power is the legitimating force for science, which implies that it is not truth and justice that reaches scientific legitimation, but rather power as such that consummates instrumental scientific legitimacy.

For Kantian and Habermasian modernity, the courage of understanding suggests: (a) the courage of truth; and (b) the courage to act. With Foucault, truth is generated by practices, mechanisms and forms of power exercised by the sciences themselves. With the advent of the postmodern criticism of reason and modern rationality, which turned into a sheer denigration of the scientific and political reason and its public use, the scope for modern as well as postmodern analysis widened with Foucault in his attempts to differentiate from both. Foucault identified the potential of modern sciences to criticize the consummation of scientific and social myths, but disapproved of the postmodern view in order to acknowledge science as making an explicit appeal to philosophy for its social legitimation. Particularly political philosophy, as analysed previously, holds itself in opposition to dialectics but is also seated in diametrical opposition to grand narratives of modernity, which either approve or disapprove of reason, formed within modern societies.

Political philosophy is another dynamic that Foucault tried to identify and innovate within his work on power relations and discourse analysis. Political philosophy does not coincide with the banality of the scientific, as postmodernists profess; it mediates the modern and distances from the postmodern theorizing of scientific knowledge, while considering postmodernist epistemology a kind of banal discourse. No wonder that his focus was on practices, systemic generation of relations and scientific analysis producing a rationale of and for political philosophy. Although Foucault was either charged with avoiding an articulation of any form of normative argument, or considered a crypto-normativist for his study of power and power relations, his sole contact with the normative can be traced in his critique of political philosophy and the epistemological and political role it is invoked to play.

For Foucault, scientific reason is the outcome, not the instigator, of practices and discourse, as well as the content of discourse. It is precisely here that a concrete epistemological deficit appears within Foucault and the postmodernists. Reason is one of the primordial elements and objects of discourse; however, the eclipse of reason produces not just a constitutive factor and the object of dialectics, but also a scientific deficit of accountability: *to whom* is *science* accountable, and how can that scientific irrationality, leading to social and political irrationality, be shunned or excluded? Among other functions that constitute a learning process for participants of discourse, the public use of reason serves as a safeguard or even public observatory of what the eclipse of reason might mean to both science and society. The eclipse of reason augurs, then, the eclipse of the public use of dialogue and exchange of argumentation on an institutional and political level, which are both mediated by the social function of the sciences. The latter appears, in Foucault's view, to share institutional domination over which scientific discourse claims an interventionist role and critical potential.

Although Foucault dealt extensively (particularly in *The Archaeology of Knowledge*) with the distortion of the social and political role of the sciences in producing mechanisms of domination and, therefore, *false science,* he failed to give a plausible analysis of how such a perspective on the scientific is to be avoided. Instead, he introduced the concept of power in marked contrast to the postmodernists (particularly Lyotard), who categorized dialectics as a superficial duality operating within the social system for the sake of social efficiency.

Conversely, Foucault remained steadfast in identifying divergences and multiple differentiations, thus tracing the conflictual potential generated by the sciences and dealt with in social systems. Although Lyotard maintained that opposition governs society, which includes a mechanism recognized as the role of knowledge in the making of society, Foucault challenged the validity and limits of such problematics. Foucault looked to how divergences turn into conflictual oppositions that generate power relations in the sciences and society. With the notion of power, Foucault avoids the cul-de-sac of consensual truth and knowledge so criticized by postmodernists. Foucault maintained that because of power, knowledge and truth are realized within social systems; whereas for the postmodern condition, truth is generated and accounted for by means of social or scientific consensus. At that point, the dialectical element, for the postmodernists, provides a moment of legitimation by composing a mechanism of arguments and proofs.

Foucault's modernism finds itself much closer to the idea of dialectics dealing or being occupied with the negative or the 'other' in science and society than with the postmodern exclusion of reason and the potential of a rational modernity. While, for Foucault, the conflictual is prioritized on account of its incorporation of a multiplicity of agonistic demands, for postmodernists the dialectical is the conformist avoidance of the divergent and agonistic pluralism, which excludes any potential for consensus as presupposing a fabricated truth. While Foucault saw the dialectical as a potential for multiplicity, the postmodernists considered it the concealment of both consensus and truth.

On a second level of analysis, Foucault's modernism is also crystallized in another crucial divergence from the postmodernists: it excludes a social explanation of the scientific and the political and places systems at the centre of epistemological understanding. The postmodernists introduce a relation of legitimation between sciences or knowledge as such, and society: 'If they [the scientists] feel that the civil society of which they are members is badly represented by the State, they may reject its prescriptions.'[20] Rejection is the point of critique for the postmodernists, but it also denotes a moment of dialecticity for postmodernism. However, if postmodernism is compared with the Frankfurt School, I maintain that the study of critical theory towards science and society remains valid because it denotes that the linear analysis of practical social and political representation within the social gives shape and substance to what constitutes science's criticality. The latter bears the potential either to legitimize or delegitimize political decisions of collective subjects for the sake of civil society's representation.

The postmodernist explanation of the critical theory of the Frankfurt School was insufficient and unrewarding. It associated the epistemology of critical theorists with a deterministic relation to Marxism, as attempting to render the autonomous subject freed from alienation or repression. It was, to a large extent, a major misunderstanding. Despite the early theorization of the first generation of critical theorists, in relation to Marxism, the epistemological innovation of interdisciplinarity was based on the idea of Kantian dialectics. The first generation of critical theorists maintained Kant's notion of reason applying to data being realized by conscious subjects through experience. Particularly in Marcuse's work, reason mediates technology as the indispensable means for innovation. In the same line of Kantian thought, Habermas' critique presents dialectics as providing the sciences with the potential of consensus, that is, not reconciliation or totalization, but consensual understanding of knowledge in relation to human interests.

The present chapter intends neither to formulate an apology for critical theory, nor to capitalize on critical theory by way of comparing the work of the Frankfurt School to similar epistemological arguments, nor to demonstrate certain deterministic similarities. However, it might be of importance for the reader of modern thought and epistemology to note that critical theory's epistemological contributions or *aporias* can be more fruitfully understood when examined through the lens of Foucauldian and postmodernist problematics. In the light of the latter's critique of modern science and technology, it becomes much clearer that the comparison should not only focus on critical theorists and Foucault along with postmodernists, but also include the divergences between the first generation of Horkheimer and Marcuse and the second generation of Habermas. While, for the early Frankfurt School, modern science is mediated and legitimated through the advent of technology, for Habermas, opposing to a large extent both his predecessors and the critique exerted by Foucault and Lyotard, technology contributes to alienated and objectifying forms of relations with nature and reciprocally among individual or collective subjects. Habermas' position, despite sharing something of the spirit of *Dialectic of Enlightenment*, did not leave any prospect for an 'other' technological advance in the service of modernity.

For the first generation, the scientific potential allowed for the avoidance of the theoretical deficit that is manifested in the proclaimed 'neutrality' of science. It also consequently avoided the legitimation deficit (as formulated by Marcuse and the early Horkheimer of 'Traditional and Critical Theory') of modern science that is unable to legitimize itself while experiencing the separation of means from ends. For Habermas, much closer in this respect to his French counterparts, the mediation of science is accomplished through communicative action among scientific and social participants.

The idea of modern science and modernity never appealed to critical theorists of the first or second generation as an idealist agenda for egalitarianism or justice mediated in humanity. Neither modern science nor modernity more broadly were ever misunderstood or even misrepresented by the Frankfurt School as an ideal social and political situation. On the contrary, long before any Foucauldian or postmodernist polemics against modernity, Horkheimer and Adorno articulated one of the most plausible warnings against modern reason turning into a tyrannical force.

It is not the point to ask to what degree the first generation of critical theorists dealt with postmodern concerns. It is not a matter of a historical continuum. Rather, the more pertinent approach would take up its problematics and consider to what extent Foucault and postmodernists formulated more or less plausible arguments for or against modernity that in essence generated the modernist idea of *ongoing critique* – either of a theoretical (that which, according to Kant, preforms and simultaneously includes experience) or of a practical (namely moral) nature. Before elaborating any course of arguments on modern science and philosophy as the bearer of political problematics, critical theorists from Horkheimer to Habermas articulated their critique of modern science through the dialectic of enlightenment 'that critical philosophy itself must dissolve if it is to restore our faith in moral idealism and social critique'.[21]

Drawing from critical theory, I think that the mediation of the demands of civil society within politics is a steady reference point for modern epistemology, particularly that of the twentieth century. If critical theory and its modern epistemological arguments are to be scientifically, politically and socially worthwhile and valid, they have to turn their attention not to the differences of epistemological trends, but to the similarities. Relatedly, the point of methodological negation and rejection of similarities appears superficial and, in epistemological terms, very convenient or even condescending: it indicates difference, through which collective subjects find a reason for existence by means of differentiation. On the other hand, tracing similarities does not necessitate totalization or an ignoring of the essence of conflict.

It mostly entails that, at first glance, negations and rejections manifest themselves as acute and insurmountable, while on closer epistemological inspection they reveal that the concerns, if not anxieties, remain the same: they attempt to realize political representation of the socially active (namely civil society) through the politically dynamic (namely the collective subject of science). In such realization, the role of science remains of pivotal importance.

Conclusions

The most modern trait of Foucault's oeuvre was the *aporias* that his arguments deliberately reach. For such an outstanding characteristic, he might be considered as the most modern among modernists and postmodernists, although as stated above he intrinsically criticized the former and delivered major criticisms of the latter. In line with Adorno and Horkheimer (they both reached conscious *aporias*, as did Foucault, that have been strongly criticized), Foucault does not write a political manifesto; he refuses to invent solutions, denounces traditional paths in epistemology and politics, and seeks an 'other' modern epistemology and modernity.[22] In particular, there are two inherent *aporias* in Foucault's modernism: first, there is no way to avoid conflicts; and second, power is socially and politically indefinite or merely lacks its own social and political *locus*. The notion of power is highly contestable and appears dubious in the sense that while power is mediated by the individual, it becomes less clear upon which object power is exercised and, last but not least, whether power is orientated towards another individual or collective representation of interests.

At some point, Foucault attempted to compensate for the bottleneck of domination and chaotic agonism that scientific or political power entails by situating power within procedures of discourse, communication and normative rationality, thus situating agonism and power within some form of valid scientific and political realm that would prove epistemologically and practically fruitful. Things did not turn out too well theoretically: the avoidance of repression that Foucault identified was linked in his late work with the theory of right. Even so, it appears implausible to argue for new forms of right that would guarantee social and scientific normativity. The recent European and global justice system defending rights did not suffice to consummate political stability and the advancement of social and scientific rationality. Even when all rights are guaranteed by means of moral justifications, the field of knowledge and the field of politics correspond with individual or collective participants who perform illocutionary acts, and produce communicative or distorted rationality.

With Foucault, the reader of modern epistemology advances a step further into political epistemology. The most important contribution towards such theorizing was the claim that science is now coherently associated with a practical aspect: its affiliation with social institutions. As such, the criterion of truth that knowledge claims to bear is situationally observable, if not historically produced.

Foucault shifts the focus from the science as such to the politics it generates, and to particular political decisions it promotes. In this way, such considerations highlight what modern epistemology is, in essence: a critique of asymmetries and distortions between science and the political. Epistemology, for Foucault, is irretrievably political and criticizes relations of domination among coerced or uncoerced participants, thereby attributing meaning to the dialectic of the scientific enlightenment. Foucault enacts a rupture both with enlightenment and with hermeneutical continuities of modernity, but the weakness of his approach is the fact that he considers power as a critique of reason that would eliminate the latter and thereby provide a significant epistemological and political move towards an anti-science and an anti-modernity.[23]

The first chart of the chapter that illustrates the varied positions on modernity of Foucault and Habermas is deliberately left unelaborated. It denotes the Gordian knot of scientific modernity between critical theorists and the Foucauldian view. The main bone of contention was the Kantian paradigm of modern critique and indicated that, for critical theory, universal norms constitute the rational basis of scientific critique, while, for Foucault, critique – to be worthy of the name – must be deprived of norms. The Frankfurt School (of the first and the second generation) unwaveringly maintained that the normativity of the sciences is not a guidance for the irrationally perplexed, but endeavours to fulfil the demand for the *ought to* which precedes or follows all social and political practice and, therefore, praxis.

For my understanding, however, it is impossible to think of modern normativity without relating it to the form of rationality that is shaped either in science or politics by means of interdisciplinarity and the dialectics of the thesis-antithesis schema. The apple of discord between Foucault and critical theorists is theorized implicitly in the quest for normativity, and explicitly in challenging the form of rationality. Although for critical theory, normativity influenced by reason and dialectics does not deterministically exclude the prevalence of irrationality, it does provide the potential of rational politics mediated by, among others, scientific reason. For Foucault, things were of a different nature and prospect: the insurrection of the subjugated knowledge is mediated through the genealogies of anti-sciences, which 'base their experience upon an immediate experience that escapes encapsulation in knowledge'.[24] Knowledge that is subjugated has to come to the fore through power, but at this moment I think there is nothing to prevent power from producing more power, despite the fact that, according to Foucault, power comes to the scientific and political fore through extended struggles and conflicts.

Nevertheless, the challenge I recognize remains: power of what kind? Or: What prevents established sovereignty from suffering a form of self-alienation through the generation of domination of a more coercive kind? Foucault attempted an answer in his 'Two Lectures'[25] by associating power with rights and truth as a modern alternative to the traditionalism of the old questions on the rights of power. But although he proclaimed to acknowledge the task of philosophy as speaking the truth, he failed to differentiate that it is *one thing to profess the power of truth and another to acknowledge the truth of power socially and politically*. All previous or later elaborations on the aforementioned subjects in Foucault's work seem insufficient to cope with the dilemma of whether the previous questions are deliberately left without an epistemologically plausible answer concerning modern science and modernity itself.

Foucault's modernism is not marked by a critique of a permanent era, but rather proposes a permanent critique of an era that

> is no longer going to be practiced in the search for formal structures with universal value, but rather as a historical investigation into events that have led us to constitute ourselves and to recognize ourselves as subjects of what we are doing, thinking, saying. In that sense criticism is not transcendental, and its goal is not that of making metaphysics

possible: it is genealogical in its design and archaeological in its method ... [I]t is not seeking to make possible a metaphysics that has finally become a science; it is seeking to give new impetus, as far and wide as possible, to the undefined work of freedom.[26]

In an overall assessment, Foucault's modernism or postmodernism considered Enlightenment as bearing an initial moment of creation that was triggered by Kant's fundamental question *'Was ist Aufklärung?'* The idea that modernity and/or rationality are initiated by one single event or view constitutes a rather theological and positivistic understanding that relates a single and, therefore, misleading cause to a whole process. The process of Enlightenment and modernity is very probably hampered, obstructed or deviated many times through its own (negative) dialectic, but even so, it constitutes a process.

The project of modernity does not begin with a sign or in a moment. It takes place persistently and unabatedly as long as societies make public use of their reason and demand rationality through knowledge and politics within social institutions. The idea of critical theory in the twenty-first century is that modernity maintains the theoretical claims of the first and the second generation for reason, dialectics and normativity, but that it should also differentiate itself from and, moreover, oppose all previous modern epistemological considerations examined so far. Scientific rationality should be generated through discourse and normativity, but it should also produce accountability criteria of dialectical development. As I have argued throughout, dialectics does not merely produce or reproduce theses and antitheses which might potentially and wilfully lead to a synthesis of arguments; it has also to introduce processes of accountability that bind science to the social and that are mediated through politics.

The latter paradigm of scientific accountability renders science answerable to society through dialectics, and at the same time decouples scientific domination from social coercion as both science and society acquire an autonomous but simultaneously dialectical potential to realize. Far from all the latter being modern exemplars of abstract and, therefore, inapplicable scientism, the previously mentioned arguments concerning accountability plausibly explain modernity by means of science where both modernity and science are considered as being processual. They are not rigorous or unwavering dogmas of many things past. The consideration of science and politics as *fields communicating through dialectics by means of accountability criteria* sets the bases for freedom and uncoerced dialogue, which might offer a path out of scientific and political self-incurred immaturity and irrationality. In the next chapter, I will examine how Luhmann's systems theory of the late twentieth century transforms the fields of science and politics into constructions of systemic reproduction, and in doing so forces dialectics into the background.

Notes

1. David Couzens Hoy (ed.), *Foucault, A Critical Reader* (Oxford: Basil Blackwell, 1991), 48.
2. Cited in Jeremy Waldron, 'Kant's Theory of the State', in Immanuel Kant, *Toward Perpetual Peace* (New Haven, CT: Yale University Press, 2006), 191.
3. Cited in Paul Rabinow (ed.), *The Foucault Reader* (London: Penguin Books, 1991), 50.
4. Michel Foucault, *The Archaeology of Knowledge* (London: Routledge, 2011), 199.
5. Rabinow (ed.), *The Foucault Reader*, 63.
6. Cited in Rabinow (ed.), *The Foucault Reader*, 22.
7. Hubert L. Dreyfus and Paul Rabinow, *Michel Foucault. Beyond Structuralism and Hermeneutics* (New York: Harvester, Wheatsheaf, 1982), 60.
8. Rabinow (ed.), *The Foucault Reader*, 70.
9. Rabinow (ed.), *The Foucault Reader*, 74.
10. For an elaboration of the concept of genealogy, see Foucault's analyses in Rabinow (ed.), *The Foucault Reader*, particularly 386 onwards.
11. Rabinow (ed.), *The Foucault Reader*, 374.
12. Theodor W. Adorno, *Critical Models* (New York: Columbia University Press, 1998), 93, my emphasis.
13. Jürgen Habermas, *The Philosophical Discourse of Modernity* (Cambridge: Polity Press, 1987), 269.
14. Habermas, *The Philosophical Discourse of Modernity*, 241.
15. Habermas, *The Philosophical Discourse of Modernity*, 242.
16. Adorno, *Critical Models*, 99.
17. Taken from the first lines of Goethe's *Faust*:

    'I've now alas!
    Philosophy, Med'cine and Jurisprudence too,
    and to my cost Theology,
    with ardent labour studied through.
    And here I stand, with all my lore,
    poor fool, no wiser than before'.

18. See the excellent arguments in Jean-François Lyotard, *The Postmodern Condition: A Report on Knowledge* (Manchester: Manchester University Press, 1997), particularly from 37 onwards.
19. Lyotard, *The Postmodern Condition*, 47.
20. Lyotard, *The Postmodern Condition*, 36.
21. David Ingram, *Habermas* (Ithaca and London: Cornell University Press, 2010), 25.
22. Apart from mere coincidences and 'light' identifications, the reader of modern epistemology cannot help but hear in Foucault's anxiety concerning modernity echoes of that expressed earlier by Max Horkheimer, *Die Sehnsucht nach dem ganz Anderen. Ein Interview mit Kommentar von Hellmut Gumnior* (Hamburg: Furche Verlag, 1970).

23 Language plays its own games: it is very tempting for the English-speaking reader to trace the conceptual and epistemological connection between 'discipline' as a scientific scope and 'discipline' as power and repression, particularly in late Foucault.
24 Michel Foucault, 'Two Lectures', in Michael Kelly (ed.), *Critique and Power* (Cambridge, MA: The MIT Press, 1994), 22.
25 See Kelly (ed.), *Critique and Power*.
26 Michel Foucault, 'What Is Enlightenment?', in Rabinow (ed.), *The Foucault Reader*, 45–6.

4

Systems theory

They can speak like Hegel. But they have no language left but the dialectical one. The countermeasure I have in mind is to make the theory decisions as transparent as possible.
 Niklas Luhmann, *Introduction to Systems Theory*[1]

Damit fehlen ausreichende Anhaltspunkte für ein Ausschöpfen des Möglichen, für Rationalisierung. Wir leben, wie man seit dem Erdbeben von Lissabon weiß, nicht in der besten der möglichen Welten, sondern in einer Welt voll besserer Möglichkeiten.
 Niklas Luhmann, *Theorie der Gesellschaft oder Sozialtechnologie*[2]

Introduction

Luhmann: farewell to the dialectic arms or the contingent steps towards knowledge

In later life, creators of grand narratives often feel obliged to provide useful handbooks or short introductions to their own systems of thought. Niklas Luhmann was no exception. In the winter of 1991–92, he delivered a series of lectures entitled *Introduction to Systems Theory*. Habermas' *Theory of Communicative Action* had already been published a decade ago, and the best way for Luhmann to establish his critique against the Habermasian understanding of social systems was by means of an introduction to systems theory.

In his work, Luhmann attempts to redefine communication, and associates it with information. For Luhmann, communication is distinct from action (*Handeln*), and the rationality of the scientific system resides in the notion of *Zweck,* or in the ends of the sciences towards action. For the first time in the epistemological history of modernity, rationality is understood as a certain scientific purpose of action and not as the critique of scientific truth and validity of reason. The schism that Luhmann brought about between 'traditional' epistemology (reconsidered now as novel) and the 'critical' theory of science (seen by Luhmann as 'traditional') was irredeemable. In the following pages, I maintain that all evidence to the contrary such a divergence was inherent to modernity.

Drawing on the Schützian model of multiple realities, Luhmann manages to blur the distinction between instrumentality and rationality by relativizing both within systemic complexity. According to Luhmann, complexity characterizes a multifaceted social system, such as science itself. However, I argue that where complexity, in Luhmann, interprets the systemic, it also employs presentism and partial situationalism to explain the essence and methodology of science as a system.

Furthermore, I think that the accountability criterion of rationality and its consequences for the sciences becomes a merging of the theoretical and the empirical in Luhmann, who elaborates on the first, and emphasizes the second. He gets rid of rationality by having decision theory prioritize the purpose, instead of the consequences, of modern science. In his conception of *Wirkungsmöglichkeiten*, or the contingencies of scientific influence, he introduces the following:

1. that ethics be annihilated within sciences, which are preoccupied with action (*Handlungswissenschaften*);
2. that the structure of action (*Handlungsstruktur*) embarks on new inquiries about the notion of scientific purpose; and
3. that the latter is founded independently of subjective criteria of purposefulness (*Zweckvorstellung*).

Luhmann seeks 'another' rationality for the sciences, which stands on the bases of scientific action and reflexivity. Although Adorno's totality indicates a *Gesamtgesehen*, a total view of the scientific, which in Habermas takes the form of rationality through norms, in Luhmann rationality is the totality of differences *not* distorted by norms. In Luhmann, norms do not allow the multiplicity of actions. Luhmann was perhaps right: I maintain that praxis *indicates* relativism or a relativistic option that facilitates communication within the scientific system, *but* Luhmann argued that the condition of praxis presupposes that communication derives from utterance, information and understanding of the transferred scientific action.

Normativity for Luhmann does not produce action within a system such as science. It is self-reflexivity, as a process far removed from any dialectical process of intercommunication among scientific participants, which indicates systems' rationality and prevents the articulation of communication within systems from becoming an abstract and unfeasible scheme. Nevertheless, whether in relation to communication deriving from the threefold schema of utterance–information–understanding or in relation to self-reflexivity, systems theory fails to define the bearer or *the actor of the previous structural processes*. Rationality, as a solitary operation towards action, might be bereft of systems' complexity and therefore of contingencies as options in Luhmannian terms, but nevertheless give a plausible representation of the objectives.

Luhmann claims that the scientific system comprises structures and *autopoiesis* as a process that solidifies the production (and not the reproduction) of the system. It also presupposes the allowance of differences and differentiations of its elements, where meaning serves as the structural invariant, and the input of information contributes to the initiation of communication within the system. To a certain extent, systems *are* differentiation. What constitutes a system is its ability to differentiate and construct a whole array of functions that allow it to 'happen'. Autopoiesis comes as a secondary innate process that solidifies that *a system produces* and, contrary to misunderstandings in Luhmann, *does not reproduce* functional and communicative processes. A system *keeps* producing itself in terms of new structures and fundamental functions, but also, on account of its own complexity, allows a variety of differentiations to exist and even change or innovate the system.

A system produces its own existence; it does not safeguard that existence unconditionally. As such, in Luhmann's understanding, this allows systemic reductions or communication deficits to distort functional differentiation, despite clear systemic contours and functions. Luhmann invented the possibilities of strategic action, and placed systems centre stage in his theory of understanding the social, instead of focusing on the lifeworld and the potentialities for communicative action as Habermas had done. Besides the subject of historical evidence in which Habermas was the first to challenge communicative and strategic action, we can certainly trace, in their exchange of arguments, one of the most fascinating dialogues on modern epistemology and modernity to have come out of the twentieth century.[3]

Luhmann's thesis on systems' differentiation signified an epistemological divergence from the social and scientific lifeworld. He avoids including the lifeworld in his theory because the lifeworld incorporates discourse and, therefore, generates disrespect or disobedience, which entail the facilitation of subjects' participation. Luhmann challenged the idea of communicative potential here in order to reach decisions in some other way – that is, apart from dialectics and disobedient negations that allow conflictual social or scientific choices related to causality. He also challenged decision-making processes that systems autopoietically construct, and exempted his epistemological theory from the traditionalism of dialectical prospects that result in limited contingencies and coerced decisions. Luhmann's presentation of scientific as well as social modernity should be regarded as decisionistic and functionally differentiated owing to systems' autopoiesis. Habermas' equivalent was of discursive interests and focused on the consequences of scientific dialectics that allows communicative action of the subjects involved to exert their accountability criteria in the direction of society and politics. What is critical in Luhmann is the autopoietic function of systems, whereas what is critical and therefore modern in Habermas is communicative action by means of dialectics.

Aside from core notional differences between the two thinkers that produced remarkable pieces of cooperative works, such as their *Theorie der Gesellschaft oder Sozialtechnologie*, Luhmann's attack on dialectics in social or scientific terms is relentless, to the extent that it often causes the student of his epistemological and social arguments to realize that his pivotal concern was in fact his fear of dialectics.[4] Luhmann owes much inspiration for his systems theory to the structural understanding of society and science. Thus, he attempts a deconstruction of the modern. In his understanding, since the Enlightenment, the modern presupposes but also produces reason, dialectics and the rationality of the sciences.

Whereas dialectics becomes conspicuous in essence and methodology because it is a *process* and not a *project* of cumulative results, Luhmann's epistemological focus remains the methodology of the sciences. The *process* of rationality that includes both means and ends in Habermas' critical theory finds its opposing argument in the Luhmannian *project* of systems' motivation. Such a project produces practice instead of communicative action, which suffices for the formation of dialectical rationality in the sciences. In strict terms, Luhmann's systems' project, which focuses on the science and maintains strong connections to both Bourdieu's and Foucault's critiques of modernity, refers to the following:

1. the structuralist approach, thoroughly elaborated by Bourdieu, as well as Foucault. *Structures* articulate a *social structure*, where in Luhmann the former develops into the environment (*Umwelt*) of the system and the latter into the society of society (*Die Gesellschaft der Gesellschaft* giving its name to his homonymous book) that comprises primarily the scientific system, among others;
2. the desubjectivized science that creates self-reflexivity as part of its autopoietic procedure;

3. the rejection of the 'traditional' rationality (in the Kantian sense of rationality) that relatedly presupposes dialectical processes of self-generation; and
4. the multiplicity of alternatives, as opposed to the exclusive dialectical processes mentioned previously. Luhmann's perception of multiplicity allows not just one alternative of the rational. The single alternative is no longer considered epistemologically in Luhmann's perspective of the modern as a single criterion of knowledge.

Luhmann's objective was to prove that the rationality of the Kantian sense is a mere disposition which harbours prejudice as an option. Therefore, he diametrically diverged from the Habermasian lifeworld (*Lebenswelt*), in which communicative action takes place and potentially leads to the formation of social and scientific rationality. Within systems' environment (*Umwelt*), rationality gives its defining lines as the experience of the potential where the latter interrupts associations and creates discontinuities as well as interdependences. His analysis of systems' environment (*Umwelt*) leans towards an anti-Kantian rather than anti-traditional conception of the rational. With Luhmann, the divergence between *Lebenswelt* and *Umwelt* became a mainstay within the epistemological terms of the twentieth century.

Systems' rationality is a shining example of epistemology in Luhmann's work, for it produces a theoretical development that is critical of Habermas' corresponding notion, prominent in its manifestation and promising in its proliferation. Although, for Luhmann, rationality, as understood in the traditional conceptions of epistemology thus far, contributes to the reduction and reductionist approach of systems' complexity, in Luhmann's modern perspective, rationality is associated with a certain rationale that binds ends to means under a positive causality, which serves the rationality of choice.

Nevertheless, Luhmann's systems theory lacks in what the German language calls *Erklärungskraft*. Luhmann's theory is consistent and methodologically grounded, but despite all evidence to the contrary and taking into consideration its academic success, it is also too narrow to include the social and the political, which incorporate *other* properties than the formalistic generation of actions, for which Luhmann fervently argued. The main argument of this chapter holds that instead of the formalism of systems theory, social enlightenment and political rationality are the outcomes of normative theory and rational praxis, which owe their validity and applicability to the formation of dialectical reason. Modernity, Luhmann claimed, lost sight of dialectical criticism and an *other* scientific civilization, which is accountable to society and which can therefore bring about enlightenment. The following pages attempt to re-examine Luhmann's conception of modernity and maintain that despite the negativity of the enlightenment, modernity never detached from pursuing an *other* scientific civilization, as explicated by Habermas.

Rationality without reason

One of the major innovations that Luhmann introduced epistemologically was his reconsideration of rationality deprived of the reductionist notion and function of reason. The other two are examined in the following sections of this chapter. I inquire into his comparative argumentation of form versus norm and his enduring elaboration of another modernity as the epistemological potentiality suggested by systems theory.

One of Luhmann's most prevailing fears might have been *die Logifizierung der Wahrheit*, namely the moment when scientific or social truth becomes an object of rationalized implementation. However, what appears problematic in Luhmann's previous argument is not even rationalization itself, but the implicit interpretation that truth can be and always is deterministically implemented. Therefore, if such a phenomenon is to happen, scientists should negotiate on the terms and conditions of implementation.

Nonetheless, I maintain that, as is very often the epistemological case with reason, it is considered a part or presupposition of a rationalization process and imposed normativity, where the claim for uncoerced dialogue that produces truth in science is rarely the case. Luhmann diagnoses in reason the end of the alternatives or the end of rational potentialities that cannot be invoked after the advent of the singular scientific reason. He fails to notice that reason paves the way for the multiplicity of dialectics where the arguments set questions but also attempt answers. Reason is not the blind answer to an imposed question, but is rather both the attempt to challenge, question and potentially provide an answer (even a consensual answer) for human interests.

Furthermore, Luhmann did not just maintain that it is systems' autopoiesis that leads to rationality. He also identified that epistemological rationality is punctuated by the concern for what is true, and accordingly he examined whether a scientific statement is valid because of its being true or vice versa. At first glance, it appears a plausible social critique, but on closer inspection it reveals that Luhmann managed to challenge not only the critical theory of the Frankfurt School, but also Kant. By characterizing the epistemological considerations of both as 'traditional' rather than critical, Luhmann necessitated some form of 'other' novelty in scientific critique and redefined rationality as the objective of social validity and scientific truth that the latter seeks to confirm. At the level of systems' autopoiesis, where communication occurs, Luhmann also identifies communication facilitated by knowledge. The problematic point in Luhmann's identification is that it relates to a symbolic level or in particular to symbolic functions of systemic structures, which exclude or eliminate the process of knowledge within the system precisely because symbols relate to a pre-modern understanding of the scientific.

For scientific as well as social rationality, being valid also entails being useful. But it is not just usefulness that guarantees the function of a system such as science. It takes other things too – such as social and scientific accountability (as shown in the previous two chapters). The accountability criterion that 'functions' for the sake of rationality on behalf of social interests renders scientific rationality self-reflective by means of dialectics, but it also renders it 'outward-looking' in social terms. What is important in Luhmann? Usefulness. What *ought to be* important though? Social accountability.

The first stress or even controversy in Luhmann's work is clearly marked: scientific usefulness versus scientific accountability. The criterion for the former becomes systems' function, whereas for the latter the formation of a social and scientific rationality by means of dialectic reason that accounts for not only its aims but also its social and political consequences. Luhmann's intention was not merely to negate dialectics, but to negate the negation that dialectics comprises and render science a system of no dialectical tension or conflict.[5] He thought that the complexity of systems allows the multiplicity of systemic facets to emerge, but also prevents the *one* dialectical solution from restricting the multiversity of the system.

In the last part of *Theorie der Gesellschaft oder Sozialtechnologie*, Luhmann rather fails to respond to Habermas' arguments on practical discourse and rationally orientated action. His 'anti-criticism' is rather weak and evasive. He avoids the main points of critique, articulated by Habermas, where system is rationally orientated, whereas, in Luhmann, it is action orientated. In order to criticize Habermas' intersubjective account of the system of science, Luhmann uses the idea of Weberian consequences as actions themselves (*Handeln*), and it is precisely at this point that systems theory makes a significant turn to the accountability criterion for the sciences (*Rechenschaft*). Action is thus placed in the position of a criterion for the sciences that develops according to socially and politically bound conditions.

Nevertheless, Luhmann does try to colonize the rationality area. An 'other' rationality is feasible and, therefore, contingent for Luhmann, when reason remains extraneous to scientific rationality, which is then freed from the sole criterion of reason, and allows a complexity of criteria within systems. For Habermas, though, systems theory is a disentangling approach to the world and the sciences precisely because of systems' complexity. Since complexity is identified as such, its realization and understanding becomes lucid. In Luhmann's theory though, complexity appears as an advance towards relativism, since it allows everything to be valid as alternatives to either practical discourse or rationally oriented action, as is the case with Habermas. Luhmann contradicts the dialectical determinism that he negates with an implausible relativism deriving from the notion of complexity.

In the light of this, there are two factors open to critique in the scientific system according to Luhmann: the first is the complex structure of the system per se; and the second is the endogenous observer of the system, which produces epistemological criticism and thus self-reflexivity. Hence the system of science attains reconciliation among opposing notions or functions within its own systemic field, and by means of complexity it considers the totality of potential events as the bearer of innovation for the system. Luhmann accomplishes two things in one blow: he discards conflictual dialectics, which he accuses of determinism between dualistic schemata, and places the scientifically unexpected within the sphere of contingent performativity that is accountable to the observer of the system itself. The analysis appears very convenient insofar as it nullifies external critique from critical theory. It is only the deficits that systems theory produces on its own: what constitutes conflict for the social system, in Luhmann, becomes the notional frustration of knowledge and science, and is a result of structural couplings.

Some tension develops, however, between Luhmann's validity of scientific truth and the underlying structuralism in his theory. This tension evolves between the desubjectivized structures of sciences and the validity criterion, which serves as the decisive factor for the *elenchus* of the performativity of scientific results towards reality. Luhmann attempts to avoid methodological dualisms of the dialectical kind for the sake of systems' complexity that provides all answers to dialectical questions. Nevertheless, it appears to me that although dualisms are reductionist, dualities that identify social or scientific subjects as the bearers of critique and validity remain socially and scientifically coherent. In Habermas' epistemological approach, multiple dualities identify social and scientific disputes as producing arguments of communicative competence and prospective consensus.

Luhmann's structural considerations of the system of science do not tally with reality and modern attempts to ground science within the social and the political. Luhmann's systems theory emphasizes a tendency of the system of science to attribute its articulation to innate differences and to the functional differentiations with other systems. Structural relations appear to blur the realization of systemic autopoiesis to the same extent that the attribute of function cannot give a plausible explanation of how the system functions. Conceptual vagueness or relativism allows all results to be acceptable and produces performativity of any social or political kind in Luhmann. The system of science, considered as functionally differentiated, generates the production of itself. However, the question remains unanswered as to whether its functional character is legitimated by societies, and whether the metamorphosis of structures into the totality of systems continues to be valid for knowledge and human interests.

Scientific truth, within structural conventions of systems, is an institutionalized label; it becomes an object of systemic differentiation or interpretation, and addresses the social system that attributes validity or even applicability. Luhmann's novel assumption grounds the system of sciences within reality, or at least presents the system of sciences as establishing a relation to reality, by doing one simple thing: identifying reality as a system, too, that can function as the environment (*Umwelt*) of the sciences that attempt structural couplings.

Adapting such considerations to reality, however, comes to seem superfluous or rather superficial. What coheres as a system is not its structural formation or symbol producing capacity, but the conscious exchange of arguments of scientific or social agents that potentially becomes socially and politically fruitful within communicative action and consensus. The regression that Luhmann so emphatically identifies within dialectics and scientific reason might produce the historically necessary step forward and towards rationality inextricably interwoven with science and social interests.

Critical theory's frame of epistemological reference follows a line of thought that acknowledges dialectics as generating communicative action, either within the scientific realm or among dialectical actors. In presenting controversial arguments, social and scientific subjects involved within dialectics create the potential for communicative consensus and accordingly *account for the validity of any consensus* reached under conditions of dialogue. For the first and the second generation of critical theory, it is not uncritical apologetics for the subject–object dualism, but rather thoughtful critique that is capable of finding the epistemological treasures of theory and experience in combination. Particularly for the first generation of the Frankfurt School, experience can only be 'experienced' by a subject, either individual or collective, and, in relation to science, critique can be exerted by scientific actors intersubjectively articulating dialectical criticism on both theory and practice.

For Luhmann, cognition of arguments is produced as a result of the influx of information within a system and because subjective cognition has access to objects external to the system. There are internal as well as external objects of cognition, which are also influential aspects of cognition itself. Epistemology is therefore the external observer of the autopoiesis of the scientific system, which allows the input of information, and which is also formed by the autopoietical function. Nonetheless, the desubjectivized system of science in Luhmann does not only create the actors' deficit. It would have been more precise to argue that systems theory is not exactly a 'desubjectivized' theory but a methodological construction, where the subject is replaced by the system. It also attributes to the system an objects' deficit because it never specifies *the object of communication*. It suggests an arranged and unhindered process of communication resulting in the performativity of the system, but it fails to grasp the object of communication itself, or in Luhmann's terms what autopoiesis addresses and which forms of structure it affects.

The second point of divergence between 'traditional' rationality in the Kantian sense and Luhmann's systemic rationality crystallizes in his position of self-reflexivity. It appears that the latter serves systems in a way that is diametrically opposed to the rationality of dialectics: it is deprived of subjects, operative in its function and performative in social and scientific results. In particular, the self-reflexivity of the scientific system can recoil to self-reference, and account for the theory of knowledge it produces. In its course of self-reflexivity, science generates its own closed system, but also allows an observer of scientific descriptions to act within the system and attributes such descriptions to epistemology. Luhmann rejects the subjectivized system of the science, but includes an observer within its domain to act for the sake of knowledge *elenchus*. He is a positivist of means and ends, but prevents his feeble or rather uncertain positivism from becoming dysfunctional with the allowance of a contingent performativity.

Although the same twofold schemas will be recurrent themes in the following sections of this chapter, one of Luhmann's significant epistemological proofs of the scientific system was his claim that science takes systemic shape through rules and successive rule following. Although his thought urged towards discontinuities of understanding, Luhmann failed to recognize the reversal of his argument: that rules are also shaped by the system of science that autopoietically produces rules and their mode of following as well. Under the same understanding, the complexity of the system of science also produces self-reflection within its endless horizon, and contradicts Kantian dialectics where endlessness implies determinism and science along with dialectics attempts to resolve scientific and social conflicts.

Luhmann's focus at this point is neither complexity nor rule following. He steadily contradicts Kant, and attempts to 're-answer' the questions concerning the nature of modernity and enlightenment by redefining what theory is. Behind Luhmann's quest for the rationality of modernity, we have to associate his suggestion of the contingency of theory by means of self-reflexivity of the system. Luhmann's attempt to alleviate social and scientific conflicts was based on the elaboration of the notion of *Zweckrationalität*. Despite orienting scientific rationality towards the implementation of certain means along with certain ends, *Zweckrationalität* permitted the contingency of results, and left a scientific space open to risks and contingent performativity.

While critical theory (primarily through Habermas) gives clear theoretical contours of the mediations between dialectics and universal pragmatics of science, Luhmann develops the idea of hermeneutical rule following and manages to alleviate the dysfunction of hermeneutics with regard to social rule following by prioritizing the notion of systemic communication. His conception of communication within the scientific (as well as the social) system professes to be the main path towards truth provided by systems theory. Therefore, Luhmann attains a merging of constructivist and hermeneutic horizons within his epistemological concerns: he combines both structural perceptions and rule following to the extent that they become scientific imperatives for the understanding of an epistemological modernity.

Form versus norm?

The system is the form. It generates the cumulative forms of 'andnesses', as Luhmann stated in his *Introduction to Systems Theory*, where the second significant step to understanding the epistemological explanation of a system, such as science, is attributed to autopoiesis as 'a circular self-production'.[6] While emphasizing in particular the innovative and even radical character of systems as forms, Luhmann distinguishes his system of systems theory from the 'traditional' perspective of the Frankfurt School.

There are clear examples in Luhmann's analyses that indicate his indebtedness to structuralism, ethnomethodology and, in an even more impressive way, to Husserlian phenomenology. Luhmann shifted the focus of attention from the subject of the phenomenological study to the phenomenality of the world, which he brought forward as forming systems' realization and action.[7] However, he grasped the epistemological deficits of systems' perception, and attempted to fill in the gaps with the following three major contributions.

(a) Systems are formed because they bear boundaries of their forms; in this way, Luhmann demonstrated systems' epistemological indispensability.
(b) Systems are produced as a result of their endogenous ability for autopoiesis; as such, he decoupled systems theory from a further epistemological explanation, which would have probably ended up questioning the systems of society or politics.
(c) The systems deprived of subjects, and of their contribution to critical observations, require operative criticism in the form of self-reflexivity of the potential observer. With this final argument, Luhmann discarded the idea of consciousness' intentional intervention into phenomenality, according to Husserl. Consequently, by failing to include critique and subjects into systems theory, he also omits norms and normative rationality and creates a systemic edifice without any accountability criteria to subjects performing critique.

Luhmann articulates an ambiguous phenomenological argument. It throws science into the world without a mediating consciousness, and maintains the functionalism of a system of phenomenality, but deprives it of the normative character of subjective consciousness. If the latter generates, by its own presence or absence, normativity (or the lack thereof), he then decides to cast aside both consciousness and normativity for the sake of the form of the system and its epistemological foundation. Taking for granted that knowledge is possible because of the closed operations of the system of science, the uncertainty of the system's entropy is mediated by means of causality. For Luhmann, 'causality is a matter that concerns the observer ... with specific interests, specific structures, and specific capacities for information processing'.[8] On the one hand, the intersubjectivity of dialectics and the interdisciplinarity of the sciences might produce the subjection of the observers under the coercion of truth recognition,[9] and the sublation of the multiple causes of the sciences, respectively. On the other, Luhmann appears to be unable to ground causality on a safe epistemological base that would allow the constellation of scientific factors and forms to produce the system autopoietically. He also neglects the asymmetry of scientific structures and causes that permit space for the observers to generate systemic self-reflection. In literal terms, by presenting systems as subjectless and without taking into consideration the discontinuities of structures, he excludes the probability of self-reflection and autopoiesis within the system and slips into contradictions.

Systems theory owes many of its central concepts to structuralism and to ethnomethodology. In particular, the logic of praxis and the logic of *poiesis* or action are placed at the forefront of Luhmann's systems theory as the most appropriate and convenient argument against the reason of theory and norms. For a moment, it seemed that structuralism might function as the political opposite of the depoliticized systems theory or even better as the political supplement to an apolitical system of science. However, things appeared more complicated and fruitful than anticipated in the beginning of the twentieth century's epistemology. Luhmann maintained a threefold case:

1. form remains one of his conceptual axes, particularly against the norms and normativity of Kant and critical theory;
2. in terms of science, he configured *poiesis* or action as the underlying contingency of forms; and
3. he departed from norms on the basis of their being 'actionless' or merely not producing any results.

With this loss of action, Luhmann identifies the failure of ethics coexisting in systemic structures, and as ethics develops independently of subjective aims it becomes invisible within the sciences. His point is that ethics is lost within subjectivity because it flourishes when the structural components of a system produce 'something more' than functional differentiation. In all probability, they produce the cumulative effect of science and knowledge. Under subjective and, therefore, distorting or limiting and limited functions of norms and normativity, such a productive outcome fails to materialize systemically.

Luhmann's aversion to norms and normativity implies a secondary epistemological divergence from the Kantian tradition and critical epistemology: it solidifies the refusal to substantiate a critique founded on criteria that are discursively produced, or more emphatically, it negated the epistemological critique in toto. Self-reflexivity of the system of science secures a significant victory over dialectics, for it corrects the dialectical juxtaposition or contradiction between *equivalent* things, arguments or objects of dispute. On the other side of systemic epistemology where self-reflexivity is questioned, the comparison of *different* systemic functions affords the system or its observer the opportunity to form and realize systemic innovations. For Luhmann, dialectics bears the following two inner malfunctions:

(a) It compares two qualitatively analogous things, when it should have taken into account asymmetries, while critical theory reverts to an ideological critique of science that is ambiguous and indistinct.
(b) It allows the potential of consensus to become a constraint on truth and, therefore, reason. Thus far, truth is prequalified as such, and reason has attributed its reasonable essence to truth on account of the consensual critique of the participants. The critical *elenchus* is eliminated and the empirical data are outdated as mere considerations towards particularized claims.

According to the latter critique, the consequential character of scientific *elenchus* is substantiated by means of action and its effects, and certainly not through verisimilar and consensual constraints of determined discussants. By epistemologically disposing of subjectivism and its supposed identification of truth, or by declaring truth of a subjectivist order, Luhmann delineates systems theory's attempt to redefine theory and action as forms of reflexive epistemological presuppositions for the accomplishment of truth.

System functionalism bears different intentions that are concretized in multiple contexts. Dialectics and normative reason are incapable of interpreting and realizing theory as a relation of asymmetry, where the emergence of systemic distinctions prevails. The symmetrical asymmetry of the system of science includes all sides of the complexity of the system, but it also permits that asymmetry is never resolved or ironed out because of the compulsory decisionistic attempt of a dialectical rationality to accommodate alternatives. At this point, Luhmann makes a phenomenological turn again, albeit one that avoids the recognition of subjective consciousness.

He indicates that as a result of how the balance of juxtaposing sides is attained within systems' complexity, the observer holds a position of *epoché*, namely of the viewer over the totality of scientific things or forms who remains aware of distinctions within a system and its forms without becoming a part of them as such. As ever, the devil is in the detail. Although it certainly did not escape Luhmann's attention that the observer stands between juxtaposed or even contradictory positions within systemic forms, he was nonetheless pushed to admit that the observer sits between opposing stools or forms of a complexity that can potentially result in systemic innovation. In Luhmann, the observer occupies the position of the critic, where the exertion of criticism in the form of self-reflective output becomes part of the systemic forms of multiple rationalities. There would not have been any better conspicuous corroboration of dialectics by its own absence.

The organization of functional decisions is mediated through factual fields of process binding decisions, and becomes dysfunctional when adopting normative binding processes that allow normative rationality to obstruct the formation of functional rationality within the system of science. Luhmann insists that the normativity of science serves normativity itself, and does not serve science, whereas system's rationality becomes a process restraining functional differentiation of the system per se. However, Luhmann fails to identify that when science discharges binding decisions from rationality, it appears that rational choice becomes an invisible and fruitless scientific programme, which makes it all the more important for systems theory to make sense of it.

In *Theorie der Gesellschaft oder Sozialtechnologie*,[10] Habermas considers complexity a distorted and inadequate attempt to realize systems theory. Once again, Habermas serves as the saviour of the methodological deficiency of theory. Hence, the totality of contingencies and technology's development appear to rescue the act of decision making, by imposing functional differentiation instead of rationally binding decisions, despite the fact that Luhmann insists on complexity being the bearer of possibilities (*Möglichkeiten*) for the system of science. Either practical discourse or rationally binding decisions provide science with a limited caliber of action and functional differentiation. The theoretical divergence between Habermas and Luhmann, namely between critical theory and the epistemology of an 'other' approach of modernity, boils down to their respective views on reason, rationality and dialectics and, moreover, to the scientific, social and political potentialities they create. For Habermas, such potentialities relate to knowledge and human interests shaped by communicative rationality, whereas for Luhmann, a system's complexity and the possibilities it allows within a *Möglichkeitstheorie* are considered indispensable to the elaboration of scientific contingencies.

Although the old distinction of the subject and the object of knowledge does not apply to Habermas' work, Luhmann's strongest point of criticism against Habermas' critical theory condenses in the latter's phenomenological *lapsus*. Luhmann attributes to Habermas the politicization of science through subjects' demands and interests and by means of the imposition of reason, which governs and limits scientific potential.[11] The latter, according to Luhmann, refers to the involvement of the above dualism in communication, thus limiting the possibilities of continuities and discontinuities, and being reduced to the practical quest for validity and consensus. The moral pursuit of truth on behalf of science can be cast aside by the epistemological search for the method for truth, where morality is substituted by epistemology. There is more behind Luhmann's understanding and prioritization of methods, theories *and* experience concerning truth: mainly the idea that if truth is dependent on theories, methods or experience, then it can be altered accordingly.[12]

Furthermore, the methodological contingency of experience, which Luhmann leaves open and uncriticized, becomes an object of symptomatic methodology that is not just situationally based, but allows ambiguity to govern the sciences and, therefore, needs the methodological stability of a system. The latter acquires positivistic interests and prejudices through the performativity of results. Methodological rigour and firmness are accomplished, but to the detriment or annihilation of a critical modernity for science.

It is at this point that the Luhmannian replacement of morality by a theory of the possibilities of knowledge renders science devoid of any political objective. Alternatively the moral deficit in Luhmann allows politics to become a field of systemic jurisdiction bereft of its potential to bind functional differentiation and to generate autopoiesis. However, if I reverse the Luhmannian epistemological concerns, it appears that critical theory can be granted a significant and innovative epistemological task that was preceded by Habermas' critique of Luhmann's systems theory.

If critical theory renders the political task of science as the major autopoietic process for the system of science, it accomplishes the fortification of the input of science towards its own complex contingencies. Critical theory allows the political to act as the accountability regulator for science that examines and intervenes into discontinuities. Such an input on the part of critical theory acts as the mediating factor that not only reinforces systems' differentiation, but also, due to differentiating processes, serves as a binding force for systems' environment.[13]

Luhmann's denunciation of consciousness, dialectics and reason, with regard to the formation of rationality, signals a new epistemological modernity where the individual is substituted by the system, the subject by the form, and the accountability of dialogue by the complexity of observations. As Luhmann himself states, such an epistemological modernity entails a loss of reality for the sake of reality being observed by the legitimizing system of science so that system binding decisions are reached. They are contingently followed by their equivalent, which are new and rationally bound, causal effects constraining the imbalance of symmetrical asymmetries within the system of science.

Another modernity?

By seeking to present the essential epistemological wholeness of an 'other' modernity, Luhmann compressed his anti-dialectical counter-enlightenment into the following three major points.

(a) Systems' rationality and its instrumental perspective (*Zweckrationalität*) of performative results can be realized under a 'subjectless' understanding that facilitates systems' functionalism and structural autopoiesis.
(b) The criteria for systems' differentiation and rationality can be separated from the initial preoccupation with dialectical reason and the force of the better argument, and can be transferred to causality and performativity.
(c) Practical questions posed by social and political morality can be discarded and ignored owing to the epistemological criticism of the systems that advance self-reflexivity.

According to the previous threefold schema, science becomes valid through the system, legitimation processes are granted to structural processes, and society is produced through communication. Particularly on the second point referring to causality facilitating performativity that functions as the precursor of a postmodern modernity, Luhmann attempts to defy not only rationality, as such, of science and society, but also modernity as the concept that configured the politics of both spheres. Rational motivation is thus bereft of subjects, dialogue and morality, and paves the way for a rather *pre-modern* science, and its observation is turned into a concrete critique. Regarding the third point, the pre-modern science that produces knowledge is mediated by the observer of the system's functions and is promoted by the observer's capacity for self-reflexivity within and because of operative functions of autopoiesis. There emerges a systemic network engaging the observer and self-reflexive autopoiesis that instigate the system's production of knowledge.

In marked contrast to systemic production of knowledge, the major points of critical theory's scientific interdisciplinarity refer to the subject as the bearer of dialectics within the process of communicative action establishing intersubjective rationality. Luhmann negates the subject, dialectics and communicative rationality in defence of the systemic observer, self-reflexivity and communication, and creates a network of performative functions for the sake of the system's maintenance defined as structural autopoiesis. To the same extent, according to the Luhmannian analysis, politics is an enclosed system of observers, self-reflexive criticism and communication therein. By *virtue of* having no access to other systems, such as science, politics produces political effects in the same way that science both presupposes and produces knowledge owing *to* its internal autopoiesis. When the contingent effects of contradictions, conflicts or risks arise within the system, 'it is science and not politics that produces the kind of knowledge which is needed in order to manage risks effectively'.[14]

It appears that Luhmann implicitly replaces the notion of rationality with effects, or seeks a firm ground of operative functions for the formation of rationality. Nonetheless, allowing science to manage risks opens the Pandora's box of conflicts among differentiated rationalities according to systems' differentiation and their exclusive rationality output. The generation of multi-systemic *rationalities* would potentially create a *rationality* deficit. Multiple rationalities within science annihilate the potential of the system to form a rational perspective that is not unequivocal but lucid and applicable, and thus accountable to the social and the political system.

By shifting the focus of epistemological attention from communicative action (producing communicative rationality of the systems) to systems' restricted performative functions, Luhmann restrains knowledge within the system of science. On the other side of systems, where politics is part of the systemic environment of the science, the system of politics is devoid of its internal and, therefore, legitimate potential to manage risks and conflicts, and to potentially produce reasonable and thereby valid public decisions. Hence, science is reduced to operative implementations of its own contingencies while being politically overburdened. Politics is reduced to functioning within its own system of operations, which *is* autopoietical but also illegitimate since science produces deliberation and decisions, while both science and politics remain socially annulled.

Such critique not only allows the construction of a pre-modern science; it also inaugurates (or re-inaugurates) a pre-scientific modernity, which claims its rational character, but still creates a pre-modern or non-legitimate and also non-legitimating science. The idea that systems theory suggests a new modernity may be politically valid and epistemologically functional, but it fails to argue for a legitimating and legitimate subject and function, respectively, that would render systems not only autopoietical but also communicative by differentiation.

Luhmann attempted to make communication the centrepiece of society or science, but as opposed to his idea of traditional epistemology, systems of science or politics generate communication internally and not inter-systemically. Politics can perform an autopoietical function for science by innovating and performing *elenchus* of scientific function. Luhmann appears to have missed the autopoietical function of politics within science. Therefore, the autopoietical function of communication refers to events, actions or structures, whereas autopoiesis renders communication, contrary to Luhmann's understanding, a social, political or scientific contingency that fails to become the coherent force of systems' formation. In contrast to Luhmann's analysis, society *is* its members, because even when communication fails or is distorted, the binding force of politics that social or scientific subjects legitimate becomes the alternative to conflicts and the safeguard of social cohesion. Politics mediates communication while communication is the second most significant social factor after the acting social agents. However, it has to be socially and scientifically mediated by politics and political arguments in the fields of society and science respectively.

Luhmann regarded the Weberian arguments and critical theory as forms of epistemological regression and traditionalism. He made every effort to present and argue for systems theory as the form of critical theory that redefines the essence of critique and places rationality within new contours. Thus, he introduced communication in marked contrast to Habermas' communicative action, and designated the presuppositions of understanding (*Verstehensvoraussetzungen*) in contrast to the ideal speech situation elaborated by Habermas.

Systems theory arranged a new modernity that countered Kant's dialectics and the idea of rational enlightenment with the argument that the system bears borders and therefore perspectives beyond them, whereas dialectics produces antinomies and conflicts of a scientifically and socially fruitless character. At that point, Luhmann presented dialectics as the constraint of reality, while presenting system's borders as the strategic factor for the creation of an environment (*Umwelt*) of other systems. Dialectics, according to Luhmann, produces unresolved conflicts, whereas the system per se and its autopoietical function generates potentials.

Luhmann dealt a double blow against both Kant and critical theory: he utilized the notion of communication to deconstruct both Kantian dialectics, which appeared inconsistent in its enlightening objective, and the Habermasian critique. Most probably, Luhmann aimed to discard communicative action as the hope of consummating a rational modernity. He only kept action as a structural prerequisite for the system and rationality as the potentiality again of a 'new' modernity, and attempted to prove that every enlightenment also entails some obfuscation.[15] However, the following elaboration of Luhmann's systems theory attempts to show that his rejection of dialectics relates to a reconciliatory but not resolving idea of implementing contradictions through epistemology. This appears implausible and, therefore, illegitimate for science, society or politics, if it is the case that the latter three conceptualizations are at all considered as systemically bordered.

Systems theory, for Luhmann, appeared as an infinite process precisely because of the perennial attempt of the system to transcend its own borders, which at the same time must be kept intact for the sake of the system's maintenance. Meanwhile, dialectics is a self-obstructing process due to its own self-produced discontinuities and negations. The main problematic with Luhmann's attempt was the system itself which only remains steadily intact and free of any exogenous processional perspective by virtue of being, in essence, a unified or total structure. Such a structure, by its own function, has to remain unfalteringly the same, producing itself for the sake of its own self-preservation and continuation.

There was a slight paradox in the above Luhmannian divergence from critical theory. While dialectics can be realized and criticized as producing negations, it appears that the borders (*Grenze*) of the system act as negations themselves of the rest of the systemic environment for each system. They produce functional differentiation due to autopoietical self-production, but it is precisely such autopoiesis, particular to each system, which engenders systemic borders and exclusion from the systemic environment by producing the system's negation. Borders are created and maintained by the negation and exclusion of the systemic 'other' and the 'outside' of the systemic.

Nevertheless, Luhmann's epistemological alternative to critical theory revived some not so novel inquiries into the constitution of the system of science. The recourse to understanding needs a scientific subject. Where consensus in Habermas is a potentiality that exceeds the frame of communicative action, and gives an additive quality to communicative rationality, in Luhmann's modernity, action is the outcome of differentiation and communication within the system, but maintains the system under a tight grip where differentiation reproduces itself through action. In Luhmann's words, 'a typical attitude of modernity becomes apparent if we describe the state of affairs … as establishing recursive autopoiesis at the level of second-order observation'.[16]

Despite the fact that Luhmann attempted to keep modern epistemology on a desubjectivized level, he met the *aporia* expressed in his own *Introduction* to *Systems Theory* – namely, 'How *can* the world observe itself?'[17] By stating this question, he acknowledged that the world *is* an *object* of observation, where the key role is played by the observer *or* by the observer of the observer, namely epistemology for its competence to formulate observations in the form of a scientific critique. Instead of the previous question, the reader of Luhmann would have expected a more consistent examination expressed in the question '*What* is a system?' But Luhmann, being consistent with his aim of reversing all theoretical certainties and consolidations, instead asked '*Who* is the system?' Although he admitted that 'The manager, the planner, is part of the system that he manages',[18] he could not avoid ending up in the *aporia* that the observation of the observation also needs an observer who, in the name of epistemology, does not shun representation by scientific subjects formulating their epistemological critique.

At first glance, it seemed that science could exert epistemological critique within its own system. But on closer inspection, the picture becomes blurred as to whether science is in the position to formulate criticism for other systems, particularly for society or politics. If it does, it develops in the service of the system, thus performing a secondary role. If it does not, it then follows a deterministic and exclusive path, which maintains society or politics or other systems as being opaque and impassable by scientific critique. The position of the observer is not a challenging or attractive position for the science, for it limits rather than expands scientific horizons and potentialities within its own systemic performativity. The systemic structure serves, then, as its own self-repression and limit. Contrary to Luhmann's argument, it constrains science *within* boundaries without any alternative for social or political expansion by means of a structural or systemic coupling that *might* entail performativity within the social and the political.

Luhmann's rejoinder derived from diametrically opposed stances. He considered epistemology as problematic for truth on account of the fabrications of science and the exclusion of the moral aspect. As stated earlier in this chapter, morality in science is annihilated within a science of action, and instead of the *Lebenswelt,* Luhmann emphasized the *Lebenspraxis*. Nevertheless, if the moral paves the way for the identification of the political, where the scientific is interwoven with social consequences and political decisions, then the force of the better argument appears to shape both political epistemology and scientific modernity. Luhmann retorted again: instead of the force of the better argument, he suggested, as had Foucault, the force of the 'only action' (*einzige Handlung*).[19]

When Luhmann grounded functional differentiation of the systems, he specified that the differentiating level of abstraction for society laid claims to the political itself. He paved the way for a political society, but what at first glance seemed an elaborate identification appeared on closer inspection to be a rather uncertain assertion. I maintain that the political is not the element that society as a system produces out of cumulative other sub-parts (as in Luhmann), which, in systemic function, produce something 'more'. As is often the case in human history, the political is the differentiation produced by many systems – economy, science or culture.[20]

Particularly for the system of science under a critical understanding that I argue for, the political output is attributed to the formation of modernity, which in many respects was facilitated by the development of the science, the exchange of scientific arguments and dialogical processes capable of bringing the scientific to the level of interdisciplinarity as the communicative process of epistemological modernity. Thus, Luhmann's epistemological construction appears to lose sight of the functional differentiation of the systems, or the way in which the political binds or even erodes systems' closedness and internal formation within the process of autopoiesis. In addition, Luhmann's idea of a system's complexity serves as the equivalent of totality. The binding force of the system's totality is the complexity of the structures of the system that develop within autopoiesis.

Had Luhmann intended to signal the importance of scientific data that constitute the system of science, this would have entailed the elaboration of critique that processes data and forms reason. However, Luhmann's understanding misses the significance of critique and produces an uncritical and therefore pre-modern system of sciences. Such an epistemological deficit, as explained previously, becomes a rationality deficit that disconnects science from society.

The task of a critical perspective is to identify that science and society change and modernize through conscious subjects and through processes that subjects adopt and put into use. They do not change through the generation of structures or systemic edifices. The conceptualization of dialectics as the path to a rational modernity does not refer to merely methodological norms or some sort of normativity. It deals with what occurs scientifically when dialectical critique is transformed into normative rationality, and potentially the practice of science into the social, thereby generating political effects.

Luhmann's systemic modernity avoids pursuing a normative consensus just because it cannot accomplish it through and *because of* the rationality deficit created within the system of science, politics or society. Such modernity undermines science as well as its own modern character in regressing to dogmatism, instead of the dialectical argument, and towards not theoretical but *hypothetical* questions on behalf of politics. Thus, politics finds itself in a state of 'normative silence'[21] that has lost contact with legitimate applicability and viability.[22] Luhmann's modernity was the particular target of Habermas' critique, mainly on account of its delegitimizing and delegitimized potentials through and because of the system of science, respectively. Precisely because of the delegitimized concept of science, and the loss of political cohesion *among* the systems, Luhmann's modernity appears a fragmented whole which seems functional, but in reality delegitimizes itself and its autopoietical consistency. The long-term tendency of modern epistemology remains the mediation of dialectics for providing science and politics with an open field for expressing negations, resolving conflicts by tackling them and reaching deliberate and uncoerced decisions of consensus.

Habermas' epistemological modernity, based on the presuppositions and accomplishment of the ideal speech situation, signals the combination and scientific coexistence of understanding and action. In the opposite case, the divergence of the two factors within the scientific produces a false or distorted consensus of an operative character, which applies distorted modes of communication to science, society or politics. The ideal speech situation aims at accomplishing a true consensus among participants where the agreement reached appears as a counterfactual situation within and between science, society or politics. Habermas departs from the force of the better argument, practical questions and rational motivation of the speech subjects in order to reach the performance of an ideal speech act. He provides the perspective of a practical hypothesis for consensus that serves as the moment of self-transcendence for critical theory (*Ausgangspunkt*).

Scientific consensus derives from communication in the form of communicative action. The obverse is not valid. Consensus is not the deterministic and indispensable *telos* of communicative action. For the latter, in Habermas' critical theory that juxtaposes the argument of shaping a rational choice theory, as in Luhmann, there is neither any initial creative moment that would render it a prejudice of causality, nor a spectacular end, as in the theorization of myths and scientific fallibilities. Thereafter, dialectics and communicative rationality formed and exerted by the science becomes an inalienably scientific and political process. It remains as such, for it initiates but also proceeds through both *a priori* and *a posteriori* means. It takes both into consideration as equivalent, namely both the theoretical claim of science or society for the exchange of arguments, as well as the interest in praxis and consensus that can realize both theory and praxis.

Luhmann's reversal of critical theory into a traditional theory takes the form of a distortion of modernity in which systems theory is presented as the novel and innovative epistemology for modernity. Figure 4.1 sketches the basic divergences.

There could not have been 'more' scientific counter-enlightenment in Luhmann and 'more' scientific modernity in Habermas. The bone of contention,

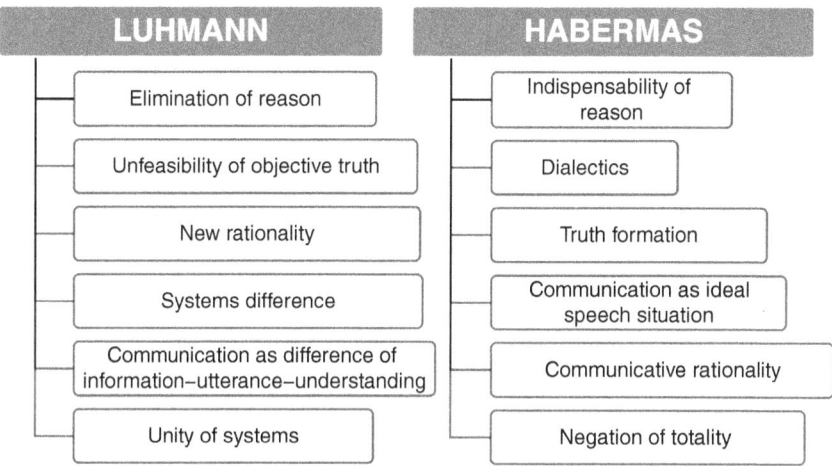

Figure 4.1 Luhmann and Habermas

although often implicitly suggested, was dialectics as both a process generating norms and a method for reaching arguments conceived *a priori*. Luhmann rejected not merely the view that arguments can be *a priori* conceived, but that they raise claims to a validity that is realized intersubjectively, and not to a preconceived systemic validity.

Luhmann insisted on systems' modernity; however, for a critical epistemology, it is the norms that hold the key to modernity. Systems produce social technology directed towards purposeful but not conscious action, *or* it is the systems' purposeful rationality (*Zweckrationalität*) that causes not only a lack of argumentative exchange but also decisionistic or operational results. In this sense, systems do appear to function, but the consequences of such functionality are deprived of their social orientation. The scientific system autopoietically generates itself; nonetheless, it appears incapable of enlightening science and moving the latter towards social accountability.

Conclusions

If we consider science in Luhmann's work as a system, in which communication governs, then the performativity of the system addresses truth or, to be more precise, the validity of truth. The communicative *elenchus* of truth is still subjectless and attributed to systemic autopoiesis. In that sense, Luhmann argues not for the contingently possible, but for the possibly contingent. This makes of its epistemological thought a convenient way of avoiding the cul-de-sac of relativism in relation to the indispensability of the validation of truth by the system, namely the *aporia* that if no truth is validated, then none exists.

Scientific truth manifests itself by means of being decided upon by the communicative structures of the system. If that is the case, then intentional scientific decisions entail purposeful results that position truth as systemically constructed and communicatively performative. Under the same understanding, scientific rationality is the contingent outcome of actions coordinated by the science that designates the criteria of rational decisions, means and ends in order to avoid discontinuities of the flow of rationality within the system. Rationality, thus, is also systemically constructed and validated, and not legitimately generated by communicative action *among* the systems.

After truth is scientifically validated, the second reversal for the system of science concerns legitimation. Science as a system cannot legitimate itself through actions and, hence, epistemology is the observer of the system of science and the presupposition or outcome of knowledge. Legitimation then becomes a possible contingency that is transformed into a contingent result of performativity, where effects are measured according to systemic communication and not according to communicative rationality of the interaction of systems.

In his attempt to relocate reason, rationality and critique outside of or within new systemic borders, Luhmann succeeds in becoming a neo-traditionalist of epistemology, grounding his epistemological critique on the contingent actions that might form an 'other' legitimation of performative presuppositions. Epistemology holds the position of a second-order observer for the system of science, but when Luhmann reverts to the weakening of reason in order to reconstruct rationality, he alters the character of epistemology into *epistemocracy*, which governs the system of science by observing and describing science itself. Knowledge thus becomes a strategic prerequisite for science, and is reduced *within* systemic borders where science aims at the performative results of autopoiesis. Luhmann delegitimizes knowledge itself, and simultaneously replaces scientific truth with the presupposition of knowledge for every single action that the system employs. The indispensable condition for the system of science is not the search for truth and its social or political validity, but rather – contrary to critical theory – the quality of knowledge, which does not intend to alter science and the system of science. He attributes three major neo-traditionalist traits to knowledge: it is now performative, systemically constrained, and instrumentally manipulated for the sake of the system per se. It is not even knowledge for the sake of knowledge; it is knowledge for the sake of the system.

Luhmann rejects the normativity of knowledge and science, for he observes that normativity is socially grounded and therefore punctuated with an exogenous intention of social or political causality to conquer or distort the inner causality and performativity of the system of science. Society and politics form their own systemic processes, which might contingently produce results that are irrelevant to knowledge's *elenchus* and critique. This triggers both de-legitimation and de-rationalization for science and politics.

Nonetheless, systems theory makes a remarkable social turn in relation to the production of knowledge, which is thus the outcome of systemic couplings of society. It is mainly the idea of the lifeworld, where knowledge develops, that renders Luhmann's differentiation of knowledge and science problematic. Although by his own admission, in *Die Wissenschaft der Gesellschaft*,[23] there are no strict borders between the two spheres, this is exactly the instigating factor of science, namely to observe the tension and draw lines of differentiation in between. He then makes the second retreat (particularly from Kant's epistemology) by accepting that the original and primary factor of knowledge is human consciousness of the *a priori* quality, which is then communicatively coupled with another consciousness to produce knowledge within the system of society that is also validated as truth.[24]

Truth is therefore a communicative medium that presumes three steps towards knowledge: (1) science is a system of observation; (2) the cognition of the knowing fact constitutes a second-order observation by epistemology; and (3) there is also a consequential level of self-reflexivity of the systems in which the cognitive and the normative intermingle in order to render truth a symbol, and attribute to it a symbolic function of knowledge.[25] Hence, a new understanding of the world develops and, according to Luhmann, a new world of the science expands too.

In contrast, communicative rationality of the science based on dialectics is not the cunning of epistemology so as to mute opposition and fabricate agreement, as Luhmann claims. Particularly as a result of its inherently open process, it allows the potential negation to substantiate dialectics and not the predefined result or project of performative autopoiesis of the system to corroborate itself.[26]

The quest for truth (and not for the validation of truth, as Luhmann sought) gives the objective world the opportunity to undertake inquiries into scientific rationality governed by reason, whereas the search for normativity attributes to science and society legitimate interests in knowledge and communicative action. Secondarily, the pursuit of truth in Habermas' critical theory is not authorized by actions ratifying communication, but rather the reverse. It facilitates communicative action to examine what constitutes scientific truth, and how it gains validity through communication and the communicative reason of science. Moreover, communicative action of the system of science with other systems within society entails that such action is the combination of theory and praxis, and not the blind product of actions of the structures, for it comprises within the lifeworld rationality and praxis of communicative reason in addition to its search for scientific truth.

There lies the functional differentiation of the lifeworld that permits society, science and politics to substantiate and advance communicative rationality. However, such differentiation takes place among intercommunicative processes for the formation and understanding of knowledge and human interests under conditions for dialogue. Instead of allowing epistemology to act on its behalf, science *maintains the claim* to form communicative rationality that constitutes simultaneously the claim of politics and society. Thus, it is not epistemology that acts as if it were in the position to articulate critique, but the communicative interplay of differentiated factors towards what constitutes the rational and the validation of communicative action within a differentiated whole.

Differentiated pluralism, which Luhmann so rigorously defended, is not the result of marginalizing or even muting normativity. It concerns the dialectical process of discourse, throughout the differentiated sphere of the social, which pursues consensus, but at the same time pursues scientific accountability towards its own established structures of autopoiesis, as well as disrespect or disobedience towards what is established socially and politically. Further epistemological debates of the late twentieth century turned to the latter topics, in particular in the field of critical realism. Such a discussion remains for the next chapter to analyse and criticize.

Notes

1 Niklas Luhmann, *Introduction to Systems Theory* (Cambridge: Polity Press, 2013), 254.
2 'There are no sufficient indications for the exhaustion of what is possible, for rationalization. We live, as we know since the earthquake in Lisbon, not in the best possible world, but in a world full of better possibilities.' Author's translation from Jürgen Habermas and Niklas Luhmann, *Theorie der Gesellschaft oder Sozialtechnologie – Was leistet die Systemforschung?* (Frankfurt am Main: Suhrkamp Verlag, 1974), 297.
3 In a letter sent to me in July 2015, Habermas gave clear indications that he was the one who initiated the discussion with Luhmann. Stefan Müller-Doohm confirmed to me in a personal message (in October 2015) that Habermas suggested to Luhmann to write a book together, which meant publishing the articles and the critiques in the Theorie-Reihe *Theorie-Diskussion*. Müller-Doohm also indicated that the formulation of the title comes from Habermas. Luhmann was not inspired by the title, but he agreed.

4 On this topic and on the comparison between Luhmann and Habermas, I have greatly benefited from discussions with Professor William Outhwaite.
5 In his words, 'Immer dann, wenn eine Verneinung auf ein weiteres Nein trifft, entsteht ein Konflikt', cited in Armin Nassehi and Gerd Nollmann (eds), *Bourdieu und Luhmann* (Frankfurt am Main: Suhrkamp, 2004), 141.
6 Niklas Luhmann, *Introduction to Systems Theory* (Cambridge: Polity Press, 2013), 52.
7 In his words, 'every distinction contains two components: indication and distinction ... The distinction contains itself, but apparently in a very specific form ... not merely some juxtaposition ... Accordingly, the re-entry of the form into the form – or of the distinction into the distinction, or of the difference between system and environment into the system – should be understood as referring to the same thing twice. The distinction re-enters the distinguished', in Luhmann, *Introduction to Systems Theory*, 60.
8 Luhmann, *Introduction to Systems Theory*, 65.
9 In Luhmann's words, 'Auf eine kurze Formel gebracht kann zwar nicht die *Wahrheit* der Zwecke noch die *Notwendigkeit* der Zwecke ... wohl aber die *Funktion* der Zwecksetzung als Reduktion der Unendlichkeit begriffen werden', Niklas Luhmann, *Zweckbegriff und Systemrationalität* (Frankfurt am Main: Suhrkamp, 1973), 48.
10 Jürgen Habermas and Niklas Luhmann, *Theorie der Gesellschaft oder Sozialtechnologie* (Frankfurt am Main: Suhrkamp, 1974), 232ff.
11 In his words, 'Freilich mag es sein, dass, wer Vernunft sucht, irgendwie an Herrschaft noch glauben muss' and 'Im Blich auf Habermas möchte ich zu bedenken geben, ob nicht auch die Ungesichertheit des theoretischen Anspruchs einer Gesellschaftstheorie nach den Massstäben der vorherrschenden Wissenschaftsauffassung einen politisierenden Effekt haben kann', in Habermas and Luhmann, *Theorie der Gesellschaft oder Sozialtechnologie*, 401 and 404 respectively.
12 See Habermas and Luhmann, *Theorie der Gesellschaft oder Sozialtechnologie*, 388–90 and mainly the following: '*Im Kontext des Wissenschaftssystems wird der Erlebnisbezug von Wahrheit rekonstruiert als Forderung entsprechender Komplexität theoretischer Strukturen und Methoden des Forschungshandelns*', 398.
13 Luhmann was well aware of such a tendency emerging in science and epistemology. In his words, 'Vor allem im letzteren sehe ich eine Tendenz zu einer *wissenschaftsimmanent erzeugten Politisierung*, nämlich der Übersetzung theoretischer Unsicherheit in politische Opposition', in Habermas and Luhmann, *Theorie der Gesellschaft oder Sozialtechnologie*, 399.
14 Christian Borch, *Niklas Luhmann* (London: Routledge, 2011), 101.
15 An idea that was elaborated in Norbert Bolz, *Ratten im Labyrinth* (Munich: Wilhelm Fink Verlag, 2012). In his words, 'Die Vorurteile der Aufklärung konzentrieren sich in dem blinden Fleck, der sie nicht sehen lässt, dass jede Aufklärung auch eine Verdunkelung ist', 42.
16 Luhmann, *Introduction to Systems Theory*, 115.
17 Luhmann, *Introduction to Systems Theory*, 118.
18 Luhmann, *Introduction to Systems Theory*, 119.
19 'Durch Einbau von Maximierungs- und Minimierungskalkülen in ein Zweckprogramm kann sicher gestellt werden, dass das Programm, obwohl der Zweck an sich viele Alternativen als Mittel zulässt, nur jeweils eine *einzige Handlung als richtig* auswählt, nämlich jene, die in dem durch das Zweckprogramm gesteckten Rahmen eine spezifische Wertrichtung maximal oder minimal befriedigt', in Niklas Luhmann, *Zweckbegriff und Systemrationalität*, 111, my emphasis.

20 See his 'Moderne Systemtheorien als Form gesamtgesellschaftlicher Analyse', in Habermas and Luhmann, *Theorie der Gesellschaft oder Sozialtechnologie*, 7–10, 24.
21 The phrase is coined and used by Darrow Schecter in his book *Critical Theory in the Twenty-first Century* (New York and London: Bloomsbury, 2013), 32.
22 Although fairly disrespectful to write, the marginalization of politics from the epistemological and social agenda might have led Luhmann to adopt major fallacies which would tally with similar understandings of epistemology and politics, such as Heidegger's support of Nazism in the 1930s and Foucault's defence of the Iranian revolution in the 1970s. It is no mere coincidence that traces if not significant elements within the latter thinkers' works of a desubjectivized epistemology and anti-dialectical critique were closely affiliated with equivalent political arguments in their work.
23 Niklas Luhmann, *Die Wissenschaft der Gesellschaft* (Frankfurt am Main: Suhrkamp, 1994), particularly 160–6.
24 'Wenn von Wissen die Rede ist, versteht man darunter normalerweise wahres Wissen', in Luhmann, *Die Wissenschaft der Gesellschaft*, 167.
25 At this point, Luhmann's thesis appears implausible and mostly epistemologically aporetic because it presupposes mysticism that is somehow eliminated in its traditional and regressive consequences by the social itself. In his words,

> '"Symbole sind Mystifikationen". Mystifikationen sind Invisibilisierungen. Invisibilisierungen verschleiern Paradoxien. Wenn wir von *symbolisch* generalisierten Kommunikationsmedien sprechen, ist darin also noch ein Hinweis enthalten auf eine paradoxe Fundierung des Wissens, aber der Hinweis ist so gefasst, dass das Kommunikationssystem der Gesellschaft ihn aufnehmen und verarbeiten kann, ohne durch die Paradoxie ins Oszillieren gebracht und blockiert zu werden', Luhmann, *Die Wissenschaft der Gesellschaft*, 189.

26 'Im dagegengesetzten Wahrheitsinteresse geht es statt dessen darum, den Gegner selbst zur Zustimmung zu zwingen, und die dafür entwickelte Technik heißt Dialektik', in Luhmann, *Die Wissenschaft der Gesellschaft*, 140.

5

Critical realism

SCIENCE, that is, knowledge of consequences; which is called also PHILOSOPHY.

Thomas Hobbes, *Leviathan*[1]

Without contraries is no progression.

William Blake, *The Marriage of Heaven and Hell*[2]

Introduction

Critical realism: the painted veil of dialectics[3]

Critical realism attempted to ground dialectics in realism. Roy Bhaskar dealt extensively with the issue, and challenged Kant's critique of science, empiricism and positivism throughout his work. He insisted on presenting the epistemological validity of structures or mechanisms which, as he maintains, encompass both perception and the laws that guide science towards predictability. Bhaskar's conception of dialectics is already apparent in his *A Realist Theory of Science*,[4] and it governs all his work until his *Dialectic*, which is probably one of his final contributions to the issue of science and epistemology. In the present chapter, I argue that his idea of predictability in science through mechanisms is of a pre-critical character and that he fails to acknowledge that norms generate rationality.

Bhaskar's counter-enlightenment epistemology, which asserts to reclaim reality, is not as explicit as Luhmann's, but his main epistemological deficit lies in his conception of dialectics as being testable within reality. Although Bhaskar claims to place dialectics within reality, he fails to grasp that his claim is not enough for an 'other' epistemology over which he also claims jurisdiction. He grounds an epistemological ontology that renders dialectics *testable but not accountable*, which leads him to form more an epistemological methodology and less an ontology of science, as he initially wished. My critique focuses on the issue that although his dialectics might generate a methodological testability, it neither signifies a commitment for science to theorize and act rationally, nor renders it accountable to the consequences of science within social conditions.

Although Luhmann will endure in epistemological history for formulating systems' theory and exorcizing his fear for dialectics, Bhaskar is part of modern epistemology because of his appreciation of dialectics, which converged with Luhmann's fear. Bhaskar joined Luhmann in tackling similar concerns of both a methodological and an epistemological character. They both deal extensively with systems, systems' complexity and reductionism. Bhaskar especially reconfigures ideas and ideals of positivism, the consideration of open and closed systems, and replaces Luhmann's systems' performativity with the notion of applicability of the scientific along with a clear focus on the nature of practice.

The present chapter explores and analyses critical realism as formed and explained by Roy Bhaskar, and criticizes his conception of dialectics as being reduced to the achievement of scientific totality. It also enquires into whether there are methodological consequences of critical realism in relation to science, or whether there are social or political stakes within critical realists' argumentation. Without opposing critical theory to critical realism, in the following sections of this chapter I develop the epistemological prospects of dialectics as providing an open field of opposing or inter-negating arguments.

The idea that the conditions of knowledge form the social theory of knowledge or, more precisely, modernize a political theory of knowledge and a critical science, serves as a stepping stone for the transition of modern epistemology to critical realism. Critical realism could be characterized as anti-Kantian and counter-empiricist epistemology. It is the first of its kind insofar as it attempts to transcend the *a priori* realization of knowledge; it is also counter-empiricist to the extent that it rejects the affiliation of knowledge with empirical law statements, which are neither confirmed nor falsified by the succession of their instances.

This chapter examines critical realism through the work of Roy Bhaskar, in conjunction with the work of other major critical theorists, such as William Outhwaite,[5] Andrew Collier and Margaret Archer. There is no convergence into a single epistemological thought that can be definitively called 'the epistemology of critical realism' of all the previous thinkers. However, they make significant contributions towards the idea that science is not a second-order observation, as proposed by Luhmann and presented in the previous chapter, but rather can trace counter-empiricist laws as major tendencies, whereas not all entities are observable. Moreover, causal mechanisms and structures are *not imagined* but dialectically conceived, and by means of social necessity they are perceived by social and scientific agents within reality.

In this chapter, I present a comparative critique: I show that critical realism, on the one hand, attempts to formulate a concrete argument of political epistemology, while, on the other hand, it places emphasis on issues that contradict the political character of epistemology in practice, in its presuppositions as well as in its consequences. Besides often being exhausted in Bhaskar's work in complicated methodological issues, as Norman Stockman rightly notes, critical realism also regularly culminates in pre-critical positions, despite its initial intentions.

In its attempt to differentiate between ontology and methodology, critical realist science considered that not *all* is method, and methodology is not *all* epistemology; structures relate to methodology to the same extent that action is central to critical realist ontology, whereas the normic condition is identified within transfactual statements. The realization that action is produced within structures immediately generates for epistemologists a dual concern: first, that we have to reveal the methodology that decodes structures; and second, that action is the royal path to ontology that epistemology seeks to describe and evaluate. Moreover, if there is any normativity governing the sciences, this can be identified in transfactuality which entails the structural relations among facts and which is elaborated in the following sections of this chapter.

The notions of realism and applicability of the sciences, which critical realism used as the Ariadne's thread that may lead the sciences to an unconditional universal statement through the labyrinth of positivism and empiricism, refer to three main scientific concerns: (a) the tracing of social conditions; (b) the consequences of the scientific within the social process; and (c) the condition of time. Under such an understanding, critical realism presupposes the multiplicity of the conditional in order to reveal the totality of the social scope that gains a universal perspective *in* and *on* the sciences and their potential. In its negating critique, Bhaskar's critical realism acted against positivism in its causal point of view, and against empiricism and the stifling of experience by redefining freedom by means of dialectics in order to disclose the differentiated element of science.

What is scientifically differentiated, for Bhaskar, holds three alternatives: (a) the classical empiricist, which is defined through regularities; (b) the transcendental idealist, which aims at formulating explanations; and (c) the transcendental realist, which occupies its problematics with mechanisms and structures. What science can do is sketch the elements of a social process, examine the constituent parts of a mechanism, explain the totality of structures, and articulate arguments. Science for critical realism *is* about structures as an open system of change, and *is* also about transcendental explanations of the social, thus forming its own ontological critique within epistemology. Bhaskar's critique then becomes more comprehensible: his focus on ontology articulates a counter-attack on positivism and renders ontology an essential concern for the sciences. His critique is neither purely transcendental nor empiricist, but a comparative study of the scientific, through both transcendentalism and the potential for the reality of practice. The means to accomplish transcendental realism become both causal intentionality of the sciences and the methodological freedom of dialectics.

In particular, Bhaskar attempted a regeneration of transcendental explanations by means of facts. He adapted explanations to social facts, and claimed that by means of explanations being related to facts, transcendentalism becomes socially productive, and is transformed within the aims of critical realism. At this point, Norman Stockman's critique of critical realism was concisely accurate: the applicability that Bhaskar claims becomes a performativity criterion, which regresses into scientific traditionalism. In the present chapter, I attempt to elucidate that the eclipse of any normativity criterion, along with the concern for applicability of the sciences, signifies a pre-critical judgement on the part of Bhaskar's critical realism.

In *A Realist Theory of Science*, Bhaskar describes the methodology of systems from a critical realist perspective. Instead of positivism imposing the method of the natural sciences on the humanities, things ought to be the other way around – namely, the dialectical method of the humanities has to indicate to all other scientific spheres their method as well as their aim. I maintain that the method that Bhaskar utilized is dialectics, and his aim is to refer to the formulation of a political epistemology, which entails neither the colonization of the sciences, nor the dictation of scientific aims by politics. The epistemological aim of critical realism calls for a philosophical critique of the sciences: if the laws that govern them are true and applicable, then sciences consummate a criterion of testability towards their scientific scope and object of reference, as well as towards the social (although both the scientific and the social are interrelated and interact with one another). When referring to laws in sciences, Bhaskar neither implicated nor explicated laws as promoting the functionalism of decision rules, but instead focused on mechanisms or structures that include perception and produce scientific laws.

On the other side of critical epistemology, which I challenge in its political substance and significance, the accountability (and not the testability) criterion both of and for the sciences is critical, and thus scientifically progressive because it encompasses the normative in more precise terms. Such normativity derives from the sciences themselves as an innate process, but it also stems from philosophy, which bears the potential to criticize science in its social and political stance and decision-making procedures. Under such an understanding, Stockman was probably wrong. There *are* scientific universals, and they are attributed to dialectics not only in its methodological dynamic according to the realists, but also in its socially and politically transformative character within science.

In order to keep anti-positivism within the range of epistemology, I argue that modern science needs the following: (a) objective theories on what the scientific consists of; (b) knowing subjects willing to inquire into the latter; and (c) the variability of scientific methodology. Although critical realism ignored the importance of extending its scope to the knowing subject, it emphasized the methodological output of dialectics for modern epistemology. Nevertheless, critical realism, particularly as presented by Bhaskar, failed to take advantage of the normative validity that dialectics offers to the object of science. As such, it deprived modern epistemology of the solid accountability criterion of critical theory that would be based and consummated on social normativity. The following sections of this chapter attempt to elaborate on these criticisms and explain the normativity deficit of critical realism, despite its initially critical as well as performative epistemological intentions.

The trickle-down theory of dialectics

This section aims to theorize the basic positions in Bhaskar's critical realism in relation to dialectics, and show that his version of dialectics fails to recognize the accountability of science that dialectics generates owing to its facilitation of the public use of reason by science. As for the conception that dialectics is also a method, it entails that because of dialectics' exchange of conflicting arguments, dialectics generates scientific and social rationality through the use of norms. In other words, the core argument of dialectics is that *norms matter*, both scientifically and socially, and, therefore, interrelatedly. Otherwise, rationality is rendered ambiguous and the social function of science, which so occupied Bhaskar's problematics, turns out to reproduce pre-critical schemata of thought and pre-modern positions on what constitutes the rational. This point develops into Bhaskar's epistemological *aporia*. Normativity and what constitutes the *ought to* for science is not a guide for the perplexed scientist, but it can serve as an accountability criterion for society and also as a principle condition for the advance of a modern science. Such an *ought to* answers to modern questions on what science is and how it relates to society, but mainly it derives from uncoerced dialogical processes and therefore claims validity and applicability.

In Foucault's and Bourdieu's theoretical development, there is a moment that is especially promising and epistemologically prominent: they are credited with placing science within society. Bhaskar's critical realism reaches three main epistemological outcomes: (a) the *transfactual* law of science, which is owing to its own character considered as *universal* law; (b) the multiplicity of method, which reaches scientific *tendencies of transduction* beyond the moments of induction and abduction; and (c) dialectics, which is maintained as a manifestation of the potential for scientific ontology.

Bhaskar's ontology reforms Heidegger's ontology and Luhmann's systems' theory, where Bhaskar defines *das Bestehende* as bearing the prospective of change through dialectics. Although Bhaskar rejects the anthropocentric idea of science, he acknowledges Heidegger's non-anthropic world of science, as studied in the everyday. It is at this point that Bhaskar misses the epistemological and social perils of the Heideggerian understanding regarding science and subjectivity, as explained in the first chapter.

Bhaskar's epistemological focus, however, remains anti-Kantian and normatively insufficient, and in this sense develops in close proximity to Luhmann's norm-free arguments. Critical realism turns its perspective from tendencies to mechanisms, and where philosophy asks the questions, science promotes the answers. Where philosophy uncovers the tendency of science, science per se reveals the mechanism of ontology of knowledge. If science, then, is the revelation of mechanisms that are indicated by tendencies in philosophy, the array of analyses with which critical realism provides us is exhausted in tracing the methodology of the science, or it merely limits science to its methodology. Bhaskar considered society a condition of knowledge, but we tend to form the impression in his work that the societal is more than a condition. In Outhwaite's terms, 'Given that we have scientific theories and that on the whole they seem to work remarkably well as an explanation of the world, what must the world be like in order for science to be possible?'[6]

One of Bhaskar's main arguments holds that even if dialectics is not mentioned in epistemology, this does not mean that it does not exist or, more importantly, that it is not applied. As with many cases elaborated in previous chapters, epistemology or science itself did not deliberately ignore dialectics but *the concept of dialectics*. I argue that dialectics is neither a method, nor a way of thinking or acting. In Bhaskar's elaboration of dialectics in *A Realist Theory of Science*,[7] dialectics is a consequential or even deterministic process including three instrumental phases of specific means that would bring about particular epistemological results: the first phase is the identification of a regularity; the second is the plausible explanation of the previous phase (but again, one should ask plausible to whom and by what means?); and the third is the corroboration or rejection of the second. In the schema following the previous analysis, Bhaskar associates the second phase with transcendental realism and, thus, the invention of explanation and testing through empirical procedures.

Moreover, in his definition of critical realism,[8] Bhaskar attempts mainly to get rid of positivism once and for all, and at the same time to rejuvenate transcendentalism. The objects of knowledge are notably structures and the object of the social activity of science. Thus he absolves positivism from its sophisticated empiricism, and turns attention to the idealism that obviously this time necessitates neither phenomena nor noumena, but real structures that are accessed, though not necessarily perceived or studied. The new idealist model that Bhaskar suggested was a substantial divergence from idealism but also a significant critique of what idealism was missing and an attempt to reclaim its validity both epistemologically and socially.

Bhaskar brings forward a second problematic divergence from existing epistemology with his notion of reflexivity. For Bhaskar, dialectics is an open process of change and appears situationally to incur changes in both ontology and epistemology. However, reflexivity in Bhaskar, despite being affiliated with dialectics, is a closed system of evolution of the self or of the structure; as such, I understand reflexivity not as counter-dialectical but un-dialectical. Both notions of dialectics and reflexivity are critical and 'critical' in the sense that means 'crucial', but still divergent and perhaps opposing: when we identify the one, we expect the other to decline or to be merely excluded from the scientific and social sphere. Reflexivity appears in Bhaskar as an excluded function of the structure, whereas dialectics is an inclusive process of science that can innovate the structure of science because of its openness to allow negations and changes.

The focus of epistemological and scientific critique in Bhaskar's critical realism remains on dialectics, for it appears to provide the exit from the methodological as well as the social monovalence: dialectics offers the sciences a political opening to society, and simultaneously allows the scientific to avoid determinism and methodological blindness. Dialectics is again an option, but at the same time it is a necessity too. It is a double opening on behalf of critical realism's epistemology: it clarifies its critical intentions by becoming a dialectical explanation, and also provides a methodological polyvalence to both sciences and society by declaring totality to be the epistemological aim of modern science. Totality is regarded, then, as a structure or system that thematizes the idea of scientific process, namely the perennial process by means of dialectics.

There are, in essence, three notions that are important for the understanding of science in Bhaskar: dialectics, totality, and universalizability. Dialectics occupies and is occupied by self-consciousness, *or* in more precise terms, it sets questions concerning method, thought, and consciousness, as well as concerning the quest for truth as the major objective of the sciences. Particularly for the latter, the dialectical element becomes the conceptual centrepiece for tracing theory along with practice, that is, both theoretical and practical reason, and it also provides claims of universal validity of all previous considerations in order not to devalue its political validity within social life.

In the following sections of this chapter, the concepts of totality and universalizability are the subject matter of analysis, but by linking dialectics with critique Bhaskar unfolds the argument that the dialectic is the element that produces critique and extends into the critique of actions. In parallel, despite the majority of desubjectivized epistemologies in modernity, as noted in previous chapters, Bhaskar's argument remains that the agent is the subject of dialectics and action. Moreover, the notion of absence is based on the idea of negation in dialectics, and action is part of the process in a praxis-generating dialectical science within society.

Bhaskar's divergence from Habermas' 'force of the better argument' indicates a major disagreement between critical realism and second generation critical theory. Habermas had tried to show that the argument is better because it comprises the reality principle that Bhaskar considers lacking in Habermas' thought. Therefore, the force of the better argument convinces people on intentions and interests, and refers not to some form of directional action, but to the account of the consequences that falls within not mere apologetics of the science, but in its capacity to form theoretical and practical reason.

Throughout the present chapter I argue that due to philosophy's essentially twofold position – that is, methodological and social-historical – it appears that philosophical arguments entail by necessity political positions. Methodological critique necessitates contradictions and negations or denials, and thus involves subjects who are accustomed to expressing negative arguments, whereas social-historical positions are never found outside of the social. They derive from and address the social. Hence, Bhaskar's critical realism formulates a dual philosophical fallacy, which it attempted to avoid even by insisting on the epistemological primacy of emancipation without ever explaining or providing a plausible analysis to define the subjects claiming emancipation and the object of their emancipatory denial.

Instead of accepting the simplified versions of either *a priori* or *a posteriori* critiques, criticism throughout modern epistemology appears to be a far more complicated process, with no easily accessible functions and consequences (especially in relation to the *a priori* version). Scientific criticism divides into the following three divergent processes that define *negation of the existent* conditions and lead to action.

(a) It is *a priori* in character, thus accepting the object of analysis beyond experience and the existent epistemological ontology. Here criticism becomes submissive and limited to intentionality and methodology itself.
(b) It focuses on the *a posteriori* understanding of the established conditions and, therefore, negates what is existent. It articulates the denial of the ontological object whereby what the subject experiences 'does not fit well' or simply 'does not work'.
(c) It formulates the negation of the existent through the *a priori*. It also negates the experience, which might provide a limited and, thus far, partly distorted vision or understanding of the totality of conceiving and acting.

Furthermore, he identifies two major points for epistemological critique: (a) the epistemic fallacy of reducing being to knowledge; and (b) the speculative illusion of the reduction of science to philosophy. Both points shall be explained in the following pages in this section. Bhaskar's conception of science is based on perceptual data. It identifies causal laws in science that involve noticing mechanisms and tendencies for their development, where such tendencies are internal to the scientific structure. Scientific laws are anti-empirical, but at the same time they reduce philosophy to the role of mediating between reality and the scientific. Bhaskar associates mechanisms and structures with the transition from the second phase of *a posteriori* understanding to the third phase of *a priori* negation. But he fails to explain why transcendentalism generates structures owing to the invention of imagined criteria. The elaboration seems weak or merely asymmetrical to what transcendental idealism is. He reduces the *a priori* to invented, but still plausible, elucidations, which entail empirical testing, although they have derived from the *a priori* conception of what science is. Nevertheless, the misunderstanding lies mainly in the identification of the second phase as being invented and imaginary.

The introduction of dialectics into critical realists' concerns brought forward their methodological and ontological mishaps. Bhaskar was right that even when we prioritize theory over social action, it is still the case that not all objects are observable. However, Kant's preposterous answer remains that critical realism appears to be characterized less by transcendental realist concerns and more by empirical idealist perspectives.[9] Critical realists attempt to formulate realist arguments, but fail to see that the notion of dialectics remains *a priori* in its formation and brings with it, in use, the gifts of social and political rationalism and normativity. Critical realism's position is that rationalism or transcendentalism present merely (!) imagined views. However, Bhaskar attempts to redefine realist arguments in *A Realist Theory of Science,* when distinguishing between the two: they are neither imagined nor imaginary.

My position towards critical realism is that the *a priori* understanding of the scientific is dialectically perceived. It precisely contradicts the imaginary for its un-dialectical nature. The imaginary appears an insufficient misunderstanding taking into consideration that Kant's transcendental perception of science develops according to the criterion of the rational and the normative as being both historically and socially situated. It is the dialectical and not the supposed imaginary essence of the *a priori* that provides science with discursively produced criteria. Such criteria of deliberation, accountability and social applicability generate theory that is not one of unobservable facts, but of processes in which humans participate socially. In such a sense, science is neither a pre-theoretical sequencing of cumulative knowledge, nor simply the secondary factor or observer of the social, but the critical and 'critical' (again, meaning 'crucial') agent or subject of the social sphere. The combination of dialectics with realist concerns would bring to the fore an epistemological critique of discursive essence along with normative consequences for the sciences, thus attempting to achieve the formation of social and scientific rationality.

Critical realism reduces the dialectical to a mechanism produced by experience. The flaw lies in reducing dialectics to a mechanism while overlooking the experience of action. Although throughout his work dialectic appears to trickle down to epistemology and ontology, Bhaskar situates epistemology constellationally within ontology, leaving neither intact for two crucial reasons. First, he questions *how* dialectics affects both spheres, and he answers by defining dialectical reason, which creates political decisions. Second, he questions *where* dialectics occurs. It is at this point that Bhaskar situates both ontology and epistemology within politics, and maintains that very few things are outside of politics. Bhaskar's main contribution to epistemology was that he affiliated epistemology with science, dialectics, society and politics, thus creating a critique of realism that had a transcendental intent.

The trickle-down understanding of dialectics presupposes categorizing the notions of structure and action, with the first referring to methodology, the second to ontology. When Bhaskar wrote that it was his intention 'to furnish the new philosophy of science with an ontology',[10] he failed to see that dialectics permeates both the structural as well as the sphere of action; it therefore incurs changes and innovations both in the methodology of science and in its ontic scope. Nevertheless, in his obituary of Bhaskar in 2014, William Outhwaite presented the double criticism that Bhaskar's concerns were, first, empiricist, and second, pre-critical (the second point finding support in Stockman). This chapter claims that Bhaskar's concerns also carried pre-modern consequences. Bhaskar seemed to avoid postmodernism, but in doing so he retreated into a pre-modern epistemology.

Relatedly, the trickle-down potential of dialectics becomes clearer at the latter (c) point mentioned previously: my position is that it is not individualism that achieves dialectics or even opposition or negation. It is rather vice versa. Dialectics generates individuation or the individual attitude without becoming an instrumental process for the sake of individuation. Dialectics rather allows the potential for individualism to 'happen'. It leaves it open and unlimited. The scientific is not the sphere of the individual potential, but is *also* as such, *along with* being a sphere conditioned within the social, and promoted by its political prospects. Otherwise, it becomes autonomized from the social and the political, where at first glance it seems free and uncoerced, but on closer inspection is punctuated with ideological concerns, and confused with provocation for its own sake. Under such an understanding of the dialectical trickle-down potential, the scientific reveals the objective reality of the subject *along with* the objective reality of the object as such.

Outhwaite was right when he focused on Bhaskar's question: 'how is science possible?'[11] Bhaskar sought to achieve a presentation as well as a critique of transcendental realism through dialectics, but missed the essential wholeness of both methodology and theory, where the latter asserts *a priori* truth, accountability and applicability; otherwise, the scientific dogma lies in the details of empiricism, claims to reality, and the relativism of no-one-true-theory. On the contrary, I hold that there is no hypothetical one-true-theory. When a theory maintains social accountability and political interests of applicability by means of dialectics, it can then provide the foundation for arguments of essential epistemological wholeness and social acceptance.

There is an element of predictability that governs scientific structures and mechanisms in Bhaskar's problematics, which the following sections of this chapter attempt to explain. Such predictability contributes to the formulation of scientific theology rather than realist epistemology, as proclaimed by critical realism. By no mere coincidence, Bhaskar turned critical realism into a religious understanding of the world in his later work. Small wonder, again, that he reverted to theology. Outhwaite was right again when, at the close of *New Philosophies of Social Science,* he wrote as follows: 'For all its elitism, conservatism and political irresponsibility, modern science, in the broadest sense of systematic study, and a politics informed by that study, is the only way we can hope to understand and retain some influence over the development of our societies.' The following sections will attempt to trace the pre-modern in critical realism, as well as the study and politics of modern science.

The double negation of dialectics

Bhaskar's work, at least in his early writings, is mainly an account of scientific activities; it is not necessarily a critique of them and it is definitely not a critique of science along Kantian lines. The next section of this chapter deals with the four phases of the dialectical process, as articulated by critical realism. The four-phase dialectical process in Bhaskar remains open to change and innovation throughout its epistemological and social course. Moreover, although Bhaskar might have disagreed, his main epistemological contribution was the concept of totality, deriving from Adorno's theorization but revived in Bhaskar's work with the emphasis on its rough edges and its negating character.

On closer inspection, totality for Bhaskar entailed the alterity or differentiation that leads to potential, but not indispensable negation. Such a negation constitutes the element of dialectics that traces the character of critical realism in being critical by incorporating the negation and being 'critical', namely crucial, owing to its capacity to generate the *totality of negations*. If the previous analysis is applied to science, it seems that dialectics is the potential for negation that science bears. Dialectics incorporates a dynamic of innovation for science and for society, in which the scientific sphere develops.

While in Hegel, dialectics proceeds from the necessary components of thesis and antithesis to a prospective or at least latent synthesis that could evolve into a consensus in Habermasian terms, in Bhaskar dialectics follows a different course. Figure 5.1 displays the basic points.

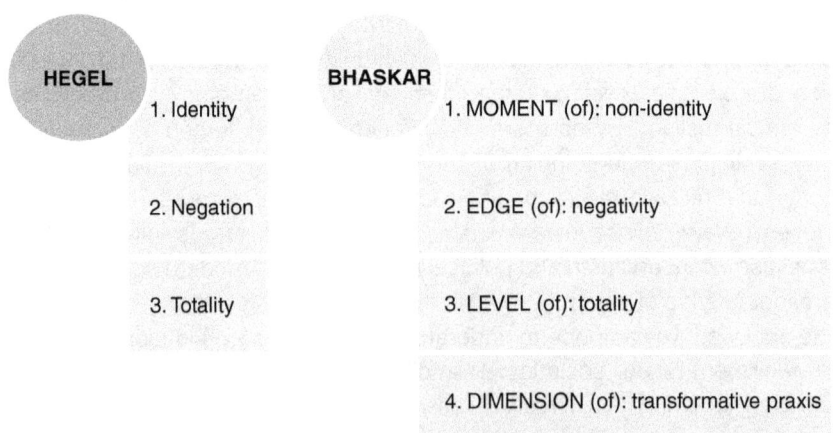

Figure 5.1 The dialectical process in Hegel and Bhaskar

Thus in Bhaskar we acknowledge a double negation in points (1) and (2), and a four-phase dialectical process, instead of a tripartite one as in Hegel. The double negation that Bhaskar offers declines the positivity of identity, and brings negativity to the point or edge of becoming a result, if not a deterministic evolution, of non-identity. However, the significant point in Bhaskarian dialectics is in (4), which introduces the transformation of dialectics through praxis. It constitutes a double transcendence of both Hegel and Kant. In the first place, praxis fills the gap left by the acting subject, and is itself subjectivized by Bhaskar providing critical realism with the task of formulating the *aporia* of a desubjectivized ontology for the sciences. In his words, 'we must see the agency as a *radically transformed transformative praxis,* oriented to rationably groundable projects'.[12]

Bhaskar's perception of dialectics transcended Hegel in terms of its double negation schema whereby the negation of identity functions as the presupposition of the dialectical negativity. Moreover, it was anti-Kantian in its essence. It declined the *commitment* to act and replaced it with what dialectics claimed to bring forward to society and science. According to Bhaskar and most notably to the majority of critical realists, dialectics claimed the transition to praxis in order to transform both the science and social concerns. The negation of identity formations seemed to be a transition beyond Kantian normativity or normative commitments, but in essence it was a transition to non-normativity. In departing from Kantian normativity, critical realists (particularly Bhaskar) present not an anti-Kantian view of epistemology, but a post-positivist analysis of theory as meaning and of knowledge as a commonsensical realization of ontology. In this way, the understanding and realization of practice is filtered through an instrumental control of predictability, where sciences play a leading role. Such a post-positivism functioned to the best advantage of positivism by rearticulating basic notions of positivism and by embellishing positivism with dialectical concerns of epistemology. Bhaskar's post-positivism marked also the (perhaps decisive) exclusive epistemological nature of normativity versus ontology, where the one develops, the other appears to be declining and falling into disuse. Normativity brings dialectics with it, whereas ontology is static scientifically and perhaps even stifling for social processes.

At this point, the reader of both Luhmann and Bhaskar could trace the spheres in which both thinkers converge, and those in which Bhaskar attempts to distinguish his own position.[13] They both consider society to be the totality of structures, in which science constitutes and articulates a significant mechanism. Such mechanisms, in order to exist, necessitate explanatory data, which they then reproduce by the totality of acts that the subjects (ignored in Luhmann's work) carry out. Subjects considered as agents, in Bhaskar, produce the social and scientific system, and at the same time transform it by the totality of acts they realize. The production of acts in Bhaskar is reminiscent of the autopoietic production of the system in Luhmann. Furthermore, Bhaskar's open or closed systems are in line with Luhmann's systems theory: events lead to a predictable or unpredictable series of other events, and regularity determinism is an advantage of causality as a form of studying intentions.

The double negation of dialectics as presented by Bhaskar, and his causality considerations, lead to a theory of dialectical totality, where dialectics is both a general critique of negations and a causal explanation of scientific intentions. The further stage of considering systems in Bhaskar and Luhmann refers to the plausibility that Bhaskar finds essential in judging the eventfulness of concepts. In his words, the concept of generative mechanism provides interpretations of the world, and '[t]he possibility of such an interpretation supplements internal consistency and contextual plausibility as a constraint on the possible forms of theoretical advance; it constitutes the ultimate goal of all theory construction'.[14] The abstract focusing on contextual plausibility bears notional similarities to Luhmann's performativity criterion.

Both Bhaskar and Luhmann replace the truth condition in science with plausibility and performativity, respectively, despite Bhaskar's declaration that 'the transcendental realist will demand that models be tested not just for plausibility but for truth'.[15] It is consistent with their mode of thought: for Bhaskar, the plausibility criterion emphasizes the theoretical burden that science has to bear, despite being insufficient or even unnecessary; for Luhmann, performativity brings systems to an end that is compatible with the scientific process of constructing systems of causes and effects. Moreover, it grounds both thinkers' epistemological arguments within the sphere of the measurable (note: the measurable, not the rationally accountable).

What appeared as the course of action of dialectics in Bhaskar, and the construction of systems in Luhmann, also bore some problematic perceptions. The *a priori* potential of perception for sciences, people and societies shows that people, sciences or scientists transform sciences and societies without any prior experience because science and society, apart from being the necessary grouping of intentional acts, are also the totality of *unintentional* acts. The latter understanding of totality means *not an unconscious* but still *not an instrumental* totality of acts bearing predefined means leading to specific ends.

To all intents and purposes, critical realism was and remains practice-sensitive and not commitment-sensitive. Realist epistemology is served not by the *a priori* intentions that form scientific thought and knowledge, but by the *a posteriori* of ontology. In this respect, dialectics as utilized by critical realists became the transcendental saviour of their epistemology. Contrary to previous epistemologies that needed empirical grounding and sought confirmation in the ontological, critical realism sought theoretical bases in transcendentalism and attempted to combine the critique generated by dialectics, a transcendental trait per se, with the realism of the ontological. In Bhaskar's *A Realist Theory of Science*, the nature of science concerns the nature of the world, and more precisely such considerations form epistemological statements within open systems, which 'situate the possibility of two kinds of possibility statements: epistemic and natural'.[16] Therefore, critical realism merged both tendencies of transcendentalism and realism, and although it continued to be occupied with epistemological agents, it focused on the structures and continuities of mechanisms within the sciences.

The pursuit of practice included the identification of actors who determine scientific and social conflicts. Social theory and perspectives generated through the interplay of structures and agents gives shape to norms as stocks of knowledge, which are universally available but at the same time maintain a temporal continuity which forms practices that accord with the social whole. Bhaskar maintains that either theory alone or practice alone is epistemologically and socially unfruitful, but in later writings he holds that practice has a degree of autonomy from theory. It appears to me that the degree of autonomy is a vague epistemological zone, which remains uncharted and undefined. Furthermore, unmediated practice, where theory is to a certain extent considered superfluous, can become a scientifically precarious condition, as well as a socially risky argument or choice.

Bhaskar posits the question: what makes a scientist, is it data or theory? The transcendentalists would argue for neither alternative. It is dialectics that makes a scientist and science as well, and Bhaskar appears explicit but cursory when he states: 'There is something like *a logic* of scientific discovery, which I am calling the epistemological dialectic.'[17] Critical realism did not deny that dialectics is charged with the job of discovering and foregrounding *alethic* or dialectical reason, as Bhaskar cites in his *Dialectic*.[18] Such an *alethic* reason contributes to or binds the realm of scientific structures, which is understood as a totality of scientific discoveries on both the theoretical and the practical level. The totality of scientific structures, mechanisms and systems of knowledge allows the potential of scientific polyvalence to be conceptualized and realized within the system of science.

If polyvalence, in Bhaskar's epistemological system, is identified with the totality of dialectical arguments, then such a meaning-attributing position reduces dialectics to an all-inclusive schema,[19] where, as Bhaskar puts it, 'in the domain of totality we need to conceptualize *entity relationism*'.[20] In his recent interview with me, William Outhwaite reconsidered dialectics within the framework of relationism by referring to common-sense ontology. He suggested that 'we don't really *need* arguments for a realist position which is shared by common sense and the practice of working scientists. Philosophical realism ... aims to be continuous ... with the sciences – complementary rather than competitive with them'.[21] In both thinkers, the relationism approach signified a 'relationalization' or relativization of dialectics for the sake of polyvalence and inclusivity. It abrogates the negating potential of dialectics, which is elaborated in the next section of this chapter. By rendering realism a complementary approach towards science, critical realism abolishes its critical power to negate and thereby to exert innovative critique of unconventional intentions.

Totality in critical realism is relationism within structures, where dialectics facilitates their reflective relations. I argue above (and in previous chapters) that dialectics is neither the exclusive reflection of a subject, nor the relations among systems. Bhaskar breaks from Kant in the search for dialectical limits, and acknowledges that dialectics in Kant is categorized as the limit of knowledge, or as the search for reason. On this point, he accuses Kant of ignoring the totality of dialectical polyvalence and throwing dialectics into the antinomic cul-de-sac. However, it appears to me that such polyvalence is the axiological reduction of dialectics to a normative silence where anything goes, whereas the Kantian perspective of tracing antinomies provides science with the normative criterion of dialectical critique.

Bhaskar attempted to ground the distinction between ontology and methodology, and emphasize ontology, but he lost sight of the perspective that it is not an 'either/or' schema that promises their epistemological realization. Epistemology cannot render the one its focal point without marginalizing the other. Since dialectics considers both ontology and methodology as the conditions of truth, it is precisely such a dual criterion for validity of truth borne by dialectics that Bhaskar fails to acknowledge. He appears to ignore one main argument: namely, that even when scientific ontology has discovered truth, this is not enough to become certain. Ontology has to be accompanied by validity, and science by accountability criteria, so as to vindicate the formation of social rationality. Otherwise, the case of scientific dialectics is lost, and science reverts to ambiguous empiricism and positivistic prejudice. Bhaskar does not avoid the latter fate, despite employing the concept of dialectics. It is a noble epistemological cause for Bhaskar to win the ontological justification of his theory, but it is not necessarily a dialectical or critical one. Science needs norms that have validity and applicability within society.

Science *is* normative, and despite Bhaskar's further theorization that dialectics is a process of regularities' identification transmitted to plausible explanations and realities of entities, dialectics is more than a method or description of epistemological steps based on realities. It is what binds sciences into a science, not as a mediating link between them or with society, but as the criterion that differentiates the hypothetical or the mythic from scientific argumentation and open learning processes of a systematic character. The first stage of dialectics is neither the regular nor the eventful scientific result of a mechanism or structure that 'involves experimental production and control, in which the reality of the mechanisms postulated in the model are subjected to empirical scrutiny'.[22] The task of science is not to discriminate between the imaginary and real mechanisms. Nor is it to produce an account of them. The task of science is to produce dialectics that would allow not testing but accountability criteria, both for itself per se as well as for the social in toto. The task of science is to exert *elenchus* on the hypothetical or the mythical, the building of rationality, and the way in which a critical science becomes the aim and the initial rationale for scientists.

The above topics do not prompt an 'either/or' dilemma, but rather provoke the following question: how is theory accomplished? There lies also the uncomfortable realization on the part of the scientist that the answer depends on what theory means and entails. Bhaskar avoided focusing on theory due to his eagerness to ground science and epistemology on praxis, thus redefining the eleventh thesis on Feuerbach. It was and remains a noble epistemological cause for the sake of the social objective of science. Nonetheless, it remains insufficient to discriminate between the dialectics that critical realists so keenly used and examined, and the positivistic perils of causality that render individualized aims and instrumental means and ends the overarching aims of the sciences. Bhaskar's notion of causality, though, bears some similarities with phenomenological intentionality. It is an abstract tendency or manifestation of human deliberation or consciousness in order for the latter to ground its epistemological concerns on the social and, therefore, to act. In Bhaskar's words, 'there could be no knowledge without the social activity of science'.[23]

Science *is* political. It is not political *ex post* because of the results it incurs on societies. It involves collectively binding decisions and acts. There is no 'individual science'; rather it is part of a whole, or, in Bhaskarian terms, a social totality. However, it is also a whole in itself, and forms the public sphere of sciences or, in other words, the totality of science that acts and interacts according to rules, relationships and interests set and pursued by participants within a public sphere. When the scientist attempts to redefine the notions of scientific results, pre-existing ends or rational-choice actions, she honours the very object that she endeavours to innovate or epistemologically negate, and declines positivism transformed into neo-positivism or post-positivism. The identification of causalities dressed as intentions and the combination of absolute means, resulting in absolute ends, simulates epistemological theology and, as I stated above, it is no mere coincidence that Bhaskar reverted to theology in his late work. What makes societies? People or mechanisms and structures? Both Bhaskar and Luhmann opted for the second alternative: structures. In Bhaskar's words,

> Societies, people and machines are not collectivities, wholes or aggregates of simpler or smaller constituents (just as intentionality is not an inner urge or push) ... In the classical world view ... all 'things' properly so-called were just more or less highly differentiated aggregates of matter, and so could be viewed either as wholes or parts (or as both).[24]

This was a monumental statement equalling Luhmann's considerations on the social set out in the previous chapter.

Nevertheless, people and societies *are* collectivities, since they identify themselves as such and not as structures; they form multiple wholes, which become coherent on account of deliberate actions based on consciousness or the intentional (in phenomenological terms). Societies are generated by conscious individuals performing intentional or unintentional acts within spheres of science, politics or culture. These *are* totalities in the Adornian sense: formed by conscious subjects who coordinate their actions as a result of conscious deliberation, and apply dialectics in all social spheres that entail political commitment.

The unity of theory and practice in practice

Shifting the epistemological attention from the knowing subject to the law-like structure of facts, as attempted by the critical realists, renders epistemology *accommodatable* to methodology and objectivism. As such, it moves science into pre-critical positions by leaving the *a priori* beyond the sphere of dialectical critique. In the previous section of this chapter, I examined the notion of the double negation that dialectics presents by challenging identity and relocating knowledge within a dialectical critical realist's explanation. That was the alterity that critical realism introduced to epistemology. However, it was a unification of 'unhappily married' elements, which amounted to a theory that included a phenomenological method and ignored the subjective component of knowledge that 'could not solve the problems of solipsism'.[25]

By considering the subject as creating solipsistic problematics, critical realism charged dialectics with an epistemological inability to treat knowledge as an accomplishment of societies or collectivities. It certainly theorized that a running start for science, developing into a concrete transformative negation, was the concept of absence meaning negation, but despite placing absence within ontology, critical realism failed to relate this to thinking and acting subjects. It was just mechanisms and structures that did all the work for sciences and societies. Thus, dialectics is neither a real nor a radical negation, as critical realism would have intended. Critical realists' perspective on what the dialectical is constitutes an uncritical critique that does not incorporate the interests of the knowing subjects who act *because of* such a dialectical negation, and absent the sequence of constraints, whether in science or society.

It was not a simple problem of epistemological dialectics, as Bhaskar set out in *Dialectic*. However, our beliefs and *a priori* certainties about the world are not shaped by the imaginary, nor are they left without criteria. Praxis is not the sole criterion of a theory. The criterion of the validity of a theory is mostly dialectics. The dialectical element renders science both critical and modern on account of the accountability potential which dialectics transmits to science. Under the accountability *elenchus*, science checks the consequences of both theory and praxis. It is not merely the dynamics of a transformative praxis that innovates and brings changes to societies; it is also the dialectical moment of negation, shaped by the *a priori* of consciousness.

Critical realism reduces dialectics to a critique of the supposedly objective, and ignores the fact that even the objective is conceived *a priori*. Despite the initial declarations of loyalty to critical reason, such a view of knowledge and science leaves the door open to social engineering and political manipulation. By limiting dialectics within what is supposedly objective, critical realism abandons the critical perspective of the scientific borne by social agents, where knowledge serves not the objectivism of facts, but the conceptual accomplishments of the knowing subjects. Although critical realists sought to avoid reducing subject to object, their perception of objectivity was in no sense a totalizing critique of the insufficient world of scientific subjectivity; on the contrary, it was a transposition of scientific dialectics from the sphere of the know-that to the know-how, from the axiological (either in terms of praxis or conscious deliberation) to the actualism of criticizing actions of oppression, not the oppressor as an acting subject.

If universality sets a limit to empirical regularity, I consider that theoretical reason implies a *commitment* to act, not praxis in itself. Thus, such a form of commitment is not a mere evasion of praxis, but allows practical reason to presuppose, without any trace of determinism, an elaboration of theory in order to accept or negate it within social conditions. What Bourdieu and Foucault attempted appears to be taken up and developed by Bhaskar's critical realism, namely that all scientific failures are attributed to the sciences' incapacity or even unwillingness to reflect upon the social and the political. In particular, scientific structures may have non-enduring universal validity for critical realists. However, what *becomes* universal for scientific mechanisms is that they *are* universal in their consequences for their agents as bearers of scientific praxis.

Bhaskar identifies two criteria of universalizability: first, the universal property of the scientific has to be theoretically grounded; and second, a reality principle governs its application by setting the cornerstone for acknowledging the real interests of the sciences instead of perceived interests. It then appears as natural that two forms of dialectical universalizability emerge, giving us the outline of Bhaskar's epistemological transition from critical theory to critical realism. The first form refers to critical reason, and the second to explanatory or totalizing critical reason. The development is not telic; rather change occurs under the guidance of the trickle-down perception of dialectics, which influences and forms both ontology and epistemology.

The epistemological discussion of multiple causations leading to multiple effects, which Bhaskar introduces in *A Realist Theory of Science*, serves to define the regularity that determinism includes and which appeals to universal epistemological intentions. His argument is directed not to realizing the universalizability of scientific validity, but rather to configuring the predictability conditions of closed systems of action according to the Luhmannian way of systems' performativity.

Although Bhaskar admits that 'Consistency with the facts is neither necessary nor sufficient for a theory',[26] the predictability criterion acts as a shield for the ambiguity of effects caused by the openness of the scientific system, which can bear enduring results of the dialectical and critical kind only under the condition of openness. In his interview with me, William Outhwaite correctly emphasized that 'systems theory moved if anything away from realism towards a more virtual and conventional understanding of systems, for good reasons within that framework'.[27]

Although drawing a parallel with Luhmann's performativity criterion is for me rather unavoidable, what becomes more impressive is the function of contingency as applied to systems perspective (just as predictability or even plausibility acts for scientific structures later in Bhaskar's *A Realist Theory of Science*). As predictability saves the lost honour of the openness of the scientific system, similarly contingency prompts epistemological solutions in order to provide epistemology with a way out from the closed systems of Luhmann. Although Bhaskar professes to decline the predictability of the sciences, he gravitates towards the admission that 'Social structures, unlike natural structures, cannot exist independently of their effects.'[28] The problematic component within this statement lay not in the idea of effects, but in the consideration of structures as socially and scientifically measurable according to effects. The (in)effective character of structures fits appropriately with critical realism's epistemological anxieties, and struggles to find a methodological basis, but disagrees with the social essence of the scientific sphere to the point where it is not assessable according to causes and effects.

In order to quantify the intangible and render the unpredictable intelligible, Bhaskar slipped to acknowledging the operative identity of the science that he persistently attempted to avoid when presenting the double negation of the dialectical critique (as analysed in the previous section). Bhaskar's notion of universality resides in the totality of the sciences performed by causalities, applicability prospects, the plurivalence of dialectical critical reason and their ontology within the social.

In an attempt to ground the applicability of the universal within the empirical, Bhaskar withdrew to the empirical, and tried to combine it with the universal within the epistemological safe haven of actualism (or the actual, as he would have preferred), implicitly including the consequences of the potential applicability of universal laws. In his words, 'the satisfaction of the CP [*ceteris paribus*] clause cannot normally be verified independently of the actualization of the consequent: hence to make it a condition for the applicability of the law is circular'.[29] To make matters simpler, Bhaskar articulated a whole series of arguments against positivism and opposed the potentiality of a normic form of scientific explanations where science becomes possible simply by acknowledging that laws of universal validity can exist 'quite independent of our knowledge of them'.[30]

Hence, Bhaskar's identification of laws makes them factors in acknowledging tendencies, causalities and intentions within the open system of science. Particularly, by virtue of being an open system, science incorporates theory, applications and ontological explanations of the domains of the real and the actual. But it is exactly at this point that Bhaskar renders the open system of science the experimental field of structures above the axiological meaning of the *identification* of events. Yet, as I tried to show previously, if the study of science is to be epistemologically and, moreover, practically rewarding, then it has to include the normic universalization of a dialectical critique and not the methodological orthodoxy of structures' identification.

Moreover, the dialectics of co-inclusion in the name of plurivalence, advocated by critical realists, stretched to the temporality of an episode from the past to the present, and also included the future as a promissory note. In Bhaskar's words, 'Dialectic depends upon the art of thinking the *coincidence of distinctions and connections*.'[31] It is a confession of an *a priori* dialectical intentionality, but maintains a sketch or description of dialectical endeavour that remains uncharted in critical realism. It is important here to give coherent and articulate explanations of how, by Bhaskar's own admission, 'dialectic is not only about change or even negation ... [but also] is concerned with presence, and the co-presence of the absent and the present ... and with alterity, [and] sheer difference'.³²

My argument is that co-inclusion and polyvalence allowed politics to configure scientific temporality instead of tolerating dialectics to engage in the unmediated past and future of the sciences. Such an all-inclusive presumption of dialectics, situated within the multiplicity of causes of an open scientific system that excludes the 'there is no alternative' formative consents, becomes then the all-inclusive theory of scientific relativism and social compromise of 'anything goes'. Regardless of the methodological paradox that Bhaskar presents, his all-inclusive dialectics neglects its negativity competence, the innovative character of dialectics does not lie in its capacity to consent but to negate, not to include but to exclude and get rid of the traditional and the dogmatic and replace them with the critical and the rational.

In the Hegelian sense, the dialectical negation is simultaneously theoretical and practical, and entails change and novelty of a transformative kind. Dialectics is the critique of myth and ideology in either the scientific or the social sphere and, according to the latter's logic, it also becomes the negation of the denial of reality and is, therefore, of a critical as well as a realistic character; otherwise, thereafter science or dialectics cannot invoke reality. It appears to me that Bhaskar focuses on the critical and renders the rational extraneous to dialectics. The double negation of dialectics maintains that being critical for theory involves negating the negative or, in Bhaskar's terms, absenting absence. He considers the Hegelian unification of theory and practice to take place not in reason but in the negativity that dialectics transfers. Nevertheless, the 'unwelcome questions' of dialectics are not by necessity situated within ontological dialectics but within epistemological dialectics, since the latter matches the desire for change within the sciences and poses questions addressing the public sphere or systems' *Umwelt* (in Luhmannian terms).

However, the Bhaskarian admission that science creates an ontology of the real and the dialectical was no mere coincidence and no small thing for a critical epistemology. Hence, science reveals itself as the dividing line between rational and irrational things, which Bhaskar names 'essential and non-essential', and as the bearer of dialectical reason, which might forget what is entailed in the need for ontology and realism. Although unfair in his critique of the essential and essentiality in science, by Bhaskar's own admission

> we must have a creature capable of dividing the world into essential and non-essential attributes, and of appreciating that the former do not always manifest themselves in actuality. With the *first referential detachment* of structures and the transfactual efficacy it affords, we get

the first taste of *alethic truth*, the dialectical reason or ground for things. And now we are doing science, from a position in which the primordial activities of referential detachment and the necessity for ontology may be readily forgotten. But also, insofar as differentiation is itself a causal act and causation is absenting, we are on the terrain of dialectic, upon which ... non-identity and transfactuality can thus retrospectively be seen to depend.[33]

Bhaskar's position crystallizes at this decisive moment when he absolves reason and de-rationalizes epistemological dialectics, thus averting its normative character and rendering it pre-critical and pre-modern. He presents a divergence of ontological and epistemological dialectics as if they were not just differentiated but opposed spheres due to their incorporation (or not) of critical reason.

Nonetheless, I argue that for critical theory and epistemology, epistemological dialectics is not a hypothetical construction of the sciences; nor is it an abrogation of ontology and realism. On the contrary, it meets accountability criteria by incorporating practice potentials of theory and a totalizing critique of the argumentation on truth presented by the sciences. Bhaskar was right when he elaborated on theoretical reason that it is the sphere that presupposes a 'criterion of actionability' that '*has a theoretico-practical duality* built into it ... [and] says the world is so-and-so ... [that] still implies a commitment to act on it'.[34]

Absence is the traditional view of science that Bhaskar deconstructs. But he falls back on 'a *systematic intermingling* of categories, concepts, critiques and figures rather than a unilinear procession'.[35] He sketches the contours of dialectical critique but leaves normativity outside of its scope, although he claims an intermingling of arguments by avoiding the unilinearity. It is precisely such a unilinearity that renders dialectics critical and rational, and thus modern: the unilinear aim of negation and rationality. In his urge to prescribe a course of action that totalizes praxis, Bhaskar moves from what he considers as dialectical form to a theorization of dialectics. He diminishes dialectics' social status by rendering it a form of praxis and *not* a form of consciousness that moves sciences and societies towards the rationality of performing reason.

However, my thesis towards critical realism is as follows: during the twentieth century, the revelation of modern epistemology, which was based on social and political interests, needs and agents' wants, was that to the extent that theory imposes praxis, so too praxis entails a commitment to theory. This revelation has put an end to complacent ontological claims on the indispensability of praxis. Praxis is scientifically, socially or politically crucial, but the human agents it involves want and have to know by their own admission why it takes place, what it does, and in so doing they revert to theoretical explanations to sustain the practical manifestations of their *a priori* concerns.

Dialectics does engage in both theory and praxis, but it does not necessitate the normativity of the rational and, therefore, it runs the risk of entangling itself in irrational considerations if it does not designate a concrete *a priori* accountability criterion, which signifies its intentionality towards social practice. Negation is the moment of the 'no-further', but it is also the moment when the *potentiality* of rationality becomes praxis by means of dialectics.

Dialectical negation leaves sciences with a void. Dialectics allows and furthers negation, but it also leaves sciences to hover over the social sphere without the perspective of forming rationality, either social or scientific. Both social and scientific rationality do not instantly and self-evidently derive from the dialectical process. Dialectics is indeed a process, and may remain so if not affiliated with the political perspective of normativity that shapes both the scientific and the social. Bhaskar was right: 'Universalizability functions as both a test for consistency/sincerity and a criterion of truth.'[36] Nonetheless, dialectical universalizability is the aim of the modern world, and particularly modern science, to come to social terms with critique, norms and innovation.

Conclusions

It was not a matter of philosophical orthodoxy, as Bhaskar claimed in his introduction to *Critical Realism*, that provoked dichotomies in reasoning. Nonetheless, he admitted that they were radical dichotomies. In his critique of Kant, in the same introduction, he presents Kant as defending transcendentalism for reasons of philosophical methodology, whereas critical realism deploys three moments of the realist argument: (a) historically transient social activities; (b) human beings as material objects (!); and (c) human beings as causal agents. The devil is in the detail again. Bhaskar rejected the Kantian notion of human beings as 'merely'[37] (!) thinkers and perceivers, and presented them first as material objects and second as causal agents.

For critical realism, dialectics included the universalizability alternative, and a totalizing praxis based on the moral imagination of reflexivity without excluding differentiation and the diversity of unity. It was a dialectical constellationality reverting to relativism, the teleology of the structural understanding of the sciences, and the lush diversity of all-inclusive dialectics deprived of its negativity and critical element. Bhaskar reconciles (albeit vaguely) the tension between theory and praxis. He presents an implicit assumption that

> T/P [theory/practice] consistency is a matter of *praxis* (in a process), which should be *practical, progressive* and *theoretically grounded*; and that both praxis and grounding should be universalizable in the sense that they be *transfactual, concrete, actionable* ... and *transformative*, i.e. oriented to the objective(s) of the praxis, which, in the field of practical reasoning, will be ultimately grounded in a theory.

But then a contradictory interpretation is also evident, when he writes: 'The simplest way of introducing the logic of consistency and universalizability is to register that you cannot say "you ought to ø" and not ø in materially the same circumstances without committing a practical or performative contradiction, i.e. being guilty of T/P inconsistency.'[38] As elaborated in the previous pages, the statement of negation of the negativity potential of dialectics, through the negation of the 'ought to', rendered dialectics uncritical and, therefore, insufficient. However, it emphasized praxis, but the uncritical character of dialectics was alone incapable of producing any normative order.

The logic of dialectical universalizability oriented towards praxis intended to correspond to the level of explanatory critical reason, which counters the consequences of irrealism for philosophy. It was a typical Bhaskarian type of dialectics – descriptive and didactic instead of providing a normative or norm-aiming description. It prioritized a commitment to praxis by intending to ground it on theory, which was again rather dispensable for the sake of praxis. Instead of a praxis-committed theory, Bhaskar provided critical realism with a theory-committed praxis, which, although claiming exclusive explanatory and non-predictive criteria for the rational assessment of theories, was situated within the causality and predictability of social and scientific reasons within structures and mechanisms.

Philosophy depends, then, upon the form of scientific practices, while eschewing ambiguities and relativism – which were not avoided after all in critical realism. Philosophical arguments are accomplished, according to critical realism, through the scientific focus on accounts of activities, not intentions or commitments to theory *and* practice. The accountability criterion of the sciences that influences all modern epistemology was no small issue in critical realism. Where philosophy appears to set the questions, science attempts to give the answers for critical realists. But that does not eliminate the fact that the point of epistemological as well as social concern is equally questions, answers, *and* to whom the latter are accountable. It is the moment of crucial divergence from Kantian epistemology and critical theory: for critical realists, the criterion of accountability was practice, whereas for critical theorists it was theory and the knowing subject that both accomplish knowledge and exert criticism on what is known through dialectics. For both epistemological tendencies, the criterion was not a solid form of epistemological concern that remains unchanged and restrictive for both science and societies. Rather, it was the base of modern science, as well as of useful theory and practice that derives from theory. Meanwhile, with critical realism, the scientific criterion reshuffled the dialectical process so that it no longer includes the formation of scientific and social rationality.

In Bhaskar's words, 'To explain a human action by reference to its rationality is like explaining some natural event by reference to its being caused. Rationality then appears as an *a priori* presupposition of investigation, devoid of explanatory content and almost certainly false.'s[39] Such a position constituted an understatement of the scientific and social potentialities that dialectical rationality bears under the auspices of *a priori* reasoning. The problem with such an argument was that, although it seems to argue for a plausible anti-positivism that maintains dialectics as a transformative scenario for science and society, it rescues positivism from its *aporias* by reclaiming determinism and teleology. Bhaskar writes as follows: 'People and society are not ... related "dialectically" ... Society stands to individuals ... as something that they never make, but that exists only in virtue of their activity.' He goes onto explain that science and society do not necessitate intentionality and self-consciousness, but constructed forms and structures that exist independently of their agents, whereby 'it is no longer true to say that agents create [them]'.[40]

My question remains the following: it is true that there is prior existence of social forms, but who can deny that people still act and mostly *react* to either social forms, mechanisms or structures as part of their conscious or unconscious, intentional or unintentional, social being and dialectical interaction? What Bhaskar fails to take into consideration is that when considering either science or society, or both simultaneously, as parts of a dialectical process, we tend to realize that human reaction to existing forms is not necessarily controllable and is certainly not predictable or predetermined. Despite Luhmannian and Bhaskarian considerations that converge to the point that 'people do not create society'[41] and attempt to remove voluntaristic misunderstandings, no one – neither individual nor scientific subject – can imagine or perceive society as a mere pre-existing condition in which people do not consciously participate dialectically, by accepting or negating the existent and by forming their conditions of social being.

Critical realism marked the transition to political epistemology of the twenty-first century, but it failed to realize that societies, and science in particular, undergo changes not through systems or structures, but through the contemplation of *someone* on the existent and coercive systems and structures. The concluding remarks that follow attempt to clarify the transition to political epistemology through critical theory and the arguments on rational theory and normative praxis.

Notes

1. Thomas Hobbes, *Leviathan* (Oxford: Oxford University Press, 2008), 56.
2. William Blake, *The Marriage of Heaven and Hell* [1790], available at www.bartleby.com/235/253.html (accessed 9 September 2016).
3. For reasons of consistency, I shall be using the term 'dialectics' throughout the chapter, as I have done for the whole book, although critical realists and particularly Roy Bhaskar used the term 'dialectic'. When the latter is used in this chapter, it refers to Bhaskar's phrasing that could not be substituted for the former for reasons of clarity and terminological accuracy.
4. See, in particular, the first pages of the book, where he states: 'In science there is a kind of dialectic in which a regularity is identified, a plausible explanation for it is invented, and the reality of the entities and processes postulated in the explanation is then checked', Roy Bhaskar, *A Realist Theory of Science* (London: Verso, 2008), 14ff.
5. William Outhwaite kindly answered my questions in an interview, conducted in 2015, parts of which shall be included in the text.
6. William Outhwaite, *New Philosophies of Social Science* (London: Macmillan Press, 1993), 18.
7. Bhaskar, *A Realist Theory of Science*, particularly 14–15.
8. Bhaskar, *A Realist Theory of Science*, 25.
9. As is excellently elaborated in Outhwaite, *New Philosophies*, 37.
10. Bhaskar, *A Realist Theory of Science*, 23.
11. Outhwaite, *New Philosophies*, 31.
12. Roy Bhaskar, *Dialectic: The Pulse of Freedom* (London: Routledge, 2008), 9.
13. Although it is not possible to examine here, the importance of the notions of time and contingency, particularly influential in their epistemological concerns and of increasing significance in the course of their work, would be another interesting point to raise in both Luhmann and Bhaskar.
14. Bhaskar, *A Realist Theory of Science*, 163.
15. Bhaskar, *A Realist Theory of Science*, 166.
16. Bhaskar, *A Realist Theory of Science*, 77.
17. Bhaskar, *Dialectic*, 34–5, my emphasis.
18. Bhaskar, *Dialectic*, 109.
19. Again, it would be interesting to note how dialectics becomes an all-inclusive theory in Bhaskar due to the inescapable conditions of time and contingency. In his words, 'The dialectics of co-inclusion is made possible by the necessary but indefinite temporal stretching of an episode, event, or period. It lies either in the past or in the present. And in the latter case it defines a boundary state between what is determined and determinate and what is, even if it is practically inevitable, not yet', Bhaskar, *Dialectic*, 143.

20 Bhaskar, *Dialectic*, 125.
21 William Outhwaite, 'Interview on Critical Realism', forthcoming in 2017.
22 Bhaskar, *A Realist Theory of Science*, 146.
23 Bhaskar, *A Realist Theory of Science*, 27.
24 Bhaskar, *A Realist Theory of Science*, 85.
25 Bhaskar, *Dialectic*, 232.
26 Bhaskar, *A Realist Theory of Science*, 138.
27 Outhwaite, 'Interview on Critical Realism', forthcoming in 2017.
28 Bhaskar, *A Realist Theory of Science*, 246.
29 Bhaskar, *A Realist Theory of Science*, 96.
30 Bhaskar, *A Realist Theory of Science*, 116.
31 Bhaskar, *Dialectic*, 180.
32 Bhaskar, *Dialectic*, 182–3.
33 Bhaskar, *Dialectic*, 212–13.
34 Bhaskar, *Dialectic*, 221.
35 Bhaskar, *Dialectic*, 184.
36 Bhaskar, *Dialectic*, 178.
37 Margaret Archer et al., *Critical Realism* (London: Routledge, 2007), 4.
38 Both cited in Bhaskar, *Dialectic*, 284.
39 Roy Bhaskar, 'Societies', in Archer et al., *Critical Realism*, 210.
40 Archer et al., *Critical Realism*, 214.
41 Archer et al., *Critical Realism*, 216.

Conclusions

This book has aimed to examine dialectics in modern epistemology and to compare it with critical theory, not 'in order to' but 'because' the latter can offer innovative means of dialectical theorizing. In this way, critical theory has the potential to advance twenty-first-century epistemology.

The prevailing idea in critical realism, as elaborated in the final chapter, was that dialectics can provide the best path to innovation in the science. The book attempted to avoid old and traditional modes such as 'biographies' of scientific terms or historical elaboration or evaluation of epistemological arguments. I also challenged the de-scientification and pre-modern approaches that have returned to the epistemological fore. It is essential for a critical theory of the twenty-first century that it can articulate a political epistemology through the dialectical potential. The book attempted to present and ground the argument that a retreat to de-theorization for the sake of the partiality of empiricism, as well as the postmodern approach, signifies not a space of postmodernity, but rather the process of de-modernization that begins with the instrumentalization of the sciences and extends to the social and the political. In order to avoid social and scientific instrumentality and pre-modern positions, the construction of scientific politics has to be criticized under the perspective of a political epistemology. Such an epistemology negates the determinism of the arguments of social structures and scientific systems, and replaces the postmodern with a dialectics of modernity that reaches all strata of scientific progress. The reverse conception, that the modernization process reaches, by necessity, all levels of the scientific and the social, is by no means valid or confirmed and, therefore, the book did not attempt to prioritize the scientific, but instead indicated the importance, and the scientific implications that scientific dialectics entails, for the social and the political.

The elimination of the negative critique that the dialectic incorporates would potentially result in theological approaches of deterministic value. When science avoids the dialectical process and methodology, scientific argumentation promotes the hierarchization of the scientific sphere that implicates the hierarchical construction of society, against the initial declarations of the postmodernists. When dialogue and dialectics as a process are extinct, science follows a rather authoritarian mode of development that unavoidably but not deterministically influences societies in all their manifestations. When theoretical dialectics is missing, what remains of praxis, if not socially blind applications, and how can science defend its dialogical and not authoritarian character? In an explicit and excellent statement on the diversity and totality of the sciences considered as *a science*, Peter Manicas writes: 'the difference among theoretical science, applied science, and technology were rapidly being eroded. There is now a growing critical literature which shows that our customary understanding of the distinctions between these is not as straightforward as one might have supposed'.[1]

What critical realism described for the social sciences can address *all* sciences, or in critical terms the totality of science, namely that meanings or theories on which sciences are based can neither be measured, tested, corroborated nor uncritically verified as if they were facts. They can only be understood and formulate *a priori* judgements that can be validated or negated within the dialectical process that is internal to the scientific and the social lifeworld. The essence of a scientific and epistemological issue is not to know all the facts because that is simply unfeasible. We cannot formulate *a posteriori* judgements because we simply cannot afford to know *all* facts. That is the real failure of science based on empiricism or positivistic prerequisites: it becomes complacent with regard to its own assumptions, and for this positivism must probably accept responsibility. Science cannot *know* facts, let alone *all* facts, but it can ask the right questions. As a process, this does not render it capable of knowing everything, but it can help to *understand* the object under investigation.

The repudiation of modernity was often accompanied, in modern epistemology, by the renunciation of the social validity of the knowing subject. Small wonder that such trends were often escorted by political statements that left little potential for rational deliberation free of scientific and epistemological primitivism and most crucially reactionary argumentation in the field of politics.

Despite lengthy debates throughout the twentieth century over whether critical theory prioritized the subject or the object of knowledge and science to the detriment of the other, it appears as simply an issue of methodology for the student of critical theory to gravitate for reasons of epistemological emphasis, if not prejudice, towards the partiality of the 'either ... or'. A systematic look over the first and second generations of critical theorists would convince even the most suspicious reader that the reasons behind such moves were analytical, and not due to philosophical partiality. Adorno in particular

CONCLUSIONS

capitulates to a great extent the essence of the balance between the subject and object of science, when their significance is mediated by the criterion of truth. By relativizing truth, science instantly puts objectivity at risk: if truth is relativized, then there is nothing to save objectivity from the same epistemological peril, and the *relativistic paradox* or *aporia* to which it led. Relativism sets itself under relativism, too, which *entails* that it is neither the subject nor the object that can subjectivize or objectivize truth, respectively. It is, rather, relativism itself that paves the way for positivism of absolute verifications as an antidote, and ignores the fact that truth exists without relativistic crutches. Adorno accepts that only dialectical critique crystallizes the scientific sphere and the dialectical negations it has facilitated.[2]

The dialectical critique of subject and object appears plausible enough to ground arguments of contradictions and create an inner dialogue of the sciences that produces both scientific demythologization and the recognition of non-identity along with the plurivalence of the dialectical other or alternative. Nevertheless, who articulates critique itself signifies once more how easy it is for realists or idealists to incline towards prejudice. Dialectical critique constitutes the antagonism of the subject and the object, where contingency (of the Luhmannian kind) serves as a manifestation of the totalitarian element within science and society as systems: what systems or structures cannot identify, they limit to the pure coincidental fact of contingency.[3]

In an impressive statement, Bhaskar writes the following: 'It is of course accepted that science may be used instrumentally in the pursuit of moral ideals, political goals, etc., but science cannot help to determine that latter. We remain free in the face of science to adopt any value-position. "Keep Science out of Politics" could be the watchword here.'[4]

I maintain that the opposite is the case: the instrumentality of sciences lies in its lack of morality and political relevance, and here the political does not imply particular scientific aims that lead to specific political goals. Science is either already political, and if it is not, then it ought to be. Value-free scientific positions are not merely ineffectual, as Bhaskar writes; they are mainly unscientific or only seemingly scientific and, therefore, pre-modern in terms of their lack of social normativity. When scientists manage somehow to keep science out of politics, they do not attain a value-neutral judgement; they just reach a pre-modern idea of science, which seeks determinism in order to establish itself socially, and which resembles theology in order to enjoy social authority.

Science is political, however, because it is a science, not because it is 'natural', 'social' or 'human'. The latter consideration suggests that the potential for science to be political and, therefore, socially sensitive and sensitized lies not in its social authority, but in its attempt to be critical, dialectical and modern. Science has a say when it is socially accountable, or when humans have the *only* say in what science ought to be, and that is the task of political epistemology to acknowledge and capitalize in its argumentation. The book approached critical realists' position[5] – namely that 'philosophical positions hardly ever *entail* political positions or *vice versa*' – from the perspective of an epistemology of and for the twenty-first century. The critical perspective I outline in the book attempts to reaffirm that when we think, we can also act, but that *thinking* entails or requires dialectics and subjects acting politically by means of putting reason into use.

Bhaskar was correct when he wrote that 'the benefit of any scientific enlightenment depends upon a *politics*',[6] but the issue, in my approach, remains: what constitutes politics? Politics is neither practice, struggles, conflicts, transformations of structures, nor social relations, as critical realists thought. Politics depends upon the public commitments of conscious subjects realizing reason and critical potential through dialogue within multiple public spheres of the lifeworld, where science takes the social position of one such sphere. Such commitments entail but do not necessitate decisions. They potentially form public decisions within collectively binding processes that reach consensus. It is the task of science, among other subjects, to allow such commitments to 'happen'.

It seems that not all things social or political can be settled scientifically. But it also appears that 'It is no more possible to have an immoral science'[7] that does not supplement its objective with a choice of ends, means, methods and dialectical criticism of itself and for society. The objective of the science is to offer an alternative way that is political by means of dialectics and the necessary negations that the latter entails. In Roy Edgley's words, 'Science essentially involves arguing against people's theories and views, that is, critically opposing them: or, as we sometimes say, *attacking* them.'[8]

It is precisely this last point that constitutes the core argument of the book in its attempt to suggest an alternative approach for modern epistemology, one with a political orientation, or for a political epistemology of modernity, if you will. My argument is that science has to recognize the political content of the scientific oeuvre, and negate political instrumentality that is coordinated and promoted within a whole range of scientific structures. It mostly assumes responsibility to present an accountability criterion of the sciences by means of dialectical criticism and counter the positivistic, the theological and the deterministic, all of which not only run through scientific modes of argumentation, but also extend to the social understanding of modernity. It was Adorno, as Bhaskar admitted, who recognized the immanence of all criticism, as well as non-identity thinking, namely the potential for dialectical negation; whereas the second generation of critical theory, in the guise of

Habermas, did not commit to non-identity thinking separated from action, as Bhaskar rather weakly criticized, but to non-identity thinking grounded on a communicative potential for science with a *commitment to realize action*.

Adorno was persistent in his *Zur Metakritik der Erkenntnistheorie* on the unavoidable process by which identity thinking develops into *Identitätszwang* for subjective reflections of pre-scientific and pre-modern forms of a theory of knowledge. The non-recognition of non-identity, or otherness, or differentiation potentials with no absolute starting point, signified a moment of failure for the rationality of the sciences through the subject.[9] It is dialectics that inspires the recognition of the non-identical, and renders it the accountability criterion of the sciences. Scientific dialectics does not ratify its conclusions and recognitions or admissions by merely negating the old, the traditional or the established. It turns out to be a much more fruitful process simply because it is a process, and not an end in itself that by knowing and understanding can overcome and innovate the mediated and the identical in science. Therefore, it bears the potential to transform the possibly closed system of science into an open process that incorporates the *not yet included through the negation of identity thinking*.

Throughout its first and second generations, critical theory emphasized the same criticism of the contingent and the identical in the form of a particular act. The identical is the expression of the 'here and now', not the general in the particular; nor is it the general concept reduced to a precise act. As such, the identical element is not the bearer of meaning, whether in its individual or total understanding. Precisely because it bears no optimum meaning, it is attributed to pure contingency, which, in its turn, serves as the excuse of all relativisms, either in science or in society. I direct the same critique towards Husserl, the postmodernists, Luhmann or the realists: that facticity and the persistent application of theory onto a particular praxis, apart from triggering perceptions of positivism and reductionism, limits meaning to the 'one and only' practical implementation, where the plurivalence, which dialectics advances and exerts *elenchus* upon, remains unchallenged. Particularly in Foucault, the exclusion of dialectics from the scientific oeuvre signifies a moment of epistemological regression to traditional and authoritarian forms of approaching the object of science. Where dialectics is barred, the balance between reflection and its objective is distorted and recalls pre-critical attempts to grasp knowledge. Where dialectics is cast aside, authoritarianism lies ahead for both society and science.

What counts as authoritarianism in similar social conditions can be viewed as the reclaim of scientific authority, where, on the part of science, the inability to react to conventionality, and the lack of self-reflection signify the moment when science is unable to act and to negate the identity of given norms and social frameworks.[10] Such an idea of power, for either science or society, can obviously become a barrier to the potential of science, as a totality incorporating differences and non-identities and working through them. As a consequence, the epistemological opposition *against* authoritarianism and the eclipse of critique does not necessarily render such an opposition a defender of critique, open dialogue and the potentiality for negations. When epistemology argues *against* prejudice and irrationality, this does not necessitate or entail that it argues *for* modernity, dialectics and communicative rationality. Arguing against the eclipse of reason does not render arguments politically and socially viable in the defence of dialectics, communicative action and normative rationality.

Where structural unity or systems constructions prevail, dialectics fails to exert criticism upon the totality of the edifice under consideration. Structural descriptions and mechanisms of understanding science become the undialectical and, therefore, uncritical alternative to the same and established theorizations of modern epistemology that fail to ground the scientific oeuvre in the search for truth. The aim of structures and mechanisms or systems is to articulate descriptions, not critical statements, to promote their own reproduction and not the negation of the object of critique. Therefore, they fail to reach dialectical processes of realizing truth.[11] Under the reductionist function of science as a structure or system of thought, the advantage becomes the reflexive analysis of the existent per se and its subsequent confirmation, not the critique by means of dialectics and the truth reached potentially. Thus, the potential of trans-individuality, in Adorno, along with the formation of general theorizations that capture the meaning of both theory and practice, stay behind their prior intentions, which are to facilitate the dialectics of subject and object. They are replaced by systems, structures, mechanisms and classificatory paradigms of epistemological reductionism (such as 'power' in Foucault).[12]

It was again the same old story throughout critical theory, namely that any fruitfulness of social or scientific intentions that epistemology can achieve lies in promoting negations. Critical theory did not aim at negation and overwhelming rejection, nor did it look to the epistemological vagueness of relativism. Critical theory of the twenty-first century, which I analyse in the present book, maintains that it is the dialectical negation, deriving from the plurivalence of meanings and understandings, that turns into conscious practice and elenchus of the social function of the science. The method and objective of science and epistemology do not constitute an affirmation, but rather form the negation and its critical merits through dialectics. That is the task of a modern science: to advance negations and refutations through plurivalent dialogue, because it is the non-identical that knowledge seeks to manifest.[13]

CONCLUSIONS

For the second generation of critical theorists, and Habermas in particular, critical temptations take the form of praxis. But the realization of theory does not suffice to praxis but to the *rational praxis* that dialectics prepares. The latter point marks the modern epistemological objective of critical theory in stark contrast to the scientific theorizing of phenomenology, structuralists, postmodernists, Luhmann and critical realists. On the one hand, all the previous epistemological movements (though not only epistemological) attempted to give an epistemologically as well as socially plausible answer to what truth is, and when problems of method arose they resorted to practice, contingency or ontology in order to ground their arguments on theorizations that included dialectics, social and scientific mechanisms or structures. On the other hand, critical theorists of the first generation emphasized the idea that dialectics is negative critique, while those of the second generation, particularly Habermas, showed that dialectics becomes ontological when providing both elements of theory and practice in a process of rationality formation. These two positions did not contradict one another, but instead endured and developed into a concrete epistemological argument that bore both the negation as the indispensable and inalienable essence of dialectics, as well as the potential for consensus and universal pragmatics within science and society.[14]

Thence, the concept of rational praxis facilitated by dialectics finds a tenable explanation in Habermas' communicative action, which transforms scientific dialectics into a field of arguments whereby each is validated by the quest for rationality within the lifeworld. One of the most significant achievements of Habermas' theory was its realization that the lifeworld is not only the domain *of* communicative action and interaction, but also the field *for* rational praxis from the part of science. Within such an understanding Habermas maintains the symmetry of theory and praxis within the lifeworld that remains open to communicative action as the potential *Versöhnung* of contradictory and even conflictual elements. The lifeworld is not, by social or scientific necessity, rational or rationality-friendly; it is transformed into the open field for rationality under the influence that communicative action exerts on both theory and praxis as dialectical potentials.

An effective critical theory for the twenty-first century requires or even necessitates enlightened action that becomes social and scientific rationality through dialectics or, for Habermas, through the context of conscious communication (despite Adorno's previous view that the unity of theory and practice is not yet achieved). The crucial element in the previous remark by Adorno lies not in the potential and unfulfilled unity, but in the 'not yet' which signifies an implicit critique of modernity and its merits.[15] Critical theorists of the first and second generations did not seek to designate the theoretical presuppositions of praxis, but rather the practical effects of both theory and methodology. Such practical effects are achieved by the dialectical porosity of the lifeworld or by its allowance for communicative action, and 'by means of the penetrating ideas of a persistent critique'[16] in order to reclaim a critical scientific civilization.

The claim that Habermas raises is that if such a scientific civilization is to be modern and critical, then it has also to be dialectical, politicized and communicative in order to avoid the *aporia* of dividing 'human beings into two classes – the social engineers and the inmates of closed institutions'.[17] In relation to science, this is the point where Adorno's and Habermas' critique meet at an epistemological crossroads, which amounts to the criteria of a scientific civilization that has to incorporate critical knowledge through dialectics. The idea of a scientific civilization becomes porous in order to accomplish an institutionalized form that reforms society and aims at rational praxis. In Schecter's critique, 'Such knowledge, institutionalized in that kind of society, would be an end in itself and tantamount to freedom rather than successful adherence to and realization of heteronomous performance principles.'[18] Such knowledge remains the task of critical theory and the aim of a critical scientific civilization to vindicate and maintain.

A modern scientific civilization dares to form normativity, in both the social and the scientific domain, by means of dialectics that serves as the main or perhaps the only safeguard of a norm-bound society, which becomes rational through the dialectic potential for negation. It would have been much more preferable for science to employ dialectics as a force for convincing people of both the necessity and the indispensability of a modernity that dares to be critical and political through science. In addition, it would have been plausible to consider that if dialectics is taken as a *method* as well as a *process* for knowledge, it can then set the objective of truth to be understood and recognized socially and scientifically by knowing subjects, and raise claims of forming conscious rationality as a dialectical project of negation realizing that totalities are untrue and can potentially lead to totalitarianism.[19]

All modern epistemological trends discussed in this book either miss or barely refer to the main difference between them and critical theory, namely dialectics. Critical theory of the twenty-first century does not focus on dialectics and science out of fear of concepts such as the sign, the system or power, and so on. It is because all such concepts and approaches respectively constitute partial if not insufficient modes for realizing modernity and rationality. What was plausible for critical theorists of the first and the second generation remains epistemologically valid, not for reasons of theoretical heritage and the remembrance of all things past, but in order to innovate within the present modernity by means of explicating the social task of science. Whereas modern epistemology attempts to attack reason and normative rationality, and to abrogate dialectics, while introducing different modes of analysis, critical theory persistently argues for rationality as invariably renewed by the process of dialectics through the negations it introduces, particularly in the field of science.

On a secondary level, it is also the task of a political epistemology to bring rationality to the scientific fore, which means prioritizing, both institutionally and methodologically, in order to meet the expectations of both modern science and society. The claim of modernity, that critical theory indicated and fostered, transcended the distinctions of past and present scientific and political justifications, and was of a threefold nature: that is, first, to exert criticism through negations; second, to formulate arguments with political impact through science; and third, to commit to rational praxis in order not to lose sight of the social constellation and of how communicative and therefore rational potential both can and should be achieved.

Nonetheless, by citing social constellation I refer to the rise of the notion of the societal as a conceptual as well as perceptual and qualitative reductionism, which curtails the potential of the political. Therefore, a political epistemology appears to present a new path, a road not yet taken or only bypassed by science and epistemology. The persistence of structures and mediated identities as sufficient epistemological analyses through modern epistemology seems to put the cart before the horse. By contrast, the schema for a critical theory of the twenty-first century need not rephrase but reclaim and vindicate the fact that knowledge is a *potential* and *a priori* realization that finds its way to both the social and the political through dialectics. Therefore, dialectics might take us, as knowing subjects, towards communicative action and consensus. Such dialectics becomes the sufficient criterion for rational consent and facilitates the admission that dialectical negations are the royal path to rational consensus. It is through transcendental truth that knowing subjects accomplish uncoerced agreement. They have first to realize negations, and then move on to consensus and rational praxis within the social and scientific (in particular) lifeworld that becomes the field for unmediated knowledge.

Notes

1 Margaret Archer *et al.*, *Critical Realism* (London: Routledge, 2007), 313.
2 In Adorno's words: 'Gerade die Objektivität der Wahrheit bedarf des Subjekts; von diesem getrennt, wird sie Opfer blosser Subjektivität',and furthermore, 'Reine Subjektivität und reine Objektivität sind die obersten solcher isolierten und darum inkonsistenten Bestimmungen. Dass Erkenntnis ausschließend aufs Subjekt oder aufs Objekt soll reduziert werden können, erhebt die Isolierbarkeit, das Zerlegen, zum Gesetz der Wahrheit', *Zur Metakritik der Erkenntnistheorie* (Frankfurt am Main: Suhrkamp, 1970), 78 and 94 respectively.

3 In *Zur Metakritik der Erkenntnistheorie*, Adorno writes: 'Den Antagonismus bestimmt das philosophische Bewusstsein als den von Subjekt und Objekt. Weil es ihn an sich nicht aufheben kann, trachtet es, ihn für sich fortzuschaffen: durch Reduktion von Sein auf Bewusstsein. Diesem heißt Versöhnung: alles sich gleichmachen, und das ist zugleich der Widerspruch von Versöhnung. Kontingenz aber bleibt das Menetekel der Herrschaft. Diese ist insgeheim stets, wozu sie am Ende offen sich bekennt: totalitär. Was nicht ist wie sie, das schwächste Ungleichnamige, das subsumiert sie als Zufall', 89.
4 Archer and Bhaskar, *Critical Realism*, 234.
5 Particularly Bhaskar's and Collier's position in Archer and Bhaskar, *Critical Realism*, 392.
6 Archer and Bhaskar, *Critical Realism*, 414.
7 Archer and Bhaskar, *Critical Realism*, 398.
8 Archer and Bhaskar, *Critical Realism*, 406.
9 In his words, 'Erkenntnistheorie, die Anstrengung, das Identitätsprinzip durch lückenlose Reduktion auf subjektive Immanenz rein durchzuführen, wird gegen ihre Absicht zum Medium der Nichtidentität', in Adorno, *Zur Metakritik*, 34.
10 Although Adorno's 'The Meaning of Working through the Past' in his *Critical Models* is a genius political text, in many points the reader will identify not only political arguments but also methodological if not epistemological arguments on the mediation of the object of politics by conscious political subjects.
11 In *Zur Metakritik der Erkenntnistheorie*, Adorno notes: 'Doch Wahrheit ist nicht – wie der Marxismus es behauptet – eine zeitliche Funktion des Erkennens sondern an einen Zeitkern, welcher im Erkannten und Erkennenden zugleich steckt, gebunden', 141.
12 Adorno writes: 'Die Dichotomie von Form und Materie bereitet unüberwindliche Schwierigkeiten in der Konzeption der „reinen Anschauung", die da zur Form geschlagen wird, ohne dass irgendein Inhalt unabhängig von ihr zu isolieren ist', Adorno, *Zur Metakritik*,147.
13 As Adorno put it, 'Man kann nicht zugleich von jenem solipsistischen Ansatz Nutzen ziehen und seine Grenze überspringen: die Konsequenzen des Gedankens müsste ihn dann schon negieren', in Adorno, *Zur Metakritik*, 127.
14 Although quite provocative (particularly for critical theorists) in its formulation, the following claim by Rüdiger Bubner was significant: 'Wenn Dialektik irgendetwas ist, so ist sie eine *Methode*. Wenn sie eine Methode ist, so ist sie ein Verfahren zur Gewinnung von Erkenntnissen ... Es gibt keine Reservate spezifischer Gegenstände, wo die Dialektik gleichsam zu Hause wäre und andere Denkweisen ausgeschlossen', in Rüdiger Bubner, *Dialektik und Wissenschaft* (Frankfurt am Main: Suhrkamp, 1974), 129.
15 In his words, 'Die kategoriale Differenz der Disziplinen wird dadurch bestätigt, dass das, worauf es eigentlich ankäme, die Verbindung empirischer Erhebungen mit theoretisch zentralen Fragestellungen, trotz vereinzelter Ansätze bis heute nicht gelungen ist', in Theodor Adorno, *Soziologische Schriften I, Gesammelte Schriften 8* (Frankfurt am Main: Suhrkamp, 1997), 212.
16 Jürgen Habermas, *Theory and Practice* (London: Heinemann, 1974), 256.
17 Habermas, *Theory and Practice*, 282.
18 Darrow Schecter, *The Critique of Instrumental Reason from Weber to Habermas* (New York: Continuum, 2010), 82.
19 In Adorno's words, 'Das Ganze ist das Unwahre', cited in Gerhard Schweppenhäuser, *Theodor W. Adorno* (Hamburg: Junius Verlag, 1996), 36.

Bibliography

Adorno, Theodor W. *Zur Metakritik der Erkenntnistheorie, Drei Studien zu Hegel, Gesammelte Schriften, Band 5*. Frankfurt am Main: Suhrkamp, 1970.
Adorno, Theodor W., and Max Horkheimer. *Dialectic of Enlightenment*. London: Allen Lane, 1973.
Adorno, Theodor W., Hans Albert, Ralf Dahrendorf, Jürgen Habermas, Harald Pilot and Karl R. Popper. *The Positivist Dispute in German Sociology*. London: Heinemann, 1976.
Adorno, Theodor W. *Soziologische Schriften I, Gesammelte Schriften, Band 8*. Frankfurt am Main: Suhrkamp, 1997.
Adorno, Theodor W. *Critical Models*. New York: Columbia University Press, 1998.
Adorno, Theodor W. *Minima Moralia, Reflections from Damaged Life*. London: Verso, 2005.
Adorno, Theodor W. *Negative Dialectics*. New York: Continuum, 2007.
Alliez, Eric. *The Signature of the World*. New York: Continuum, 2005.
Andersen, Heine, and Lars Bo Kaspersen (eds), *Classical and Modern Social Theory*. Oxford: Blackwell, 2007.
Andriopoulos, Dimitrios. 'Epistemological Concepts and Problems in Plato's Dialogues'. *Philosophical Inquiry* 36, 1–2 (Winter–Spring 2012), 51–70.
Apel, Karl-Otto. *Analytic Philosophy of Language and the Geisteswissenschaften*. Dordrecht-Holland: D. Reidel, 1967.
Apel, Karl-Otto (ed.). *Hermeneutik und Ideologiekritik*. Frankfurt am Main: Suhrkamp Verlag, 1971.
Arato, Andrew, and Eike Gebhardt (eds). *The Essential Frankfurt School Reader*. New York: Continuum, 1998.
Archer, Margaret, Roy Bhaskar, Andrew Collier, Tony Lawson and Alan Norrie (eds), *Critical Realism, Essential Readings*. London: Routledge, 2007.
Arendt, Hannah. *Between Past and Future*. London: Penguin, 2006.
Austin, J. L. *How to Do Things with Words*. Cambridge, MA: Harvard University Press, 1975.
Benhabib, Seyla. *Critique, Norm, and Utopia: A Study of the Foundations of Critical Theory*. New York: Columbia University Press, 1986.
Benhabib, Seyla, Wolfgang Bonβ, and John McCole (eds). *On Max Horkheimer*. Cambridge, MA: The MIT Press, 1993.
Benhabib, Seyla, and Fred Dallmayr (eds), *The Communicative Ethics Controversy*. Cambridge, MA: The MIT Press, 1995.
Bernstein, Jay (ed.). *The Frankfurt School, Critical Assessments*, vols I–VI. London: Routledge, 1994.
Bernstein, Richard J. *The Restructuring of Social and Political Theory*. Philadelphia, PA: University of Pennsylvania Press, 1990.
Bhaskar, Roy. *A Realist Theory of Science*. London: Verso, 2008.

Bhaskar, Roy. *Dialectic: The Pulse of Freedom*. London: Routledge, 2008.
Bhaskar, Roy. *Reclaiming Reality*. London: Routledge, 2011.
Bleicher, Josef. *Contemporary Hermeneutics*. London: Routledge and Kegan Paul, 1980.
Bolte, Gerhard. *Von Marx bis Horkheimer*. Darmstadt: Wissenschaftliche Buchgesellschaft, 1995.
Bolz, Norbert. *Ratten im Labyrinth*. Munich: Wilhelm Fink Verlag, 2012.
Bonβ, Wolfgang, and Axel Honneth (eds).*zialforschung als Kritik*. Frankfurt am Main: Suhrkamp, 1982.
Borch, Christian. *Niklas Luhmann*. London: Routledge, 2011.
Bottomore, Tom, and Rober Nisbet (eds). *A History of Sociological Analysis*. London: Heinemann, 1978.
Bourdieu, Pierre. *Science of Science and Reflexivity*. Cambridge: Polity Press, 2004.
Bourdieu, Pierre. *Acts of Resistance*. Cambridge: Polity Press, 2004.
Bourdieu, Pierre. *Pascalian Meditations*. Cambridge: Polity Press, 2006.
Bourdieu, Pierre, and Loic J. D. Wacquant. *An Invitation to Reflexive Sociology*. Cambridge: Polity Press, 2007.
Bourdieu, Pierre. *In Other Words*. Cambridge: Polity Press, 2007.
Bourdieu, Pierre. *Outline of a Theory of Practice*. Cambridge: Cambridge University Press, 2013.
Bronner, Stephen E., and Douglas MacKay Kellner (eds). *Critical Theory and Society: A Reader*. London: Routledge, 1989.
Brunkhorst, Hauke. *Theodor W. Adorno: Dialektik der Moderne*. Munich: Piper, 1990.
Brunkhorst, Hauke. *Habermas*. Leipzig: Reclam Verlag, 2006.
Bubner, Rüdiger, Konrad Cramer, and Reiner Wiehl (eds). *Hermeneutik und Dialektik*. Tübingen: Mohr, 1970.
Bubner, Rüdiger. *Dialektik und Wissenschaft*. Frankfurt am Main: Suhrkamp, 1974.
Bubner, Rüdiger. *Essays in Hermeneutics and Critical Theory*. New York: Columbia University Press, 1988.
Buck-Morss, Susan. *The Origin of Negative Dialectics*. New York: The Free Press, 1979.
Carr, David, and Edward S. Casey (eds). *Explorations in Phenomenology*. The Hague: Martinus Nijhoff, 1973.
Caws, Peter. *Structuralism*. New York: Humanity Books, 2000.
Clam, Jean-Joseph. *Sache und Logik der Phänomenologie Husserls und Heideggers*. Altenberge: Akademische Bibliothek, 1985.
Collier, Andrew. *Scientific Realism and Socialist Thought*. Hertfordshire: Harvester Wheatsheaf, 1989.
Connerton, Paul. *The Tragedy of Enlightenment*. Cambridge: Cambridge University Press, 1980.
Cook, Deborah. 'Adorno, Foucault and Critique'. *Philosophy and Social Criticism* 39, 10 (December 2013): 965–81.
Craib, Ian. *Modern Social Theory*. London: Harvester, 1992.
Crowell, Steven Galt. 'Husserl, Heidegger, and Transcendental Philosophy: Another Look at the Encyclopedia Britannica Article'. *Philosophy and Phenomenological Research* 50, 3 (March 1990): 501–18.
Couzens Hoy, David (ed.). *Foucault, A Critical Reader*. Oxford: Basil Blackwell, 1991.
Dallmayr, Winfried (ed.). *Materialien zu Habermas' 'Erkenntnis und Interesse'*. Frankfurt am Main: Suhrkamp Verlag, 1974.
Deleuze, Gilles. *Difference and Repetition*. New York: Continuum, 2001.

Deleuze, Gilles. *Desert Islands*. Los Angeles: Semiotext(e), 2002.
Deleuze, Gilles, and Felix Guattari. *What Is Philosophy?* London: Verso, 2011.
Dilthey, Wilhelm. *The Essence of Philosophy*. Chapel Hill, NC: The University of North Carolina Press, 1956.
Dilthey, Wilhelm. *Gesammelte Schriften, V. Band*. Stuttgart: B. G. Teubner Verlagsgesellschaft, 1964.
Dilthey, Wilhelm. *Introduction to the Human Sciences*. Detroit, MI: Wayne State University Press, 1988.
Doxiadis, Kyrkos. 'Three Versions of 'Power' in Michel Foucault's Work'. *The International Journal of Interdisciplinary Social Sciences* 4, 8 (2009): 115–22.
Dreyfus, Hubert L., and Paul Rabinow. *Michel Foucault, Beyond Structuralism and Hermeneutics*. New York: Harvester Wheatsheaf, 1982.
Dubiel, Helmut. *Wissenschaftsorganisation und Politische Erfahrung*. Frankfurt am Main: Suhrkamp, 1978.
Eickelpasch, Rolf, and Armin Nassehi (eds). *Utopie und Moderne*. Frankfurt am Main: Suhrkamp, 1996.
Elam, Mark, and Margareta Bertilsson. ' "onsuming, Engaging and Confronting Science; The Emerging Dimensions of Scientific Citizenship'. *European Journal of Social Theory* 6, 2 (2003): 233–51.
Farber, Marvin. *The Aims of Phenomenology*. New York: Harper Torchbooks, 1966.
Filmer, Paul, Michael Phillipson, David Silverman and David Walsh (eds). *New Directions in Sociological Theory*. London: Collier-Macmillan, 1972.
Foucault, Michel. *The Order of Things*. New York: Vintage Books, 1994.
Foucault, Michel. *The Politics of Truth*. Los Angeles, CA: Semiotext(e), 2007.
Foucault, Michel. *Archaeology of Knowledge*. London: Routledge, 2011.
Foucault, Michel. *The Courage of Truth*. Hampshire: Palgrave Macmillan, 2011.
Gadamer, Hans-Georg. *Truth and Method*. London: Continuum, 2004.
Garfinkel, Harold. *Studies in Ethnomethodology*. Cambridge: Polity, 2011.
Gellner, Ernest. *Spectacles and Predicaments*. Cambridge: Cambridge University Press, 1991.
Gensicke, Dietmar. *Luhmann*. Stuttgart: Reclam, 2008.
Gmünder, Ulrich. *Kritische Theorie*. Stuttgart: Metzler, 1985.
Gripp-Hagelstange, Helga. *Niklas Luhmann, eine erkenntnistheoretische Einführung*. Munich: Wilhelm Fink Verlag, 1995.
Habermas, Jürgen. *Knowledge and Human Interests*. Boston, MA: Beacon Press, 1971.
Habermas, Jürgen. *Theory and Practice*. London: Heinemann, 1974.
Habermas, Jürgen, and Niklas Luhmann. *Theorie der Gesellschaft oder Sozialtechnologie – Was leistet die Systemforschung?* Frankfurt am Main: Suhrkamp Verlag, 1974.
Habermas, Jürgen. *Zwei Reden*. Frankfurt am Main: Suhrkamp, 1974.
Habermas, Jürgen. *The Philosophical Discourse of Modernity*. Cambridge: Polity Press, 1987.
Habermas, Jürgen. *Strukturwandel der Öffentlichkeit*. Frankfurt am Main: Suhrkamp, 1990.
Habermas, Jürgen. *Moral Consciousness and Communicative Action*. Cambridge: Polity Press, 1990.
Heidegger, Martin. *Brief über den Humanismus*. Athens: Roes, 1987.
Harrington, Austin. *Hermeneutic Dialogue and Social Science: A Critique of Gadamer and Habermas*. London: Routledge, 2001.

Held, David. *Introduction to Critical Theory: Horkheimer to Habermas.* Cambridge: Polity Press, 1990.
Helle, Horst-Jürgen (ed.). *Georg Simmel: Introduction to His Theory and Method.* Munich: Oldenbourg Wissenschaftsverlag, 2001.
Heritage, John. *Garfinkel and Ethnomethodology.* Cambridge: Polity Press, 2010.
Hobbes, Thomas. *Leviathan.* Oxford: Oxford University Press, 2008.
Hodges, H. A. *Wilhelm Dilthey: An Introduction.* London: Kegan Paul, 1944.
Hohendahl, Peter-Uwe. *The Institution of Criticism.* Ithaca and London: Cornell University Press, 1982.
Hohendahl, Peter-Uwe, and Jaimey Fischer, Jaimey (eds). *Critical Theory, Current State and Future Prospects.* New York: Berghahn Books, 2001.
Honneth, Axel. *The Critique of Power, Reflective Struggles in a Critical Social Theory.* Cambridge, MA: The MIT Press, 1991.
Honneth, Axel, and Hans Jonas (eds). *Communicative Action.* Cambridge, MA: The MIT Press, 1991.
Honneth, Axel, Thomas McCarthy, Claus Offe and Albrecht Wellmer (eds). *Cultural-political Interventions in the Unfinished Project of the Enlightenment.* Cambridge, MA: The MIT Press, 1992.
Horkheimer, Max. 'Bemerkungen über Wissenschaft und Krise'. *Zeitschrift für Sozialforschung I*, 1/2 (1932): 1–7.
Horkheimer, Max. 'Hegel und das Problem der Metaphysik'. *Festschrift für Carl Grünberg zum 70. Geburtstag.* Stuttgart: Kohlhammer, 1932.
Horkheimer, Max. 'Zum Problem der Voraussage in den Sozialwissenschaften'. *Zeitschrift für Sozialforschung* II (1933): 407–12.
Horkheimer, Max. 'Die Philosophie der absoluten Konzentration"'. *Zeitschrift für Sozialforschung* VII (1938): 376–87.
Horkheimer, Max. *Die Sehnsucht nach dem ganz Anderen, Ein Interview mit Kommentar von Hellmut Gumnior.* Hamburg: Furche-Verlag, 1970.
Horkheimer, Max. *Sozialphilosophische Studien, Aufsätze, Reden und Vorträge 1930–1972. Mit einem Annhang über Universität und Studium.* Frankfurt am Main: Athenäum Fischer Taschenbuch Verlag, 1972.
Horkheimer, Max. *Critical Theory: Selected Essays.* New York: Herder and Herder, 1972.
Horkheimer, Max. *Aspects of Sociology.* London: Heinemann, 1973.
Horkheimer, Max. *Critique of Instrumental Reason.* New York: Continuum, 1974.
Horkheimer, Max. *Eclipse of Reason.* New York: Seabury Press, 1974.
Horkheimer, Max. *Gesammelte Schriften, Band 3, Schriften 1931–1936.* Frankfurt am Main: Fischer Taschenbuch Verlag, 1988.
Horkheimer, Max. *Gesammelte Schriften, Band 4, Schriften 1936–1941.* Frankfurt am Main: Fischer, 1988.
Horkheimer, Max. *Between Philosophy and Social Sciences: Selected Early Writings.* Cambridge, MA: The MIT Press, 1995.
Hoy, David Couzens, and Thomas McCarthy. *Critical Theory.* Cambridge: Blackwell, 1996.
Husserl, Edmund. *Cartesian Meditations: An Introduction to Phenomenology.* Hague: Martinus Nijhoff, 1988.
Husserl, Edmund. 'Phenomenology'. *The Encyclopaedia Britannica Article* (1927): 237–55. Accessed 13 September 2012.
Ingram, David. *Habermas and the Dialectic of Reason.* New Haven, CT: Yale University Press, 1987.

Ingram, David. *Habermas*. Ithaca and London: Cornell University Press, 2010.
Jacoby, Russell. 'Phil Slater, Origin and Significance of the Frankfurt School'. *Telos* 31 (Spring 1977): 198–202.
Jameson, Fredric. *Late Marxism, Adorno, or, The Persistence of the Dialectic*. London: Verso, 2000.
Jameson, Fredric. *A Singular Modernity, Essays on the Ontology of the Present*. London: Verso, 2002.
Jenkins, Richard. *Pierre Bourdieu*. London: Routledge, 2002.
Kant, Immanuel. *Toward Perpetual Peace*. New Haven, CT: Yale University Press, 2006.
Keat, Russell. *The Politics of Social Theory*. Oxford: Basil Blackwell, 1981.
Kellner, Douglas. 'Critical Theory Today: Revisiting the Classics'. *Theory, Culture, Society* 10, 2 (1993): 43–60, accessed 2 April 2001.
Kelly, Mark G. E. *The Political Philosophy of Michel Foucault*. New York: Routledge, 2012.
Kelly, Michael (ed.) *Critique and Power*. Cambridge, MA: The MIT Press, 1994.
Krais, Beate. 'Habitus und soziale Praxis'. *Institut für Sozialforschung, Mitteilungen* 13 (2002): 111–27.
Krause, Detlef. *Luhmann – Lexikon*. Stuttgart: Lucius and Lucius, 2005.
Laslett, Peter, and W. G. Runciman (eds) *Philosophy, Politics and Society*. Oxford: Basil Blackwell, 1967.
Luhmann, Niklas. *Zweckbegriff und Systemrationalität*. Frankfurt am Main: Suhrkamp, 1973.
Luhmann, Niklas. 'The Future of Democracy'". *Thesis Eleven* 26 (1990): 46–53.
Luhmann, Niklas. *Die Wissenschaft der Gesellschaft*. Frankfurt am Main: Suhrkamp, 1994.
Luhmann, Niklas. *Introduction to Systems Theory*. Cambridge: Polity Press, 2013.
Lyotard, Jean-Francois. *The Postmodern Condition: A Report on Knowledge*. Manchester: Manchester University Press, 1997.
Maciejewski, Franz (ed.) *Theorie der Gesellschaft oder Sozialtechnologie*. Frankfurt am Main: Suhrkamp Verlag, 1974.
Marcuse, Herbert. *Reason and Revolution*. London: Routledge, 1968.
Marinopoulou, Anastasia. *The Concept of the Political in Max Horkheimer and Jürgen Habermas*. Athens: Nissos Academic, 2008.
Milner, Marion. *The Suppressed Madness of Sane Men*. East Sussex: Routledge, 2009.
Mischel, Theodore (ed.), *Cognitive Development and Epistemology*. New York: Academic Press, 1971.
Misgeld, Dieter, and Graeme Nicholson (eds), *Hans-Georg Gadamer on Education, Poetry, and History, Applied Hermeneutics*. New York: State University of New York Press, 1992.
Moeller, Hans-Georg. *Luhmann Explained*. Chicago, IL: Open Court, 2006.
Morris, Michael. *An Introduction to the Philosophy of Language*. Cambridge: Cambridge University Press, 2011.
Moss, Lenny, and Vida Pavesich. 'Science, Normativity and Skill: Reviewing the Anthropological Basis of Critical Theory'. *Philosophy and Social Criticism* 37, 2 (2011): 139–65.
Müller-Doohm, Stefan (ed.), *Das Interesse der Vernunft*. Frankfurt am Main: Suhrkamp Verlag, 2000.
Müller-Doohm, Stefan. 'Thinking from No-man's-land. The Life and Work of Theodor W. Adorno'. *Studies in Social and Political Thought* 11 (May 2005): 91–103.

Müller-Doohm, Stefan. *Adorno: A Biography*. Cambridge: Polity, 2009.
Nassehi, Armin. 'What Do We Know about Knowledge? An Essay on the Knowledge Society'. *The Canadian Journal of Sociology* 29, 3 (Summer 2004): 439–49.
Nassehi, Armin, and Gerd Nollmann. *Bourdieu und Luhmann*. Frankfurt am Main: Suhrkamp, 2004.
Natanson, Maurice (ed.), *Phenomenology and the Social Sciences*, vols I and II. Evanston, IL: Northwestern University Press, 1973.
Negt, Oskar. *Der Politische Mensch*. Göttingen: Steidl, 2010.
O'Connor, Brian. *Adorno's Negative Dialectic, Philosophy and the Possibility of Critical Rationality*. Cambridge, MA: The MIT Press, 2004.
Outhwaite, William. *Understanding Social Life: The Method Called Verstehen*. London: George Allen and Unwin, 1975.
Outhwaite, William. *New Philosophies of Social Science: Realism, Hermeneutics and Critical Theory*. London: Macmillan Press, 1993.
Outhwaite, William. *Habermas: A Critical Introduction*. Cambridge: Polity Press, 1994.
Outhwaite, William (ed.), *The Habermas Reader*. Cambridge: Polity Press, 1996.
Outhwaite, William. 'The Concept of Critique in Critical Theory'. Paper presented at Sussex University, July 1998.
Outhwaite, William. 'The Myth of Modernist Method'. *European Journal of Social Theory* 2, 1 (1999): 5–25.
Outhwaite, William. 'The History of Hermeneutics'. In Neil J. Smelser and Paul B. Baltes (eds), *Encyclopedia of the Social and Behavioral Sciences* (6661–5). London: Elsevier Science, 2001.
Outhwaite, William. 'In Defence of Social Structure'. *Studies in Social and Political Thought* 4 (2001): 3–15.
Outhwaite, William (ed.). *The Blackwell Dictionary of Modern Social Thought*. Oxford: Blackwell, 2003.
Outhwaite, William. *Habermas: A Critical Introduction* (2nd edn). Stanford, CA: Stanford University Press, 2009.
Outhwaite, William. 'Roy Bhaskar'. Unpublished paper given by the author, 2015.
Outhwaite, William. 'Forth Years of Critical Realism'. Unpublished paper given by the author, 2015.
Outhwaite, William. 'Interview on Critical Realism'. Forthcoming in *Philosophical Inquiry*, 2017.
Pivcevic, Edo. *Husserl and Phenomenology*. London: Hutchinson University Library, 1970.
Privitera, Walter. *Problems of Style, Michel Foucault's Epistemology*. New York: State University of New York Press, 1995.
Rabinow, Paul (ed.) *The Foucault Reader*. London: Penguin Books, 1991.
Rogers, Mary F. *Sociology, Ethnomethodology, and Experience*. Cambridge: Cambridge University Press, 1983.
Rose, Gillian. *The Melancholy Science: An Introduction to the Thought of Theodor W. Adorno*. London: The MacMillan Press, 1978.
Runciman, W. R. (ed.) *Weber: Selections in Translation*. Cambridge: Cambridge University Press, 1993.
Rush, Fred (ed.) *The Cambridge Companion to Critical Theory*. Cambridge: Cambridge University Press, 2004.
Schecter, Darrow. *The Critique of Instrumental Reason from Weber to Habermas*. New York: Continuum, 2010.

Schecter, Darrow. *Critical Theory in the Twenty-First Century*. New York and London: Bloomsbury, 2013.
Schirmacher, Wofgang (ed.) *German 20th Century Philosophy: The Frankfurt School*. New York: Continuum, 2000.
Schuler, Philipp. *Rationalität und Organisation – ein Vergleich zwischen Max Weber und Niklas Luhmann*. Munich: GRIN Verlag, 2007.
Schütz, Alfred. *Collected Papers*, vol. I: *The Problem of Social Reality*. The Hague: Martinus Nijhoff, 1962.
Schweppenhäuser, Gerhard. *Theodor W. Adorno, zur Einfürhung*. Hamburg: Junius Verlag, 1996.
Scruton, Roger. *Kant: A Very Short Introduction*. Oxford: Oxford University Press, 2001.
Shakespeare, William. *The Complete Works*. Hertfordshire: Wordsworth Editions, 1996.
Simmel, Georg. *On Individuality and Social Forms*. Chicago, IL: The University of Chicago Press, 1971.
Skinner, Quentin (ed.). *The Return of Grand Theory in the Human Sciences*. Cambridge: Cambridge University Press, 1994.
Skuhra, Anselm. *Max Horkheimer*. Stuttgart: Verlag W. Kohlhammer, 1974.
Smith, Daniel W., and Henry Somers-Hall (eds), *The Cambridge Companion to Deleuze*. Cambridge: Cambridge University Press, 2012.
Speck, Joseph (ed.). *Grundproleme der grossen Philosophen*. Göttingen: Vandenhoeck, 1991.
Stockman, Norman. *Antipositivist Theories of the Sciences*. Dordrecht: D. Reidel, 1983.
Strawson, P. F. *Meaning and Truth*. Oxford: Clarendon Press, 1970.
Thompson, John B. *Critical Hermeneutics*. Cambridge: Cambridge University Press, 1981.
Thornhill, Chris. *Political Theory in Modern Germany: An Introduction*. Cambridge: Polity Press, 2000.
Torgerson, Douglas. 'Between Knowledge and Politics: Three Faces of Policy Analysis'. *Policy Sciences* 19, Dordrecht: Martinus Nijhoff (1986): 33–59.
Tyfield, David. 'Modern Science and the Capriciousness of Nature'. *Journal of Critical Realism* 7, 1 (2008): 161–169.
Vandenberghe, Frederic. '"The Real is Relational": An Epistemological Analysis of Pierre Bourdieu's Generative Structuralism'. *Sociological Theory* 17, 1 (March 1999): 32–67.
Vierkandt, Alfred (ed.). *Handwörterbuch der Soziologie*. Stuttgart: Ferdinand Enke Verlag, 1982.
Wagner, Peter. 'An Entirely New Object of Consciousness, of Volition, of Thought'. Paper given at Sussex University, July 2001.
Wellmer, Albrecht. *Kritische Gesellschaftstheorie und Positivismus*. Frankfurt am Main: Suhrkamp Verlag, 1969.
Wellmer, Albrecht. *Critical Theory of Society*. New York: Herder and Herder, 1971.
Wellmer, Albrecht. *Methodologie als Erkenntnistheorie*. Frankfurt am Main: Suhrkamp Verlag, 1972.
Welton, Donn (ed.) *The Essential Husserl, Basic Writings in Transcendental Phenomenology*. Bloomington, IN: Indiana University Press, 1999.
Welz, Frank. *Kritik der Lebenswelt, Eine soziologische Auseinandersetzung mit Edmund Husserl und Alfred Schütz*. Opladen: Westdeutscher Verlag, 1996.

White, Stephen K. *The Recent Work of Jürgen Habermas*. Cambridge: Cambridge University Press, 1989.
Wiggershaus, Rolf. *Theodor W. Adorno*. Munich: Verlag C. H. Beck, 1998.
Winch, Peter. *The Idea of a Social Science and Its Relation to Philosophy*. London: Routledge, 2008.
Zimmerli, Walther Ch. (ed.). *Technologisches Zeitalter oder Postmoderne?* Munich: Wilhelm Fink Verlag, 1988.

Index

absence 161–3
accountability 36–7, 102–4, 107–9, 116–19, 142–4, 155–6, 161–3
  political 53–5
  in the sciences 3–5
  systems 112–14
action 111–13
  in ethnomethodology 35–7
  in structuralism 53–5
Adorno, T. W. 8–10, 27–9, 31–2, 65–6, 69–70, 87–9, 97–8, 112–14, 171–5
applicability (of the sciences) 140–2
Auschwitz 69–70, 88–90
autopoiesis 113–17, 121–3

Bestehende (das) 144
borders (of a system) 129–32

causality (in Luhmann) 120–3
common-sense 33–4, 36–8
communicative action 12–15, 44–5, 127–9
complexity (systems) 112–14, 131–3
concepts 22, 70–1
conceptual differences 72–4
conscious subject 87–90
consensus 64–6, 132–4
contingency 158–61
critical theory 7–9, 66–8, 75–7, 107–9, 118–20
criticism (in Foucault) 93–6
  dialectical 170–3
  scientific 146–9
critique 1–3, 74–5, 96–7

  in Bhaskar 145–8, 150–2
  of dialectics (in Foucault) 83–4, 88–90
  epistemological 86–7
  in Foucault 82–4
  totalizing 156–8

Dasein 41–3
deduction 13–14
dialectics 3–4, 13–17, 44–8, 75–7, 79, 82–5, 97–9, 161–3
  in Adorno and Foucault 87–9
  in Bhaskar 144–6, 150–3
  in critical realism 147–9, 162–4
  in critical theory 46–8
  cunning of 46–8
  in Foucault 89–93, 100–3, 171–2
  in Gadamer 43–6
  Hegelian 73–5, 160–2
  in Heidegger 40–3
  in Kant 127–9
  in Luhmann 123–5
  poststructural 70–2
  as a process 114–16, 168–70
  in Simmel 26
  social 75–6
  structural 57–60, 67–8
  for structuralism and poststructuralism 52–4
dialogue 82–5, 107–9
differentiated pluralism 136
differentiation (systems) 113–16, 124–6
  in Bhaskar 150–3
  scientifically 141–3
Dilthey W. 19, 21–2, 24

discourse 87–8, 90–2, 96–8,
    102–3, 114–18
discursive reason 85–7
doxa 60–1

eidetic reduction 31–3, 39
elenchus 53–5, 76–7, 96–7, 123–5, 155–7
Enlightenment 81–3, 114–15, 120–3
    in Luhmann 124–6
Entwurf (Kantian) 10–12
environment (systems) 115–17,
    118–20, 124–9
epistemocracy 134–6
epistemology 1, 82–5
    in Bhaskar 139–42
    of critical theory 3–5, 103–5
    in Husserl 28–30
    in Luhmann 130–2
    modern 1–3, 4–6, 146–8,
        170–1, 173–5
    political 6–8, 105–7, 141–4, 162–5,
        170–2, 175–8
    of praxis 93–5
    in structuralism and
        poststructuralism 75–8
    traditional (in Luhmann) 112–13
Epistemon 72–3
epochè 26–9, 31–3, 39, 124–6
ethnomethodology 35–8, 122–5
Eudoxus 72–3

Frankfurt School 2–5, 7–9, 27–9, 32–4,
    65–7, 102–5

Gadamer, G. 43–6
Garfinkel, H. 35–8
Geisteswissenschaften 20
Gesamtgesehen (in Adorno)
    2–5, 112–14

Habermas, J. 2–5, 11–14, 44–7, 59–60,
    65–6, 83–5, 129–32, 171–5
habitus 53–4, 56–9, 62, 67–9

Handeln 111–13, 117–19
Handlungsstruktur 112–13
Handlungswissenschaften 112–15
Heidegger, M. 38–42
hermeneutics 43–6
Horkheimer, M. 2–5, 8–10, 21–2, 65–6,
    77–8, 103–5
    on philosophy 6–7
Husserl E. 26–33, 39

ideal speech situation 132–4
imaginary (the) 147–50
imagined (the) 147–9
individualism 149–51
instrumentality 165–8
intentionality 26–7, 30–1, 34,
    40–1, 72–4
interaction 25–6
interdisciplinarity 13–15, 84–5
intersubjectivity 26–7, 37–9, 48–9
    in Husserl 30–1
    in Schütz 33–4

Kant, I. 1–3, 61–2, 74–5, 81–3, 99–101,
    103–5, 128–9, 147–9, 162–3
knowing subject 27–8, 37–9
knowledge 90–1

Lebensanschauung 24–5
Lebenspraxis 130–3
lifeworld 27–30, 40–2, 66–7, 113–16,
    136–8, 172–4
linguistic turn 44–6
Lyotard, J. F. 102–4

Marcuse, H. 8–10, 31–3, 103–5
Marxism (of the Frankfurt
    School) 103–4
mathesis 90–3
mathesis universalis 35–6
meaning 22
Merleau-Ponty, M. 38–40
methodology 25, 28, 79–80

INDEX

in critical realism 140–2, 153–5
in Husserl 30–2
in Simmel 26–8
modernism 102–4
   in Foucault 103–4, 106–8
modernity 83–7, 88–90, 92–3, 97–9, 107–9, 120–2, 168–70
   epistemological 131–2, 167–9
   Foucauldian 97–100, 114
   Habermasian 97–9, 101–3
   Kantian 100–2
   in Luhmann 114–16, 125–6, 128–31
   systemic 131–3
Möglichkeitstheorie 124–6

negation 57–8, 171–4
non-identity thinking 170–3
normativity 101–3, 106–8, 112–14, 116–18, 143–5, 173–5
   in ethnomethodology 37–9
   in Luhmann 112–14, 122–4, 134–7
   of the sciences 24–6
noumena 21, 26–7

observer (of a system) 118–20, 130–3
one-true-theory 149–50
ontology 39–41, 45–6
   Bhaskar's 139–41, 144–6, 156–8
   in critical realism 140–3, 153–5
   of the science 160–3

performativity 100–2, 117–20, 141–3
   in Bhaskar 151–3
phenomenality 120–3
phenomenology 26–33, 45–6
philosophy 6–8, 41–3, 144–6
   in critical realism 162–5
   for critical theory 75–8
   for Marcuse 7–8
   political 87–9, 101–3
   in poststructuralism 69–70, 72–4, 76–8
polyvalence 153–5, 160–2
positivism 6–8, 158–9

for Bhaskar 145–7
in Deleuze 70–1
postmodernism 99–102, 148–9
poststructuralism 68–71, 75–7, 94–7
power 90–2, 95–7, 101–2, 105–6
   systems of 95–7, 121–3
practice 53–4, 67–8, 75–9, 87–9
   in Bhaskar 151–3
   structuralist 87–90
practices 54–6, 87–8, 101–2
   archaeological and genealogical study of 86–8
praxis 40–2, 157–8, 161–2, 168–9, 173–5

rationalities (in Luhmann) 126–8
rationality 66–8, 111–14, 134–6
   in Adorno 88–90
   communicative 135–7
   Kantian 82–4, 115–16, 120–1
   political 115–16
   in Schütz 34–5
   systems 115–18, 120–2
   traditional 115–16
realism (of the sciences) 140–2
   critical 145–7
reality principle 146–7
reason 46–8, 73–5, 83–5, 116–19
reflexivity 145–7
relativism 14–16, 47–8, 56–7
   in Foucault 93–4
repetition 70–4
representation 71–4, 94–6

Schütz, A. 33–5
science (modern) 5–7, 143–5, 155–7, 168–9, 171–3
   in Bhaskar 145–7
   in critical theory 2–5, 7–9, 14–16
   in Deleuze 74–5
   for the Frankfurt School 15–17
   in Habermas 11–14
   rigorous 61–4

self-reflexivity 36–8, 68–9,
  113–15, 120–2
Simmel, G. 19–20, 24–6
social character of the sciences 2–5,
  18–20, 23, 35–6, 102–4, 140–3
structuralism 56–8, 67–9, 75–8
  in Luhmann 118–19, 122–5
structure 84–6, 155–8, 171–3
structures 58–9
subject-object 8–10, 12–17, 55–9, 77–9,
  94–6, 119–21, 167–9
system 113–16
  construction 171–3
  functionalism 123–5
  of power 95–7
  of rules (or practices in
    Foucault) 86–8

taxinomia 90–5
totality 145–8
  in critical realism 154–6
transcendental reduction 30–2
transcendental subjectivity 48–9
truth 39–41, 64–5, 78–9, 88–93, 134–6

in Adorno 69–71
in Bourdieu 62–4
condition in Bhaskar 152–3
in critical theory 8–11
in Foucault 91–3, 100–3
in Gadamer 43–5
in Habermas 65–7
in Heidegger 38–42
in Luhmann 118–20, 135–8

Umwelt 115–17, 119–20
universalizability 145–8, 158–9, 162–4

validity 33–4
Verstehen 20, 34–5

Weber, M. 22–4
Weltanschauung 22
Widerstand 44–5
Wirkungsmöglichkeiten 112–13

Zweck 111–13
Zweckrationalität 120–2, 126–7, 133–5
Zweckvorstellung 112–14

EU authorised representative for GPSR:
Easy Access System Europe, Mustamäe tee 50,
10621 Tallinn, Estonia
gpsr.requests@easproject.com

www.ingramcontent.com/pod-product-compliance
Lightning Source LLC
Chambersburg PA
CBHW070239240426
43673CB00044B/1846